WEST VIRGINIA USA

WEST VIRGINIA USA

JERRY WAYNE ASH AND STRATTON L. DOUTHAT

photography:

BILL KUYKENDALL AND HARRY SEAWELL

First Printing, September 1976

Second Printing, November 1976

International Standard Book Number (Standard Edition) 0-917040-00-7

International Standard Book Number (Deluxe Edition) 0-917040-01-5

Copyright 1976, Seawell Multimedia Corporation

Parkersburg, West Virginia 26101

Library of Congress Number 76-11298

All rights reserved.

Printed and bound in the United States.

by Waverly Press, Inc.
Baltimore, Md.

*In the soft light of dawn, a delicate
mist lingers in the hollows of Ritchie County.
Dawn colors also beautifully tint a Hardy
County farm landscape (overleaf picture) in
the rugged South Branch Valley.*

The publishers owe special recognition to the following: Mary Sonis, whom we always asked when nobody else knew the answer! Jim Comstock, editor of the *West Virginia Hillbilly,* who furnished leads for research and visual material. Ken Hine for his highly qualified assistance with design and layout. Dr. Mahlon C. Brown of Marshall University, and his history students for assistance in assembling the Chronology section. Bob Spence of *The Logan News,* who helped with photographs and information. Joe Sakach, for making his collection of rare books available. O.O. Brown, who contributed from his collection of old river photographs. Henry McCoy and the Sistersville Library for making the *Walter McCoy Collection* of photographs available. The Departments of Commerce and Natural Resources *Wonderful West Virginia* magazine, the West Virginia Geological and Economic Survey for information, materials, and scientific data about West Virginia. The West Virginia Federation of Women's Clubs for their invaluable support. The West Virginia Jaycees for their statewide support and enthusiasm. Photographers Tom Evans, Arnout Hyde, Jr., Jack Lowe, Ric MacDowell, Jim Osborn and Gerald S. Ratliff for their top-notch work. And the late Ward B. Fletcher, Sr. whose early-1900 photographs bring back a colorful era; and Kate Long for devoted advice and encouragement.

SEAWELL MULTIMEDIA ™ CORP

Parkersburg, W. Va. 26101

*A white-tailed doe cautiously surveys a
Canaan Valley meadow.*

INTRODUCTION

I'm not sure which is more traumatic—the country boy's first trip to the city or the city boy's first trip to the country. But what is originally a shock can become a rewarding experience due to our inherent ability to adapt to different environmental conditions, or to *change* them. Historically, mountaineers have had frequent need to resort to this ability and to make the best of it, often in the face of adversity.

Most of us in America haven't really managed the *time* to find out exactly where we live or exactly what our neighbors are like. We have a tendency to confine ourselves to our incidental surroundings and to limit our social contact to people with tastes and status that are within a range identical to our own.

The makers of this book set aside the time. Even a book cannot convey what a satisfying experience this can be, but we're making a sincere attempt to share as much as we can with you.

Jerry, Strat and the others took the time to listen to scores of contemporary West Virginians—all of whom possess a different, personal point of view of their environment and of who they are as West Virginians. The only common trait we were able to sift out of all of this can be described in one word:

Pride.

Bill Kuykendall drove thousands of country miles into every county in West Virginia, recording not only photographic images, but audio tapes as well. His mission can't be measured fairly in statistics, but it can be measured in journalistic performance. He waited, in every case, until he was confident that he had the story focused in his mind as well as

on film. Though he didn't *write* them, Bill was responsible for the discovery of a large number of tales that ultimately found their way into the book.

Jerry's and Strat's pursuits were executed in much the same manner. Instead of forcing rushed interviews, they *listened* until they were satisfied that the stories had fully surfaced.

Our patient researchers (as well as these two authors) found new inroads to the past—often through the keen wit and wisdom of some of the old-timers who lived a part of it.

In periodic joint editorial meetings, all of us tossed in new ideas for evaluation and development. The net result is a book that virtually wrote itself—and—a formula for other volumes in the APPALACHIA USA series.

Some of the contents are sketched in bold strokes to establish specific backgrounds, but whether or not you're as seriously interested in West Virginia as we are—I think you'll thoroughly enjoy some of the characters you'll meet between these covers.

Harry Seawell

The Great Kanawha River, once the scene of Indian paradise, now mirrors both industrial wealth and the glittering city of Charleston.

Overwhelmed amid change (overleaf), an Indian tribe parades through Clarksburg's ironic surroundings in the early 1900's. Ward Fletcher's camera captures the fearless chief's tolerance of machinery, but not the soul of his defensive squaw.

MOUNTAINS AND MOUNTAINEERS

Rebirth of a wilderness

The American people have had "wilderness in their backgrounds for so long. They are so much a part of it. They need a wilderness resource for their peace of mind, for their ease of conscience. We've got to have some wilderness."

He was quoting a professor he once had, "one of the great ones," and it gave special meaning to the two-day journey we made through a slice of Maurice Brooks' beloved Appalachian mountains.

What better way to understand the importance and the emotions and the wonder of these mountains than to travel with this man? Seventy-five-year-old Maurice Brooks' keen mind and recollections were the extension of a West Virginia family that for more than a century had observed and cared for every living thing to be found from the valleys to the mountain ridges.

It was a clear, bright December morning as we left Terra Alta for Canaan. And Professor Brooks soon began preparing us to view that mountain and that valley through the perspective of three-quarters of a century of drama that included both tragedy and triumph.

"This high country around Canaan had the greatest spruce forest this state has ever seen," he said. "None other like it has ever occurred this far south."

He was beginning to describe a virgin spruce forest of some 100,000 acres, with giant trees that averaged from 150 to 300 years old in a wilderness that had stood untouched for millions of years.

Red spruce is an extremely slow-growing tree, able to grow on the thinnest type of soil, but hardy and able to grow to glorious heights in about 150 years. The trunks are straight and taper very little as they reach skyward, making it possible for lumbermen to cut "five clear logs" from one trunk, each nearly the same diameter.

During the millions of years of spruce growth at Canaan, the forest had grown so dense there was hardly room to walk between the giant trunks.

Earl Hedrick's farm on the North Fork of the Potomac's South Branch is on historic soil cultivated by early German settlers. Seneca Rocks (part of the Spruce Knob-Seneca recreational area) tower in the shadowy background.

Professor Brooks was like a human encyclopedia on Appalachian nature. He picked up a piece of three-toothed cinquefoil, a true Appalachian plant that grows from

Canada to Georgia. Finches survive the winter on its seed. General George Curtin established the logging camp at left in 1902 at the confluence of the Cherry and Gauley rivers. Brooks said that railroads were usually the only connection the logging towns had with a doctor—or anything else—from the outside world. (The town of Curtin is now relocated, on the Cherry, in Webster County.)

The sun's rays were shut out for unmeasured time and falling needles from the spruce had accumulated a "duff" layer that was eight feet or more in depth.

That was the kind of forest primeval that the first lumberman found at Canaan and on Dolly Sods. And in one brief generation from 1885 to 1910, it was brutally clearcut, fires started, and wilderness became wasteland.

The troubles of the spruce forest actually began during the Civil War. Confederate soldiers camped on Cabin Mountain on the east side of Canaan Valley. They "let fire out," as Professor Brooks put it, and thousands of acres were burned on the east side of the valley.

Then in 1884 another large section of the spruce was damaged by an infestation of beetles. Experts estimated that

some 100,000 spruce were killed and that laid the wilderness open to another fire in the deep duff layer.

But the biggest and final blow to the virgin spruce forest came in 1885 when the Western Maryland Railroad laid tracks into Davis and an unprecedented logging boom began.

Consider the awe with which those early loggers must have viewed the great spruce forest. . . with trees so close together they had no place to fall.

From Allegheny Backbone Mountain on the one side to Dolly Sods on Allegheny Front, it was almost a pure, compact stand of giant spruce.

The productivity of this forest was spectacular. At a time when five or ten thousand board feet of hardwood per acre was usual, this spruce forest yielded 80,000 to 100,000 board feet per acre.

It was clearcut. It probably would have been clearcut under any circumstance, but Professor Brooks noted that clearcutting was the only way to harvest spruce.

"They're not strong enough to stand alone. If they had practiced good selection cutting, the others would have blown down in the first strong wind."

Professor Brooks had first seen Canaan Valley in 1912 at the age of twelve. He saw some of the remaining virgin spruce before it was cut. And he saw the timbering operations.

"The E.D. Babcock Lumber Co. mills were still running full blast and I tell you it was an experience to be in one of those mills. It was big business. They would cut 100,000 board feet on an average per day.

"I'll never forget the sign that was over the door of each entrance . . . it made an impression: 'A place for everything and everything in its place.'

A Davis logging crew posed for a group portrait in a Canaan region virgin forest nearly a century before Professor Brooks stood before Bill Kuykendall's camera in a re-growing Canaan woods.

"Those operations were absolutely spotless and they were completely ruthless as far as leaving anything on the soil."

Professor Brooks once heard the chief forest engineer, V.V. Babcock, say that the Davis lumbering operation was the finest job he had ever worked with: "We didn't leave one stick of lumber on it big enough to make a 2 x 4."

"That was his idea of a really fine forestry job," Professor Brooks said.

We had stopped at a roadside pull-off along Route 219 just a few miles into Tucker County. We surveyed the mountains and valleys and gaps below.

"To change the subject for a minute, I want to point out that in the fall of the year, one of the great shows in the Alleghenies is the fall migration of hawks

from about September 15 to September 25.

"Thousands of migrating hawks fly through these mountains and this is one of my favorite spots. They come down this ridge on this side . . . invariably on this side of the ridge, and on a good day when there's a good breeze coming in from the northwest or southwest they'll be flying right at treetop level.

"I've seen groups of hawks of two or three hundred coming through here at this point. And a quarter of a mile away you'll never see one. You might stay over there for ten years and not see a migrating hawk. If you were down there in the valley or over on the next ridge you'd never see one.

"They come through this narrow little pattern here because they've found that the air currents, when the breezes are right, will just buoy them along and you'll never see them jerk a wing. They sail along. They've learned to go south on the wind and they might travel forty miles along these mountains and never beat a wing . . . no energy spent a'tall.

"The red-tailed hawk is a permanent resident of West Virginia, and is much more common in fall migration. Nearly every day's hawk counting at Dolly Sods in fall will record some of these."

"These broadwing hawks are going to Central America and they've got a long way to go. I've literally spent days on this pull-off and usually you can count on three hundred, five hundred, or even a thousand hawks on a good day. Of course, hawk watching is another story. We'll talk more about it on Dolly Sods."

Our Travelall moved lazily on as the beautiful pictures of West Virginia landscape passed by and Professor Brooks painted other pictures not so pretty.

In Canaan 100,000 acres of virgin spruce forest were timbered out, leaving the deep duff layer to dry out, become volatile and produce a fire that burned nine months, threatening the few residents who were left in Davis and completely removing from the rocky earth every living thing.

I asked Professor Brooks to describe the impact the scene must have had on the mind of a young boy, the son of a naturalist:

"Of course, I grew up in a family of scientists. I started as early as I can remember camping and fishing in West Virginia and I got a tremendous liking and respect for this mountain country and undisturbed wilderness.

"The trauma of seeing this territory after it was lumbered and burned out was very great . . . I don't quite know how to describe it."

We were approaching Davis now, and young trees, beginning to look mature, lined both sides of the highway.

"But one of the things that's causing me as much pleasure as almost anything is to see the rebirth of this country here now as the strip mines are restored and as the Western Maryland Railroad (and they're doing most of it in here) replants thousands of acres in forest; the realization that in another twenty or twenty-five years, this mountain that I saw as horrible bare rocks will have another good stand of timber . . . that realization gives me great pleasure!"

We were entering the town of Davis now and Professor Brooks remembered:

"The whole town of Davis would have burned to the ground if the local people hadn't saved it. They dug a six-foot trench around the town and kept it full of water which they carried up from the Blackwater River.

"The fire kept on burning until there was nothing left but bare rock . . . no duff layer, nothing. It was the most God-awful desolation I have ever seen."

He had painted us a terrible scene and the obvious question came blurting out: "Do you mean to say no one in 1912 was the least bit concerned about the environmental impact . . . there was no resistance?"

"No one had ever heard of resisting that sort of thing in those days," Professor Brooks responded. "The word 'conservation' was new to all of us at that time.

"We just became aware of it in 1908 when President Theodore Roosevelt held the famous White House Conference on Conservation. He asked each governor to be represented at that conference.

"My dad was a state delegate then and he went to the conference . . . came back talking about conservation. No one had ever heard of the word before!"

During those few first years when conservation was first considered, West Virginians believed it was not a practice that could be seriously applied to this territory.

"They didn't think it was practical for these mountains because the important job was to get the lumber out. It was the same attitude that the coal strippers had ten or fifteen years ago."

We lunched in Davis and then drove into the Canaan Valley. We stopped at another overlook and the scene was beautiful . . . the forest was back! Not the way it was . . . because there will never be another virgin forest like the one man destroyed . . . but the next best thing, the result of a man-made miracle . . . a project that few believed would work.

Burned-out Canaan began to acquire little lichens and mosses by 1919 and 1920. Soil began to accumulate ever so slightly in the crevices of the rocks and

ferns began to grow. But the real salvation came in 1933 when another President Roosevelt, Franklin Delano, established the Civilian Conservation Corps.

The "CCC boys," as they were called, performed valuable services all over West Virginia, but none more significant than the reforestation project that began in Canaan in 1935. At the height of the Canaan project, there were three CCC camps housing some 500 boys and men.

"Many people thought it was the most foolish waste of money that ever was," Professor Brooks said. They didn't believe reforestation of Canaan's vast wasteland was possible.

But day and night the CCC boys worked. They hauled truck loads of soil up out of the valley. The boys followed the trucks and put two bushels of soil in each crevice where a tree was to be planted. By 1942, when World War II spelled the end of the CCC, 175,000 spruce and red pine trees had been planted on Canaan Mountain.

We looked spellbound from one mountain to the other. There it was. Professor Brooks put it into words:

"Today it's a flourishing forest. It's literally the rebirth of a forest area . . . it's a different forest, but it's back in forest again and it's potentially productive. That's just one of the many incredible benefits to West Virginia brought by the Civilian Conservation Corps!"

We call it wilderness now, and in the modern sense it is. But in the true sense the East has no real wilderness.

"This is not a wilderness a'tall," Professor Brooks said. "It's been cut over . . . burned . . . all kinds of things have happened to it.

"But there's a new definition of wilderness now. It says if left alone and protected, it will grow back into a wild area similar or equivalent to what it already was."

That's the only "wilderness" left after two hundred years in Eastern America . . . not a wilderness preserved, but a wilderness recreated.

We drove through Canaan and up on Dolly Sods. Dolly Sods is a high mountain plateau where the elements are severe. Reforestation hasn't quite managed the same progress there.

Grey-white rocks are still prominent and trees struggle in crevices to survive the cold winter wind, clipped bare on one side by nature's windy pruning shears.

The aftermath of lumbering and fires must have been something like Dolly Sods.

We talked of many things on Dolly

A dirt road winds through replanted spruce toward the summit of Spruce Knob Mountain (highest point in the state). Above, weather-beaten spruce survive the elements on the rocky peaks of Dolly Sods.

Sods—the huckleberries, the spectacular hawk migrations along its southern slopes, the jagged rock cliffs on the distant mountain range and the many mysteries they hold in plant and animal life. We talked of the need for the preservation of just a little of our wilderness heritage, and we talked of the realistic necessity for compromise.

We watched a spectacular fiery sky at sunset, first in the west, then above us, then all around.

Then we descended the other side of the mountain into Petersburg for a night's rest. Tomorrow we would see something even more miraculous — a virgin forest

Next day we stopped in one community and visited at a primitive general store and trading post. After making our way past the inside-out deer hides stretched out on the front porch, I was shown for the first time that romantic mountain root, "sang."

Ginseng was selling for $73 a pound,

but Professor Brooks (after explaining that the real value of "sang" was as an aphrodisiac) pointed out that one piece of root symbolized a man of extreme sexual prowess . . . "that should bring a premium price from some braggart Chinaman!"

I included that root in the mere ounce I bought and later read with interest Professor Brooks' accounts of sang hunting in his book, The Appalachians.

"Sang," he wrote, "holds a very special place in (mountain people's) traditions and their hearts. In an economy that was largely conducted by barter and trade, and in which hard money was a rarity, ginseng could be sold at all times for cash. When taxes had to be paid, a few days of sang digging would raise the necessary funds.

"Added to the economic importance of ginseng was a touch of romance; its roots, properly dried and handled, would be sent to faraway China. (Mountain) people had few ties to foreign lands, but this was an authentic bond between unlike people. What these unseen Chinese did with the roots, once they were transported, was a mystery, but since all things must have an answer, the sang diggers dismissed the matter by saying that Orientals used the plant as a medicine. And, if one stretches a definition, they were right. Medicines are supposed to restore health and happiness in their users, and ginseng must certainly have fulfilled these functions.

"The Chinese held to a doctrine of signatures: if a plant resembled an animal or a portion of one, that plant must be beneficial to the animal or organ."

"Sang" roots resembled man, sometimes in erotic proportions.

"I have often wondered what some of my stern and highly moral sang-digging

ancestors would have done had they known the ultimate use to which their finds were put," Brooks continued. "On careful consideration, I believe they would have gone right on selling sang."

We were heading for "high Cheat" as this story was told and Professor Brooks began to speak of the ruggedness of the mountains and the weather and the people there.

He talked of the heavy snows and strong winds that often beset the ridges of "high Cheat," making winter a "silent season," without the singing of even the hardiest of birds.

Gaudineer Knob, the location of our remnant of virgin spruce forest, was not far ahead now and Professor Brooks pointed to a fairly large house at the fork of the road.

"That's Traveler's Repose. There's a good story about that place. It seems that during the Civil War, mail was carried along the old Staunton-Parkersburg Turnpike from the upper Shenandoah Valley to the Ohio River settlements.

"One winter a new carrier took over the job and facing some pretty tough weather ahead, stopped at Traveler's Repose. Not relishing the idea of pressing on he just stayed there for the winter. Presently, the people in Parkersburg got

impatient for their mail and got word to the carrier through messages to Pittsburgh and Washington. Receiving the messages, the carrier sent a letter to the Postmaster General which still hung on his office wall the last time I was there. Among other things it said, 'If the floodgates of hell were to open, and it were to rain fire and brimstone for six straight weeks, it wouldn't melt all the snow on Cheat Mountain, so if the people in Parkersburg want their damned old mail, let them come and get it!'"

After lunch we headed up on Gaudineer Knob. Soon we would see the only stand of virgin spruce left . . . left for us to view only by a miraculous accident.

The sign read:

"The life and death struggle of a primeval forest can be observed along this trail. Natural forces, unaided by man, are at work within this forest area. Individual trees do not live forever, but the life of a forest goes on and on. What are the chain of events that lead from life to life?"

The chain of events that led to the preservation of this small corner of the original virgin spruce however, made me wonder if the hewer of the sign didn't mean to say "unhampered by man" rather than "unaided."

"In 1859 there was a lumber company in Richmond that bought a piece of timberland on this Shavers Mountain that started near Glady and extended up to about here, seven miles, about 59,000 acres," Professor Brooks said. "And they hired a young surveyor who took about two years to survey the thing. By that time, the Civil War was on so they didn't

Frozen spruce trees glisten in the winter sunshine in the Monongahela National Forest.

do anything with it for awhile.

"One day an old Virginia surveyor, an ex-Army officer, was looking over the surveys and made an interesting discovery. He found that the original surveyor had forgotten about the declination of the compass needle. It was a mistake of about four degrees, not allowing for the error of magnetic north.

"Under an old Virginia doctrine of vacancy, he applied for ownership of that four degree wedge from about Glady to this point. His claim was upheld in court and he owned about 900 acres of virgin timber, part of which was spruce."

That wedge was left uncut and became a "seed forest" for a natural reforestation of thousands of acres of spruce. Some of the trees at the end of the wedge at Gaudineer Knob are about three hundred years old, and I was thinking of the reverse of Dolly Sods. This must have been the way it was *before* the lumbering and before the fire.

The U.S. Forest Service was successful in purchasing about 130 acres of the wedge and today we have one small, but precious chunk of the past, not vast enough to be a forest, not remote enough to be a true wilderness, but just enough to give us the faintest idea of what we have forever lost—our *first* wilderness.

After two days and seventy-five years, we were filled with anticipation as we drove into Gaudineer Knob. After all that sunshine, we now had rain. As we drove through the now-dense forest we saw snow on the ground, surprising leftovers from some days-ago storm, preserved from the sun's rays by the thickening spruce growth much the same as the dampness of that eight-foot duff layer of the virgin wilderness Professor Brooks had seen so many years ago.

We hurried down the path to where the virgin spruce towered . . . saw them with roots gouging into rocky crevices, some close enough together to give us images of the compact spruce forest of the past, some leaning precariously as though the three hundred-year life cycle was about to reach its end. Millions of seedlings here and there were awaiting the chance to take the place of their ancestors; in another part was a huge fallen tower of a spruce decaying and making possible food for future life.

As we stood silently in that virgin stand, we felt as if we were present in a whispering cathedral: sounds from the past—the damp, silent drip of rain on the forest floor, the axes and teams of horses, the bustling mills, the roar of fire, the smolder of smoke, the clunk of a CCC boy's shovel — filtering through our minds—realizing that except for this small remnant and the loving labor of man, we could be witnessing the end.—JA

New timber stands blanket the high country in Fayette County and surrounding mountains. More than half of West Virginia's 21,170 square miles is restored to useable timberland.

The emergence of an uncommon breed

Back in 1776 when General Washington was trying to defeat King George's redcoats and establish our independence from the crown, the soldiers he cherished most were those buckskinned backwoodsmen of western Pennsylvania and West Augusta—Washington's name for what is now known as West Virginia.

At that time, however, not many of these rugged men lived in the "dark, bloody ground" west of the Appalachian crestline. Most of them made their homes in western Pennsylvania and almost all of them were Scotch-Irish who had emigrated from northern Ireland. They were excellent woodsmen, experienced Indian fighters and sure shots.

In addition, and to Washington's satisfaction, they considered themselves to be Americans rather than colonists and, practically to a man, hated the British.

According to Dr. O. Norman Simpkins,

Eight million immigrants, dreaming of freedom and prosperity, were processed through New York's Battery Park between 1855 and 1890. Many were bound for West Virginia's coal fields, oil fields, farms and factories. Charles Ulrich masterfully captured the emotions of these new Americans— particularly their patience—in this painting which he titled, "In the Land of Promise: Castle Garden." The Alfred Koerners (right), a German family in Helvetia, were photographed in 1955, some 85 years after the Randolph Co. community was settled by a group of bewildered Swiss families. J.H. Diss Debar, the State's immigration commissioner had mis-informed the Swiss that this rocky, timberland wilderness would be just like Switzerland.

these mountain men were the first Europeans to settle West Virginia and these hard-working, fun-loving people had plenty of reason to hate the British and to seek the isolation of the Appalachian wilderness.

"These people had been taxed to death back in Ireland," said Simpkins, who heads Marshall University's Sociology and Anthropology Department and is considered to be one of the country's foremost experts on the origins of the Appalachian culture. "A half a million of them left northern Ireland between 1707 and 1776."

Simpkins says these Scotch-Irish were lowland Scots who had been lured to northern Ireland by the British crown with the promise of free land. But after they got to northern Ireland, the British reneged and these proud people who had held off the Romans, the Normans, and for years, the British, were forced to become sharecroppers who quaked at the footstep of the British landlords.

"They came to this country to avoid political persecution," he said. "They were freedom-loving people who had been misled and lied to and who certainly had no reason to love the British."

"When they arrived here," Simpkins said, "they found the Eastern Seaboard was already taken. So they settled the back country, along the Piedmont and in western Pennsylvania, where they acted as a buffer between the Indians and the English. A generation later, their descendants began pushing off in flatboats from Fort Pitt and floated down the Ohio into what we now know as West Virginia."

"There were some German and English settlers too," he said. "And in addition to coming down the Ohio, these early settlers also came into the state from the Eastern Panhandle and the Shenandoah,

A rainbow lights the Mason County sky above Joel Flaxer's farm. Some hundred and thirty miles to the east of Flaxer's, the Germany Valley weather changes on a moment's notice. Originally settled by John Hinkle in 1760, the valley was soon populated by German immigrants attracted to its beauty and rich farmland. The region took its name from the nationality of its inhabitants who continued to observe their Old World customs.

where they portaged across to the New River and then made their way to the Kanawha."

The first settlements usually were located at the mouths of streams such as Point Pleasant where the Kanawha empties into the Ohio. Guyandotte, at the mouth of the Guyandotte River just above Huntington, was an early settlement as at was Fort Lee, now called Charleston.

"These people wanted to be left alone," says Dr. Simpkins, a Scotch-Irishman who was born on a farm in Wayne County. "They didn't want to pay any more taxes. They wanted to be free to live their lives on their land without any interference from a government."

Some historians say the Appalachians were first settled by runaway indentured servants—castoffs who were "the scum of London." Dr. Simpkins literally snorts at the idea.

"That's a lot of hooey. If the scum of London had gotten over here in the mountains fighting Indians, they'd have all been killed off. And besides, most of the early names in the region were of the Scotch-Irish naming pattern rather than the cockney London pattern."

Two well-known Scotch-Irishmen who first explored this region were Daniel Boone and Simon Kenton. What they found was a wild beautiful land of vast forests and giant trees, of abundant game and fish-filled streams.

Mike Snyder, a former advertising agency account executive, entered the blacksmith trade after a host of occupations. His artistic iron work is an expression of himself and his experiences. Before and after each day at the anvil, Mike tends his flock and does other chores on his Randolph County farm.

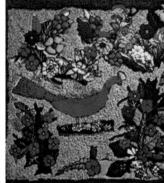

At chore time (above) a Tucker County youth rounds up a stray calf. For more than a century Helvetia families (right, reading from top down) have preserved old country cooking, music, farming techniques, crafts. Traditional Alpine art adorns the Helvetia Crafts Shop door. Ruth Roten (below), a jeweler who teaches and exhibits. Fiddling at an Aunt. Minnie's farm musicians' competition, Stumptown. Hand-hooked rugs once covered floors, now hang on walls (Art and Craft Fair, Cedar Lakes). Wheeling Symphony captivates sell-out crowds at Capitol Music Hall. A young visitor at Coolfont resort near Berkeley Springs. Brian Van Nostrand's distinctive pots are thrown from clay he digs, fired in a kiln he made and heated with wood he cuts from his land in Hacker Valley. Dr. Margaret Ballard (at home in Monroe Co.) is restoring the log cabin seen in the background. The Postmistress at a post office in Monongalia Co. tends her flower boxes. Top right: Auctioneer Morris Whipp practices his trade in Mineral Co. The young lady (below) defies the rain at the State Fair in Lewisburg. A master craftsman of hand split cedar shakes at Cedar Lakes Fair. The stained glass sunburst (at bottom) exhibited at the Art and Craft Fair at Cedar Lakes.

At first, the Indians posed almost as much a problem as did the elements. Kenton once was chased naked in the dead of winter from Fort Lee to Point Pleasant. Lewis Wetzel, another famous early settler, was captured by the Indians when he was a child and spent the rest of his life seeking revenge.

These hardy folk were not easily discouraged, however. Hundreds of them poured into the area after the Revolutionary War. They killed game and fought off the Indians with their long-barreled flintlock rifles, built homes from the logs of giant oaks and poplars and carved out homesteads. They usually marked their claims by slashing trees with their short-handled iron axes, called tomahawks by the Indians, who would eagerly pay several beaver skins for one of these handy instruments.

"Most of the settlers weren't writing-minded and didn't bother to record their claims back in Richmond," observed Simpkins. "So, when the lawyers came in, many of them lost their land. Both Boone and Kenton lost large claims this way."

Dr. Simpkins says the Scotch-Irish were natural forest dwellers and excellent animal raisers.

"They were hard workers but they didn't like sustained labor. They would work hard for awhile and then take some time off to relieve the tension. They loved music and whiskey. They introduced the Irish pot still to this country and made whiskey both for their own consumption and for cash, of which there was very little back then; most people bartered and swapped labor."

More and more settlers arrived during the early years of the Nineteenth Century. After the Civil War, the Eastern industrialists began a serious, systematic

harvest of West Virginia's vast lumber and mineral resources. They brought in the railroads and built them with cheap labor supplied by thousands of workers from such Middle European groups as the Italians, Poles and Czechs.

Blacks were among the early settlers who came to western Virginia. They were instrumental in the salt industry which flourished around 1800 and helped the European pioneers in their battles with the Indians. The main influx of Negroes, however, occurred after the Civil War when they migrated to West Virginia or were brought in as part of the many labor gangs which built the railroads and later began mining the coal.

The second wave of immigrants, which followed the war, was composed largely of urban-oriented people. Towns and cities began forming as the industrial revolution picked up steam and began shaping the West Virginia we know today.

"By now everybody's so intermarried that we're all mixed up," says Simpkins. "Almost anybody can say he's Scotch-Irish or German or English or whatever."

But one thing's for certain: today's West Virginians spring from a proud heritage and from a proud people whose heroic feats and indomitable nature promoted the state motto "MONTANI SEMPER LIBERI."—SD

Highway building in West Virginia, 1913. Black workers found common labor jobs in construction, as well as the logging, oil and gas, and coal industries in the first part of the 20th century. At right, William Roff, the son of a Swedish immigrant and glassworker, followed in his father's footsteps with a 35 year career in glassmaking. He retired from Weston's West Virginia Glass Specialty Co. the day this picture was made.

RIVERS AND RIVER LORE

Water highways to wealth and paradise

The rivers were essentially the first interstate highways. Many of the first settlers came to western Virginia in canoes, the same way the Indians traveled this wild, rugged land for as long as they could remember. The canoes soon were joined by keel boats and flatboats. The advent of the Nineteenth Century brought the steamboat which, in turn, gave way to the gasoline and diesel-driven towboat and steel-hulled barge.

During the days West Virginia was being settled, however, the flatboat was the most feasible form of river travel. By 1760, some 10,000 people lived in western Virginia, many in settlements which sprang up along the mouths of

Barge tows pass on the Ohio at Paden City. Diesel towboats move nearly two hundred million tons of goods and raw materials annually on West Virginia's navigable waterways—the Ohio, Monongahela, Kanawha, Little Kanawha and Big Sandy Rivers. One compact tow boat can push enough weight to sink a lake freighter.

streams. It wasn't uncommon for riverside residents to count seventy flatboats in a single day as they floated downstream laden with livestock and household possessions.

Packet boats began appearing on the Ohio by 1794. A year earlier, the Virginia legislature had passed the first act for clearing and extending the Monongahela and West Fork rivers for passage of canoes and flatboats. Four years later, in January of 1800, the Virginia Assembly declared the Monongahela a public highway.

The flood of settlers increased after the turn of the century, and with it—a growing demand for boats. A shipyard sprang up in Wellsburg during this period and it wasn't long before both Wheeling and Wellsburg became important boat-building centers.

From 1806 until 1850, Wellsburg was one of the largest boat-building ports in America. A number of seagoing schooners were built there during the early days, and later, when the steamboat ruled the river, such famous steamers as the *Arcadia de Kalb* and the *Liverpool* were launched at the Brooke County boatyard.

The first steamer built at Wheeling was the *George Washington* on which

the Ohio's first floating ball was held the evening of May 12, 1816.

Most historians date steamboats from Robert Fulton's experiments in 1807, but not the residents of Shepherdstown. They claim a fellow resident, James Rumsey, had propelled a boat with steam at least twenty years before Fulton.

But regardless of who perfected the idea, steam revolutionized the rivers. It wasn't long before floating palaces were carrying cargo and passengers up and down the Monongahela, Kanawha and the Ohio. The Kanawha, which had provided General Andrew Lewis' troops with a way west in 1774, was crawling with steamers less than a century later. The first steamboat reached Charleston in 1823. By 1850, residents of the area depended almost entirely on the steamers for supplies and transportation.

A short time later, luxurious excursion boats plied the rivers. During the early 1900's people flocked to the riverbanks beckoned by the mellow tunes of the steam calliopes on the showboats. The years passed and trains and autos gradually choked off river travel, but not river trade. Industry depends heavily upon water transportation. The Ohio and

Harman Blennerhassett

Margaret Blennerhassett

Kanawha, between them, carry nearly 100 million tons of freight each year.

The mountain tributaries function in a different, but important, role. Trout fishermen from throughout the East migrate to West Virginia every year. White-water canoeists and raft riders from the States and Canada are addicted to adventure on the frothy-white, fast waters of streams such as the North Fork, the Cheat and the New River.

The New River, itself, is the second oldest river on the planet and a true geological wonder. Anyone who has ever sat beside its boulder-laden waters, listened to the soothing roar and watched the red-tailed hawks soar overhead and the spray rise above the rocks will never forget the experience. No poet—no photographer—no composer—no artist—will ever capture the effect. —SD

Almost heaven

Looking back on the long and varied list of players that paraded across our frontier stage two centuries ago, it's hard to find a more fascinating or tragic figure than Harman Blennerhassett, the aristocratic Irish romantic who scandalized his family by marrying his young niece, and then fled to the furthest reaches of the New World in hope of finding an island of serenity where he and his bride could live happily ever after.

"Ever after," however, was to fall something short of eternity for this pair of unlikely lovers. It was less than eight years before the sunlit idyll had faded and they once again had to flee.

But this was all yet to unfold back in the summer of 1798 when Harman and

Margaret Blennerhassett stepped out of the keelboat from Pittsburgh and onto the dock at Marietta, where the arrival of two such luminous personalities was greatly appreciated by the old French port's relatively large and sophisticated intellectual community. The Blennerhassetts had planned to venture on down the river but were so heartened by their warm reception that they decided to settle in the area.

At the time they arrived in this country, after a seventy-three day Atlantic crossing, Blennerhassett was thirty-one and his bride had just turned nineteen. He was a tall, thin man with weak eyes who cut an impressive figure in his blue broad-cloth coats and silk stockings. His wife, also tall, was an intelligent and beautiful woman with blue eyes, brown hair and a ready smile.

This elegant couple took Marietta by storm. Blennerhassett, though educated as a lawyer and ill-prepared for frontier life, was a brilliant conversationalist and a lavish spender, and Margaret could analyze Shakespeare's plays and discuss French literature.

Blennerhassett had just sold the family estate in Ireland for the princely sum of $165,000. In addition to his fortune, he was traveling with an extensive library, purchased in England before his departure, and with many boxes crammed with scientific equipment and chemicals for his experiments.

The newlyweds were enthusiastic about the primitive beauty they found in the Ohio valley and about their new friends. They were especially eager to

Blennerhassett Island, formerly known locally as Backus, Long, or Belpre Island, was called "Isle de Beau Pre" by Harman Blennerhassett.

38

forget the recent past and the scandal that ensued after their marriage in the spring of 1796. (Blennerhassett was visiting his sister on the Isle of Man, and as a favor to her, traveled across the English Channel to escort his niece home from school. They were married during the journey.)

The Blennerhassetts, who had sat in Parliament for five hundred years, were shocked and outraged. They immediately ostracized the couple, forcing Harman and his bride to turn to America for acceptance and serenity.

Wanting to be free from prying eyes, the couple purchased a one hundred seventy-acre site on the upper end of Backus Island, a long, narrow strip of land in the Ohio River, twelve miles below Marietta and some two miles below the city of Parkersburg, which was then just a scattered assortment of rough hewn log cabins. They paid $4,000 for the land and immediately moved into a block house constructed by soldiers during the Indian wars a few years earlier.

Blennerhasset quickly set about building a mansion with a ten-room central section and circular wings that contained a spacious library and laboratory. Built at the astronomical cost of $40,000, the tall, white house was furnished with imported couches, rich tapestries and gold gilt mirrors. Its large, airy halls were soon ablaze with lights and filled with music as the Blennerhassetts entertained their friends from Marietta and nearby Belpre.

The graceful lines of the foundation of Blennerhassett's mansion reappear, much as they may have looked during the original construction in the late 1700's. The site was unearthed by a West Virginia Geological and Economic Survey team in 1974.

The house also boasted two large porticoes from which the couple could watch their English gardener tend the two-acre flower garden. They whiled away many other hours watching the endless line of keel boats floating down the Ohio toward the ever-expanding frontier.

Ten slaves took care of a one hundred-acre garden, cattle, dairy and large peach orchard, and several servants took care of the Blennerhassetts and their two sons who were born on the island. For a while, things went well. Margaret nursed the children and sewed while Harman delighted his guests with original compositions on the bass viol and cello or with his latest experiment with that new phenomenon, electricity. He favored special friends with relics and trinkets from the ancient Indian burial ground on the island and spent many evenings studying the heavens with a powerful telescope.

Although Blennerhassett was a scholar and an accomplished drawing room conversationalist, he was an inept and impractical businessman who was constantly being bilked by his neighbors.

By 1806, when Aaron Burr came along trying to raise an army supposedly to conquer Mexico and claim a part of the Louisiana Territory which the United States had acquired from France only three years before, Blennerhassett was in a financial bind and was looking for a way to recoup his losses. Burr's grandiose scheme immediately appealed to him, especially the part about potential fortunes and the promise that he would be made ambassador to England.

He poured thousands of dollars into the venture, which called for raising an army of five hundred men and constructing a flotilla of fifteen boats to take them to New Orleans. Burr drilled the men on the island while the boats were being built near Marietta.

President Thomas Jefferson got wind of the plan, however, and ordered authorities along the frontier to stop Burr and Blennerhassett. Burr was in Kentucky recruiting troops at the time and was temporarily out of reach. When Blennerhassett learned of Jefferson's decree, he hurriedly left his island home and headed downriver to join his co-conspirator.

He departed on December 9, 1806, just one day before the Wood County militia, under the command of Colonel

Hugh Phelps, attacked the island and routed the thirty recruits who were awaiting the completion of the boats. Mrs. Blennerhassett and the children boarded a keelboat on the 11th and headed for Kentucky. Although she didn't know it at the time, Margaret would never again set foot in her beloved island home.

The militiamen stayed on the island and set up a makeshift courtroom in the mansion, which they soon wrecked. Most of the damage came after they broke into the wine cellar and staged a two-day drunken brawl.

Blennerhassett, meanwhile, was reunited with his family and they traveled on downriver to the Mississippi Territory. Burr was arrested, escaped and was arrested again. In March of 1807, he was taken to Richmond to stand trial for treason. Blennerhassett was en route back to his island when he learned that he, too, had been indicted for treason. He immediately proceeded to Lexington where he gave himself up and hired attorney Henry Clay to defend him.

Burr assisted in his own defense and was finally acquitted. During the trial, Blennerhassett was held in prison and often used his scientific skills to purify the air in his cell by mixing oxygenized muriatic acid gas. Blennerhassett became enraged during the trial, especially when some of his friends testified that he was a harmless, bumbling sort of fellow who "had every sense but common sense."

The treason charges against Blennerhassett were finally dropped after one of the government prosecutors characterized Burr as a "destroyer" who had gone to Blennerhassett's idyllic island retreat and "changed paradise to hell." Blennerhassett was released on bail and ordered to appear at Chillicothe, Ohio on January 4, 1808 to face misdemeanor

charges. But he was never called to appear. He and Burr parted company upon their release although not before Blennerhassett told the former vice president he expected to be reimbursed for some $50,000 he had invested in Burr's plan.

Blennerhassett then returned to his island where he found his slaves had fled, his property had been confiscated by creditors and his house had been plundered, even to the point where the window casings had been ripped out for the lead weights. Using the rest of his fortune, he took his family to the Mississippi Territory where they ran a cotton plantation until the bottom dropped out of the cotton market a few years later.

By then, Blennerhassett was almost broke. He had recovered only a fraction of the money owed to him by Burr and was plagued by repeated heartbreaking financial failures. Margaret and Harman finally were forced to go live with his relatives in England. They were living in quiet retirement on the Island of Guern-

Margaret Blennerhassett fled to Marietta on the night of December 10, 1806. The Wood County militia was dispatched by President Jefferson to foil Mexican Venture plans made by Aaron Burr (right) and her husband.

sey when, in 1831, Blennerhassett died following a series of strokes.

Margaret returned to New York City in 1840 and, along with sons, Harman Jr. and Joseph Lewis, petitioned Congress for reimbursement of the losses she incurred when the militiamen wrecked her home. The petition described her as living "in a state of absolute want." But she was never to reap the rewards of her petition. Just as it appeared Congress would act on the matter, Margaret became ill and died, on June 16, 1842.

The mansion, meanwhile, had disappeared. The Blennerhassett dream home was burned to the ground in 1842, reportedly in an accidental fire set by trespassers. Nature soon reclaimed the willow-fringed island and today only the buried foundation stones remain of Harman Blennerhassett's hope of finding a happy haven in America. — SD

Yellow death on the John Porter

Everyone is "wearing a clothespin on his nose at Paducah until the *John Porter* and tow passes down there. Old Pap Paxton has had a bale of cotton pushed into each of his ears and his nose plugged. They are scared yet down there."

That, according to the *Louisville Courier,* was how many people felt in December of 1878 about the steamboat *John Porter* after a summer voyage that brought a cargo of yellow fever up the West Virginia shores of the Ohio River, leaving twenty-three crewmen and sixty-six residents of Gallipolis, Ohio, dead.

The river tug carried the name of her owner, Captain John Porter, a life-long riverboat man—a West Virginian who would later earn a happier claim to fame as the "Brick King," literally paving the way for the motorcar era in the United States.

Because John Porter was involved in varied enterprises, he was not aboard as his tug left New Orleans in late July for what was to become "the yellow fever trip."

The disease had struck the Gulf coast city just days before the *John Porter* headed north with thirty-five men and eighteen barges. Two days later the ship fireman became ill; his hands yellowed and swelled. As the boat churned up the Mississippi, several of the crew became victims of the dreaded disease which, at that time, was mysterious and incurable.

The dead were buried at the river's edge as the *John Porter* steamed ahead and the crew kept secret the events on board, fearing people might panic and refuse them port or passage.

By the time the vessel reached the Ohio River, the fever had assumed epidemic proportions and the story leaked out, spreading rapidly upriver to every point where the *John Porter* might dock.

Armed men began to line every wharf along the West Virginia and Ohio shores, preventing any attempt to tie up. Doctors and health inspectors boarded the *John Porter* in several towns, but citizens wanted neither the dead nor the dying brought ashore to contaminate their communities. Now and then she would nose shoreward to ask permission to bury the dead, but each time the privilege was refused. That forced several night dockings along some remote West Virginia shores where the. crew would tie up long enough for a quick burial and services.

By mid-August the *John Porter*, hampered by low water, finally passed by a relieved Gallipolis, Ohio, where residents feared a wreck or some other disaster might send contaminated debris and humans ashore. Then the tug broke a rocker arm and floated back to the wharf at Gallipolis.

A quarantine was thrown up around the boat and tow. Many fled to the hills or barricaded themselves in their houses. Businesses were closed. Pots of tar and sulphur were burned in the streets in the futile belief that the offensive fumes would kill the germs of yellow fever.

Although the rocker arm was repaired quickly, the few remaining crewmen fled with their paychecks and sixty-six towns-people died with the fever before an October frost put an end to the epidemic.

The *John Porter* continued to ply the waters of West Virginia for many years after "the yellow fever trip," but river residents everywhere viewed that tug with unpleasant memories. The *Courier* printed this report the following April:

"Anybody who ever looked at the *John Porter* through a telescope is barred from society out of towns on the Kanawha River."

Captain John Porter is still best remembered in Ohio by a monument in the Gallipolis city park which has a crow-bar-shaped steel rod rising from it. The inscription reads:

"This iron stick is the broken rocker shaft of the Steamer *John Porter* which brought yellow fever from New Orleans to Gallipolis in 1878, causing sixty-six deaths."

But in West Virginia, it's a church bell that remembers Captain John and his role in perfecting vitrified brick which allowed some of the state's cities (Charleston, Wheeling and New Cumberland) to be the first in all America to have paved streets, long before the automobile was conceived.

Porter is credited with establishing the name "Brickyard Bend" for that twelve-mile stretch of Ohio Valley from Newell to New Cumberland in West Virginia's Northern Panhandle.

He gave brick streets to the Mountain State in the 1870's; later paved the streets of Steubenville, Ohio, and Pittsburgh, Pa., as well as many other Eastern cities.

In 1872, the Brickyard Bend area shipped 11,000,000 bricks and as the demand grew, the Porter family began shipping bargeloads of brick down the river to Louisiana.

Although John Porter devoted the rest of his life to the brick business on shore, he never really left his beloved river, maintaining a fleet of tugs and

barges and using the Ohio to transport his product far and wide.

The bell in a church tower in the community of Congo (part of Brickyard Bend) rings out testimony to that fact. The bell is all that's left of the tugboat *John Porter*—the town gave her permission to permanently come ashore. —JA

"I still remember him standing on a box to reach the whistle!"

Rick Neale is a latter-day Tom Sawyer—a Vienna, West Virginia boy who grew up on the river and dreamed of the day he would become a riverboat pilot. But while Mark Twain's book ended before Tom could make the grade, Rick was piloting powerful boats almost

before he could read.

"I guess I was about seven the first time I ever handled a boat," he said. "I remember we came to a bend and I wasn't strong enough to handle the rudder. The boat spun around two or three times."

It wasn't long, however, before Rick could handle the 42-foot diesel well enough that his father, Charles Neale, would let his son take over for long stretches. By the time he was ten, Rick was working as a deckhand for the family tugboat company and by the time he was fifteen, he was the youngest commercial pilot on the river.

Now nineteen and a student at Marshall University, Rick still works as a harbor pilot every chance he gets. In this capacity, he picks up barges from long-hauling riverboats and delivers the barges to destinations, usually industrial plants, along a 40-mile stretch of river on either side of Parkersburg. The barges most likely are loaded with materials such as iron ore, gasoline or coal, and Rick may be towing as many as fifteen in front of his tugboat. The deliveries are made during all hours in all sorts of weather and call for expert handling skill and knowledge of the river, both of which Rick has in abundance.

"Rick is a beautiful pilot," says his friend, marine telephone operator Elizabeth Stiers. "He should be—he was taught by 'Speck' Criss."

Captain Criss, now in his nineties, has been a riverboat pilot for better than seventy years. In addition to teaching

(Clockwise from top left) Rick Neale in pilot house; 1905 letterhead of the New Martinsville-based Eisenbarth-Henderson Floating Theatre, the "largest, the finest, most elaborate"; the steamer Senator Cordill, with a 1924 freight bill for "one carton of dry goods—60 cents plus 10 cents charges"; modern day deck hands working in the rain on the towboat "Western"; the stern wheel packet "J.K. Bedford", which left Marietta with a cargo of apples and wrecked on February 27, 1912, at Bean's Landing, Ohio; looking across the Ohio at the city of Huntington in 1872. A logging raft (center), composed of logs fastened together, is on its way down river. The loggers lived aboard in temporary housing until the rough lumber reached its destination. The old photographs are from the collection of O.O. Brown of Paden City.

Rick the tricks of the trade, he also filled the little boy's ears with tales of steamboats, floods, wild storms and wrecks.

"I still remember him standing on a *box* to reach the whistle!" says Criss with a chuckle. "Rick was just a little fellow but he really knows his stuff now. I believe he could take a boat anywhere."

Rick was a skinny high school freshman when he first began handling the family tugs without supervision. One summer he spent all but two nights on the river.

"I used to do my homework in the pilothouse," he said. "And I still do, for that matter. The river can be really nice at night if it's not foggy or raining. Sometimes I'll listen to the radio from New Orleans and just enjoy being out on the water."

The river is always changing, however, and nobody knows better than Rick just how treacherous the Ohio can be. He still has vivid memories of one blustery April afternoon in 1974.

"It was one of the worst days I've ever seen on the river," he said. "We'd just made a delivery to a dock at Porterfield, Ohio and were coming back up river. The swells were from 10 to 15 feet high and we were just right at the head of Blennerhassett Island when we saw some people in a 12-foot outboard.

"My chief deckhand, Orville McCoy, said something about how nobody should be out on the river in such weather when a swell suddenly capsized the boat."

Rick turned his tug toward the boat and went to the aid of the woman and two men who had all been tossed into the river.

Dianne Jones of Parkersburg remembers her shock when she realized who had rescued her.

"I just couldn't believe that young boy was the pilot," she said. "He had handled the boat so easily and I had always thought of rivermen as being big, strong rough-talking people . . ."

Rick and Orville were given Coast Guard citations for their part in the rescue. But they didn't feel like heroes— they were merely following the unwritten code of the river: you always help someone in trouble.

River life is a family affair with the Neales. Rick's father runs the business and fills in as a pilot; his mother is the company dispatcher and his little sister has worked as a cook on one of the tugs.

Rick has been awarded a college scholarship for outstanding grades, but his heart is still on the river: the squawking radio, throbbing engines and gentle smack of the waves against the boat have gotten into Rick's blood. He can't imagine spending his life anywhere except in the glass pilot house of one of the family's green and yellow tugs.

"I plan to spend my life in the pilot house," he says. "I guess my diploma will make a nice wall decoration."

Meanwhile, Rick is still looking forward to visiting Tom Sawyer's old stomping grounds.

"I've taken barges to Pittsburgh and Cincinnati," he said. "I've also been on the Monongahela, Allegheny, Little and Big Kanawha, Elk and Muskingum Rivers, but I'm still looking forward to the Mississippi."—SD

The end of a long day's work and the beginning of a long night's work—Orville McCoy, Rick Neale's chief deckhand, is silhouetted by the "Jane Neale's" searchlight as he checks mooring lines on a twilight run.

ROCKS AND BONES

West Virginia's birth certificate

When nature gave birth to West Virginia, she endowed it with a wealthy inheritance of underground resources. After nature opened this savings account, she let it draw interest for hundreds of millions of years. Long since, mankind has fallen heir to this estate and will have spent it all in just a few centuries.

This leaves us with two choices:

We can try to outsmart nature.

Or, we can try to understand her better and utilize her gifts more efficiently.

Our story sets the stage for the sciences with the latter choice, and offers a condensed narrative of the state's spectacular geological birth.—Editor

West Virginia's mineral bearing rocks can be traced back to a dark, silent world at the bottom of a prehistoric sea. Though silent, except for the sigh of the wind and an occasional rumbling of volcanos, her origin was not without life and not uneventful. No fish swam in the earliest of these seas. But the *muddy bottom* that would later turn to stone and eventually become the basal part of West Virginia's mountain chains was crawling with creatures—assorted gastropods, later versions of which we call snails; beautifully designed brachipods which bear some resemblance to many of today's shellfish; crinoids, the heads of which greatly resemble flowers and which are often called sea lilies; corals and other colonizing creatures and simple algae and bacteria.

This earliest sea was void of fish and other vertebrate animals. The air above was void of fowl. These would come in a later chapter of evolution, but West Virginia's geologic birth was taking place in that primitive sea bed some 500 to 600 million years ago.

Today, localized areas along the eastern fringe of West Virginia's beautiful Appalachians, from which all younger sediments have eroded, show well-preserved, fossilized remains of these ancient creatures of the sea.

This is West Virginia's birth certificate, graphically inscribed in stone and, for the most part, serving as a secure foundation for the thousands of feet of rock since formed.

The rocks westward from the valley and ridge section, across the mountain plateau and western hills sections, contain fossil evidence of other more recent events. Coal seams outcrop in the hills, but others are deeply buried, as are beds formed from evaporating seas, ages before the development of coal swamps and large amounts of petroleum and natural gas.

Most people think of West Virginia in terms of its surface geography—beautiful, tree-covered hills, meandering streams, scenic snowscapes, waterfalls and rivers. It's hard to envision the state as it was between 200 and 300 million years ago when it was a swampy, pond-studded plain with a tropical climate that nurtured giant seed ferns, horsetails and foot-long cockroaches that roamed blissfully among these and the 100-foot tall forerunners of our present lycopodiums or ground pine.

Hard to imagine, yes, but true nevertheless. The evidence is readily available if, like Bill Gillespie or Wiley Rogers, you know where to look.

Gillespie is the State Assistant Agriculture Commissioner and he has been the paleobotanist, a person who studies fossil plants, at West Virginia University since 1957. Most weekends find him somewhere around the state poking into the shales uncovered by strip mining or into the exposed hillsides along one of West Virginia's highways.

He searches for fossil plants imprisoned in the rock. Through these pages of the past, he can recreate the days when gigantic cockroaches ruled the insect kingdom, when tremendous dragon flies glided through the moist atmosphere and when small amphibians plodded slowly from pond to pond.

First came the plants, however, and West Virginia, with the nation's most complete section of exposed Pennsylvanian Age rocks dating back about 300 million years, is a virtual fossil treasure house.

The United States Geological Survey is now measuring and mapping the rocks minutely as a basis for establishing a type section against which all others can be equated and evaluated. Gillespie is doing the fossil plant work for the project and he reports that finds are numerous, interesting and varied enough scientifically to serve as the basis for identifying the various zones.

"In many places," says Gillespie, "these ancient rock formations are stacked like pancakes. It's like having a vertical view of a chapter in evolution. One mountain, for example, has forty-three coal seams and fossil plants occur in association with at least half of them."

During the Pennsylvanian Period, what is now West Virginia was a low-lying delta on a super continent near the equator. It abounded with lush, tropical foilage. By the end of the period, the super continent had begun to pull apart and North America slowly moved to its present position. During this time, the peat swamps were being converted into beds of bituminous coal and amphibians were the largest vertebrates on the land. The fossilized remains of these ancient, lizard-like creatures can be found in nearly all museums. One, on display at Marshall University, was unearthed at Sandstone, near Hinton, and Rogers says it is one

Plant fossils (clockwise from the top left): trunk of a tree common during the Coal Age; spore extracted from Pittsburgh coal; portion of a Coal Age seed fern; ancestor of present day Red Oak; leaf of a Coal Age seed fern; pollen grain found in a pre-historic clay deposit; spore entrapped in Freeport Coal.

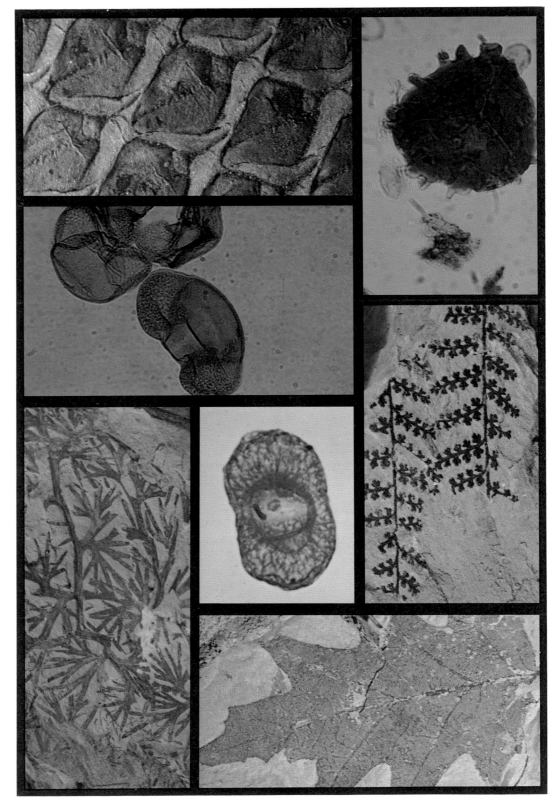

of the earliest amphibian remains ever discovered in West Virginia.

A couple of massive mastodon jawbones—with teeth as large as teacups—can also be seen at Marshall. These stem from the Pleistocene or recent ages, time extending up to 8-10,000 years ago, but Dr. Rogers, who teaches geology at the University, says such finds are relatively rare in West Virginia.

"There are few fossilized vertebrates in the state," he added. "Unlike the plants, most of the higher forms were eaten when they died or their bodies decayed."

But although there are few rocks younger than Pennsylvanian in West Virginia, the record from western states indicates clearly that the amphibians were followed by the lumbering but terrible lizards called dinosaurs, then birds, snakes, early mammals and finally the mammoth mastodon and the ground sloth.

When the first white explorers arrived a few centuries ago, these early inhabitants had given way to the buffalo, timber wolf and panther which man has now removed from the area.

If there's a shortage of vertebrate

North central and eastern West Virginia photographed in infrared from LANDSAT. Coal, oil and gas-producing regions appear to left of the Appalachian mountain limestone region. Cheat and Monongahela rivers (dark blues) appear in upper left, with I-79 (light grey) running southward to Braxton Co. Rt. 19 continues to Nicholas Co. (lower left). From Elkins (center-light grey) the Tygart Valley (pale red) runs southward. The Potomac's North Branch runs from upper center to upper right. Hampshire Co. is in the top right corner. Clouds appear as white specks.

fossils, however, there's certainly no dearth of fossilized plants. Gillespie and other paleobotanists can easily trace the development of the early vegetation. And in so doing, they can also determine many of the mechanisms behind the formation of West Virginia's vast mineral deposits—limestone, sandstone, oil, natural gas, salt and coal.

Coal, however, lends itself more easily to such examinations and it is with coal and the associated rocks that Gillespie works most.

The best fossil leaves are those trapped in the first wave of sediments which became the shales just over the coal beds.

He says that geologists often have to rely on fossil plants as guides to rock age and sequence in the Appalachian coal measures. The plants have changed through time and studies show that these changes are all that is needed to zone the rocks into rather narrowly defined vertical units. He also says that the spores and pollen from these ancient plants are entrapped in the coal seams and associated shales and that they can often be used to identify specific beds. As many as 5000 spores are routinely recovered from each gram of coal.

The luxurient tropical forests of the Pennsylvanian Age contributed untold tons of plant debris to the swampy areas as the gigantic fifteen-foot seed ferns and hundred-foot high lycopods died and toppled into the stagnant water of the surrounding swamps, where they were gradually changed into peat.

During the final stages of peat formation, erosion slowly piled tons of sediment over the ripe peat. As the weight above it increased, the peat became even more compacted and was slowly transformed into lignite or brown coal. Later, after more weight and ensuing

heat and pressure, the lignite was transformed into bituminous coal.

Then, as millions of years passed, the low-lying delta was elevated upward above sea level by the movement of the earth's crust. Gigantic mountains were thrust up in the eastern portion twelve thousand and more feet in height. These have been worn away through the ages and their drainage streams have cut down into the low-lying, coal-bearing sediments. The net result is the beloved West Virginia hills with their hidden fortunes.
—SD

$20,000 for a pile of dirt

Who made these great earthen mounds? What people made these great earth circles, and why?

That was the question a young army officer at Fort Randolph (now Point Pleasant) asked the great Chief Cornstalk just before his death.

Cornstalk replied, "There has been a legend among my people they were built by some great white race who lived here before."

According to the legend, the great white race had built the huge earth mounds, greatest monuments in the East, from plans in a book that had eventually been lost when the white men disappeared.

Archeologists in West Virginia have long since discovered that the mound builders were of the same Mongoloid stock as Cornstalk and his people. The great burial mounds were a spectacular page of Indian history, and the Indians were unaware of it.

There is, therefore, a poetic justice in the fact that the very earth the Indians once cherished and worshipped now provides the clues necessary to reconstruct the history, the heritage and the facts that the Indians themselves had failed to record.

"Digs" in West Virginia by professional archeologists have been going on for three-quarters of a century, but it has been only in the past dozen or so years that the state has supported extensive research.

Dan Fowler, head of the archeological section of the West Virginia Geological Survey, describes the work as one of solving an exciting puzzle.

"When we unearth an arrowhead, a skull or some other artifacts, it's like a clue leaping from the past to tell us about the people who roamed this land before us, people who called it home, who suffered here, loved here, lived here.

"We know so little about these people. We don't even know their names. We don't know what they called themselves. We're not even certain of their language. We don't know their religions. We can only speculate what their beliefs were, their practices, their games, their daily activities and methods of living.

"We do believe they were as human as we are, and through the discoveries of archeologists, we are beginning to appreciate a people that were in many ways like us. They were West Virginians, mountaineers who cherished the same pride of living here. They loved to see the spring blooms and to visit the great waterfalls. They were attracted to these mountains for many of the same reasons we are today."

Scientists believe Indians were in West Virginia as far back as 13,000 years ago. Many "fluted spear points," indicative of these ancient Indians, have been found throughout the state.

Some of the oldest sites were found along the ancient New River and Kanawha River with one site at St. Albans, excavated to a depth of 19 feet, which revealed Indian culture of 9,000 years ago.

Petroglyphs (primitive art carvings in rock) reveal some of what must have occupied the minds of West Virginia Indians for centuries.

The wealth of information being discovered by archeologists not only dispels Cornstalk's legend of a super white race, but also puts to rest a white misconception about West Virginia — that these mountains were never really "home" to the red man.

"We call it the great hunting ground myth," Fowler said. Since early white settlers saw no evidence or remains of permanent Indian villages in West Virginia, they assumed the occasional "savage" encountered here was simply using the state as a traditional hunting ground. There were a few recorded instances of settlers discovering evidence that tended to refute the "hunting ground" theory, but Indian villages did seem to be nonexistent.

Archeologists, however, have concluded that the coming of the "corn revolution" among Indian tribes allowed greater concentration of Indians for longer periods in one place. That gave way to the strengthening of tribes and wars began to occur.

West Virginia, according to well-documented research, became the territorial conquest of the great "Five Nations," the League of Iroquois, and in the years prior to the settlement of West Virginia by white man, most Indians had been driven out of the area and feared to return.

But the remains of great Indian villages in West Virginia are so evident today that many can be seen from the air in the form of lush green patches, the result of many years of solid waste disposal at the outer edge of some Indian village or other.

And at some sites, Fowler recalls walking on soil that would literally "crunch beneath your feet," the result of an accumulation of bones and seeds, nuts and pottery, stone tools and hundreds of other discarded artifacts that may have collected for many years before the land finally gave out, causing an Indian village to move on to new territory.

The most spectacular remains of Indian culture in West Virginia are the great Indian burial mounds, sophisticated earthworks that reached 50 feet or more in height and several hundred feet in diameter.

Most well-known of these is the Grave Creek Mound at Moundsville in the Northern Panhandle.

The first reliable measurement of the Grave Creek Mound was 69 feet high by 295 feet in diameter at the base. It was a burial mound that included several other structures such as a moat, dug completely around the mound, and a causeway connecting the mound with the outer area.

George S. McFadden purchased the mound property in 1874 and later considered it a "white elephant" because he was paying taxes on unusable land.

McFadden considered leveling the mound to "improve" the property, and told the historical society of his plans. The society appealed to teachers and pupils in 1891 to help raise money to save the mound, but only $431.88 was raised.

For some unknown reason, however, McFadden did not destroy the mound, and in 1908, State Superintendent of Schools Thomas C. Miller, declared Nov. 5 as "Mound Day" and pupils solicited $1,400 to save the mound. The asking

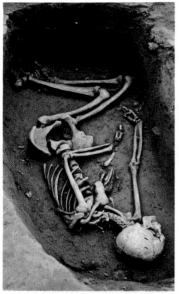

price, however, was $20,000 and Governor M. O. Dawson was successful in getting the state legislature to appropriate $18,600 to the cause.

The Grave Creek Mound was under the supervision of the warden of the nearby state penitentiary until 1967 when it was transferred to the Department of Natural Resources. Efforts continue to develop the mound into a major tourist attraction.

Moundsville is a good illustration of another fact about West Virginia archeology . . . a great deal of the state's past civilization lies beneath our own. The Grave Creek Mound was threatened by the new civilization around it. Other pages of the past lie buried beneath buildings in many of our larger communities.

"A good place to live for the Indians is also a good place for us to live," Fowler said. "A good place to live is sheltered, level, with a water supply and other natural resources that make life pleasant."

Early settlers often chose the very clearings that had been hewn and burned out by the Indians—"old fields" they called them.

The Indians, the settlers, and present day mountaineers found all that in West Virginia. And that's no legend.—JA

Excavations at Buffalo Indian Village (Late Prehistoric) and the Fort Ancient Indian site on Blennerhassett Island provided the State with invaluable artifacts (from top left): flexed Indian burial; excavation trench with post molds showing Indian stockade; burials; 1974 Blennerhassett Island survey; skeletons in common grave; 19th century print of Grave Creek Mound; petroglyphs found near Jane Lew; clovis points from the Parkersburg area.

PIONEERIN' PREACHIN' AND POLITICKIN'

Life on the frontier reaffirmed their suspicions of government and sorely tested their faith.

The people who pushed their way into the rugged wilderness of western Virginia brought with them a simple, Calvinistic faith and a strong hatred of government—two traits that were to shape the state's history from the very beginning.

Many of these early folks were Scotch-Irish and their distrust of government stemmed from centuries of persecution and exorbitant taxation under the British. Their Calvinistic leanings essentially came from their Presbyterian background.

Life on the frontier reaffirmed their suspicions of government and sorely tested their faith. Not only did danger lurk around every bend but so did temptation.

During these early days, the community of Berkeley Springs in the Eastern Panhandle was known as "Sin City" and the roughhewn log taverns scattered along the Midland Trail were the talk of the territory. A motley assortment of travelers assembled at these taverns each evening and the whiskey always flowed freely. Gambling and fighting were frequent pastimes. Many pioneer men took pleasure where they found it and more than one traveler had his journey cut short by the razor-sharp blade of a hunting knife.

Organized religion was non-existent west of the mountains until the early days of the nineteenth century. Many communities then began erecting meeting houses for worship. The services were usually nondenominational with the sermons delivered by laymen.

Political activity was disorganized and usually confined to local issues during the early days. Only qualified male landowners could vote and most pioneer men were too busy defending their families against Indians and filling the family larder to do more than hurl a few curses in the direction of Richmond every now and then.

But time brought change. As the Indians were driven out, homesteads were secured and the settlements became towns. People began to take a greater interest in their state government.

What they found so disturbed them that in 1828, a full thirty-five years before the final formalities of statehood, the residents of central and western Virginia voted to call a constitutional convention. Most of the people in western Virginia wanted more representation and more control over their local governments. Some were even beginning to talk about creating a new state west of the Alleghenies.

Meanwhile, a wave of evangelical preachers, mostly Baptists and Methodists, began combing the hills and hollows for converts. They converted thousands and thus sowed the seeds that grew into the state's present-day religious patterns.

It was during this period in 1840 that Alexander Campbell, the titular head of the Christian Church, founded Bethany College near Wheeling. One of Campbell's followers, William Dyke Garrett, typified the hundreds of heroic circuit-riding ministers of that period.

After his conversion and baptism, "Uncle Dyke" Garrett spent the next seventy years traveling over the mountains of southern West Virginia bringing comfort and hope into saddened homes, burying the dead, performing marriages and preaching sermons wherever a group would assemble to listen.

He rode through the rugged country day and night in all weather and even-

tually earned the title of "Shepherd of the Hills." Possibly his best-known convert was Anderson "Devil Anse" Hatfield, the infamous feud chieftain. Uncle Dyke baptized Hatfield in Main Island Creek in 1910 and was instrumental in bringing love and peace to the people of the hills. —SD

Sauerkraut and pickle beans

The Reverend W. C. Dunson has been a circuit-riding preacher in West Virginia for fifty years. He could tell some interesting stories himself but . . . ,

"I used to enjoy listening to some of those older ministers when I was young, ya know."

The first year, he preached with two other ministers in a revival at Auburn, in Ritchie County. The three ministers stayed with the good people of that community during the lengthy revival and became acquainted with a retired Methodist preacher in the town, Reverend A. L. Ireland.

"He had the greatest array of stories of his ministry of anybody I ever listened to," Dunson recalled.

One story the old preacher told was of a similar revival meeting in Flatwoods, in Braxton County, where three ministers of different faiths were sharing the religious duties.

Everything was going fine at the Flatwoods meetings except for one "fly in

A restored pioneer home that once withstood the threat of famine, Indian attack, outlaws and disease now rests in the secure surroundings of Twin Falls State Park in Wyoming County.

the ointment." A young couple kept courting heavily in the back of the church.

"They sat back there, and they'd hug each other. They'd steal a kiss now and then. In fact, they were attracting more attention than the service."

The three ministers didn't know quite how to deal with the situation and one day the Baptist preacher said, "Ireland, I delegate you to rebuke that couple tonight if they continue the way they've been going."

The Methodist preacher said, "Yes, Ireland's the man oughta do that." So, Ireland agreed. But he made his fellow preachers promise to follow up his every statement with "Amen."

The next night the meeting was going well, but "if anything, that couple did get a little bit more loving than usual."

The Baptist preacher finished the sermon and nodded to Ireland to say a few words.

Just as Ireland took the platform the couple was in an embrace. He fixed his eyes on the couple and that caused all the people in the audience to look the same way. "And just about the time they came out of their trance everybody was gazing at them."

Ireland began his monologue:

"Ta-a-a-lk abou-u-u-t su-u-u-gar and ca-a-ane molasses," he said, "But th-a-at's the swe-e-etest thing," (with a drawn-out nasal twang) "that's the sweetest thing I ever saw in my life. It's a good thing it's wintertime and not summer or that'd melt and run all over the floor and people'd get their feet in it.

"Young couple, you don't know it, but you have a bad case. There's only two remedies I know of. One's to go over to Oakland, Maryland, or some other place where a couple can get married real quick.

"And if that's impossible, then lay in a good store of sauerkraut and pickle beans and eat plenty of that so that you can get some of this sweet stuff out of your system."

He went on and then looked around at the other preachers to find them doubled with laughter and unable to utter the promised "Amens."

Now, in Flatwoods in those days, the mail usually arrived at about 11 a.m. and it was the custom of many townspeople to gather at the post office to exchange information.

The next day everyone was at the post office when the loving couple came, separately, to pick up their mail. Each had several small packages delivered to them. When they opened them up, they were each one filled with sauerkraut and pickle beans!

That's the kind of fun and community camaraderie one found in the country church of yesteryear when the itinerant West Virginia preacher often spent as much time getting there as he did tending to the needs of his flocks.

The circuit-riding preacher usually made appointments at each of his churches.

Reverend Dunson's first charge was at Troy in Gilmer County. In 1926, that circuit was made up of eight churches, six in Gilmer, one in Ritchie and one in Lewis County.

"At the time I went out there they were in the process of grading some highways through the county. There was only a half-mile of paved road in Gilmer.

"And every direction I went out from Troy, they had graded that new road, but hadn't put on a hard top or anything. Well, you know, in that Gilmer County mud—there was just no bottom to it."

Reverend Dunson rode the circuit horseback and preached sermons at two churches each Sunday. That meant each church "got preaching" once each month which was a great deal more often than in an even earlier day when a circuit-riding preacher might not be seen for six months or more.

In those times, the preacher's arrival was quite an occasion with dozens of young couples quite anxious for wedding ceremonies, church elders in a big hurry for a good revival meeting to rekindle backsliding souls, and mourning families thankful that the preacher had finally come to hold proper services for those who had "passed on."

Many West Virginians still know of the "Sarvice Berry Bush" which got its name from the fact that it blooms in the spring when the itinerant preacher might finally reach one of his snowbound flocks to hold all sorts of religious "sarvices."

The arrival of the preacher on horseback was a big occasion in rural West Virginia even in Reverend Dunson's day. He recalls the country church as the social center where young men met and courted young girls and where saint and sinner alike gathered since "old-time religion" was just about the only entertainment all year.

Dunson remembers his long-ago church audiences as great opportunities to preach not only to the "pillars of the church," but also to the sinners who may have attended for social reasons.

"My second charge was at Alton in Upshur County," he said. "I just got there in the beginning of the Depression. I couldn't even afford a horse; I walked the circuit. I had four churches."

One was twelve miles from his home church. He would walk on a Sunday to one church four miles away, preach, walk eight miles in the afternoon to the

next church, preach, and then walk the twelve miles back home the next morning.

Preacher Dunson eventually got an automobile to do his circuit-riding. "And from that time on I never spent a night away from my family."

Though retired for many years, he still "rides circuit" to fill in for a Preston County charge that includes three churches and many special services.

With all those sacrifices, the circuit-riding preacher has received his rewards.

"I just came to the conclusion that if I got any peace out of life, if I found any meaning in life, I was going to have to do what the Lord called me to do. I thought I would have to make sacrifices. But the Lord works those things out. When you give up something for Him, you gain much more than you give."—JA

The country lawyer makes his point.

Henry Gassaway Davis was a lively old Scotsman who had started railroading in Europe. He came to this country and got in on the ground floor of railroading as a close personal friend of Andrew Carnegie.

After investing in western Maryland and eastern West Virginia coal land, he helped build the Western Railroad into Elkins, West Virginia and later built for himself a magnificant mansion in that community.

He became a wealthy man, was Postmaster General of the United States at one time, and in 1904, he was the Democratic candidate for Vice-President of the United States.

Davis had a daughter, Hallie, who married Stephen B. Elkins, a wealthy man in his own right. Elkins was a Coloradan by birth and came to West Virginia when the coal business began to expand.

Henry G. Davis proposed that a companion home be built for the newlyweds next to his own Elkins mansion and bought fifty acres of wooded land near the edge of the town which now forms the nucleus for Davis and Elkins College.

Elkins became interested in politics, like his father-in-law, and was elected to the United States Senate on the Republican ticket. He had served one term in the Senate and was due for re-election at a time when the state still elected its United States Senators by vote of the State Senate, not by popular ballot.

When it came time for his re-nomination, the President of the State Senate, a Republican, made his speech with oratorical flourish:

"Senator Elkins *loves* West Virginia. He lo-o-o-ves its people. He lo-o-o-ves its rivers and forests. He lo-o-o-ves its land. And I, therefore, am proud to make this nomination for his re-election to the United States Senate to represent the great state of West Virginia."

The minority leader in the Senate was W. E. R. Burns from over in Braxton County, a shrewd country lawyer. He took the floor and said, "Mr. President, I want to congratulate you on your eloquence. And I am happy to tell you I concur with your every word. Senator Elkins *does* love West Virginia. He lo-o-o-ves its forests. He *owns* its forests. He lo-o-o-ves its railroads. He *owns* its railroads. He

lo-o-o-ves its coal mines. He *owns* its coal mines. And, Mr. President, he loves you!"—JA

Women who endured and conquered

There wasn't a job or task an early pioneer woman couldn't or wouldn't handle. Far from being "stuck" before a roaring fire cooking meals and mending clothes, she was just as likely blazing trails into unexplored wildernesses and plowing earth for newly-settled farms.

Besides the hardship of backbreaking manual labor, many frontier women had to face the terror of Indian attack on their families. Others watched their husbands and children brutally slain and scalped or captured. Some were carried off themselves and subjected to torture and years of imprisonment in an alien culture in strange lands.

One of the first families to settle permanently in western Virginia was the William Morris family in the Great Kanawha Valley, near the mouth of Kelly's Creek about twenty miles above the future Clendenin settlement that grew into the present city of Charleston.

In those pre-settlement days, lone cabins were easy prey for roving bands of Indians, but one Indian who ventured into the Morris cabin one day was met with an unexpected attack with an unlikely weapon. As the redskin advanced into her kitchen, Mrs. Morris grabbed a heavy iron skillet and beat him over the head until she had driven him out the door and slammed it behind him. Enraged, the Indian raised his rifle and took aim at the cabin door but the leader of his marauding band ordered him not to

shoot this brave and worthy woman.

However, most tales of Indian noblesse have been obscured by grimmer stories of suffering and death passed on by surviving witnesses.

Nearly twenty years before the Morris family settled on the bank of the Kanawha, Mrs. Mary Ingles and her sister-in-law, Mrs. Betty Draper, were traversing land never before seen by the white man. Not only were they the first persons of their race to see the Great Kanawha, but they were the first white women to see any part of the present states of Ohio, Kentucky and Indiana.

In the summer of 1775, a group of Shawnees attacked the settlement of Draper's Meadows where the two women and their families lived. Mrs. Draper was some distance from her house when she saw the Indians approaching. She ran to the cabin, grabbed her baby and made a mad dash to escape out the back door. As a shot from an attacker's rifle shattered her right arm, she dropped the baby; picking up the child with her other hand, she started running again. But she was overtaken and witnessed her infant's brutal murder as its head was smashed against a log. Terrorized, she and Mrs. Ingles with her children were taken captive.

To avoid delay, Mrs. Draper with her shattered arm and Mrs. Ingles in an advanced stage of pregnancy, were allowed to ride.

Their route took them down the New River, then through Mercer, Raleigh and Fayette Counties to the Kanawha River, through the Kanawha Valley to the great "Buffalo Licks," a short distance from the present day boundary of Charleston. Here they stopped briefly to help make salt at a site eventually destined to become the greatest salt-making center in the world and where Mrs. Ingles' great grandson, Dr. John P. Hale, would be-come the greatest individual salt tycoon in the entire region.

On the night of the third day of their hazardous journey, Mrs. Ingles gave birth to a daughter without any medical assistance and with only the ground for a bed. But next morning she mounted her horse, baby in arm, and kept her place in the captive march; had she failed to keep pace—death would most certainly have come.

The captives were separated and sent to different settlements. Mrs. Ingles was sent to Boone County, Kentucky where she immediately planned an escape with a companion—a Dutch woman from Pennsylvania.

Leaving her baby behind—knowing it faced certain death, but also knowing success would be impossible carrying the child—she chose escape. Keeping the Ohio River in view, they made their way homeward. Eating roots and grass, sleeping in hollow logs, under cliffs or in the open woods—they traveled nearly five hundred miles on feet that were badly bruised, bound in torn pieces of cloth from their dresses and held on by strips of leatherwood bark.

By the time they reached the Kanawha River their bodies were drained, but they continued on to the mouth of the Coal River. Upon reaching Paint Creek, they decided, for some unknown reason, against taking the more direct route back to Draper's Meadows and chose the hazardous New River Gorge.

The gorge severely taxed the waning strength of these women, but even more alarming to Mrs. Ingles, her traveling companion's nerves were becoming more and more taut. At what is now the Virginia—West Virginia line, the Dutch woman decided cannabalism was the only answer to survival. The two women, dazed and numb with shock and over-exposure, entered into deadly combat until Mrs. Ingles broke loose and bolted to freedom continuing her journey alone.

It was late November when she collapsed near the home of Adam Harmon just fifteen miles from her former home.

Six years later, Betty Draper was ransomed from her Indian captor and came home to live with her husband and family.

Mrs. Ingles was blessed with many more children and lived on to her eighty-fourth year.

But other early pioneer women met with more tragic fates.

For every woman like Jenny Wiley of Walker's Creek who survived the nightmare of capture and endured slavish labor to escape the Shawnee and return to her husband, there was a widowed husband and father who would never again see his wife and never know her destiny.

For every Mary Kinnan, of Tygarts Valley, who saw her children and husband massacred and was tortured with the constant reminder of her baby's scalp, there was an early woman pioneer who perished with her family.

For every tale of misery and suffering, torture and death inflicted upon the early settlers, there was an incident of humane and noble treatment by Indian captors. Margaret Handley Paulee Erskine of Greenbrier County was captured by the Shawnee, but the Chief, White Bark, adopted her as a member of his family and she was accorded all due respect. In all four years of her captivity, Mrs. Paulee said she was never molested by an Indian man—chastity being a dominating quality in the Indian male.

In the repeated retellings of stories, some early pioneering women grew to legendary stature. Peggy Higginbotham, who lived in the late 1700's to the middle of the 1800's was such a person. She was the daughter of Moses "Mosey" Higginbotham, an early settler in what is now Monroe County. Peggy was said to be "a woman over six feet tall who could outride and outrun any man in the settlement."

Mosey used to keep a pet panther chained near his barn. He could only be approached by Mosey or Peggy and he was not very friendly at that. One day he turned on his master and received a wound from the man's hunting knife. "Old Mis-Step," as the panther was called, escaped the stockade but continually stalked the paths of Mosey and Peggy.

Peggy narrowly escaped death one night while walking her small dog, who sensed the nearness of the big cat and slunk close to her. She accidently stepped on his foot and the dog let out a cry which frightened "Old Mis-Step" away. Peggy repeatedly trod on her dog's foot all the way back to the settlement to ward off the panther.

On another occasion, "Old Mis-Step" had Peggy cornered at a creek bank. She had only a pine branch to defend herself, but thrashed away with her fragile weapon until she beat the animal into the creek and drowned it.

Whether doing battle with panthers or Indians, pioneering women were continually challenged and proved themselves strong, courageous and clever. Certainly many feats have gone unrecorded and names have been forgotten, but the traits of endurance, pride, and adaptability exhibited by these women were passed on to their children.

These women found their days and their lives full—dangerous, exhausting, yet certainly satisfying, as they pulled

together with their fellow pioneers toward the dream of settling this rugged, wild territory.

Years later, in a different century, another West Virginia woman was pioneering a new territory—2,000 feet above the ground.

Pearl White, raised in the hills of Ritchie County, was a pioneer in the field of aviation and the first woman parachute jumper in this country.

Now residing in Parkersburg and acting as the district Civil Air Patrol Commander, she can tell dozens of stories of her daring flying days.

"I wasn't quite sixteen years old. I was going to school in Washington D.C. I saw an ad in the paper—learn to fly for $45—so I decided that was a good deal. I went out to the airport and signed up to learn to fly . . . forgot all about business college.

"With a lot of luck and a lot of extra rides, I soloed in two and a half hours which of course is a record. I learned to fly the C-2 Aeronca: twenty horsepower, top speed, 55 miles an hour. We didn't have tailwheels on them then so you had to get out and pick up the tail and turn it around. It was held together with what you might call bailing wire."

The plane Pearl learned to fly in was nicknamed "The Flying Bathtub" and with good reason.

"It was built down on the ground, had a big stomach and built sort of like a bathtub. It was a very light plane— there wasn't much to be heavy about. We didn't have all the instruments that

In the early 1930's, the OX-5 engine was Pearl White's favorite. The Challenger (pictured) qualified her for membership in the OX-5 Aviation Pioneers Club.

Pearl greeted enthusiastic spectators at Beacon Airport, Alexandria, Va. after her first parachute jump. She had planned to fly in the Air Show that day, but instead she strapped herself into two parachutes and floated to a gentle landing.

they have today—radio gear and what have you. We didn't have *any* radio gear —period.

"You just came in, took a look at the wind sock, saw which way the wind was blowing and saw if there was anyone in the pattern. If there wasn't you came in . . . nobody guided you in. In those days you flew by what they call 'the seat of your pants.'"

Those were exciting daredevil times and spunky men and women like Pearl were taking the country by storm. In fact, "barnstormers" was the nickname given to these hair-raising stunt pilots who performed from one end of the country to the other.

Pearl was making quite a living and quite a name for herself jumping and flying in air shows. She was at the height of her career the day she ran into another American legend and fellow aviatrix, Amelia Earhart.

"I met Amelia Earhart in New York. She kind of took me down a little bit though. On that particular day I was stunt flying—I was performing and when I came down, I was kind of a smart aleck.

I was very young and all—the publicity had gone to my head. I had a swelled head and we had heard about her, so I said, 'Well, what'd you think about my flying?' And she said 'Well, if you live long enough, you might make a good pilot!'

"It was like stickin' a pin in a balloon. It was the best thing that ever happened to me because I never forgot it and it helped me out a lot in settling down."

Pearl came back to her home state to perform at the Pennsboro Fair in Ritchie County in the early '30's and in 1935 she made a parachute jump at the Ohio River Festival in Ravenswood.

That was an extremely foolhardy jump because the year before, Pearl White had made a similar jump at Galax, Virginia—her 27th jump—and woke up a week later in a hospital with her back broken. She spent three months in the hospital and six months in a cast but there she was a year later, risking her life again.

Indomitable, spirited, brave—the list goes on as does the roll call of names— women who came to this land, settled

it, fought for it, died here—but passed on their spirit and ways to those daughters they had borne here. Pearl White, a daughter of these West Virginia hills, carries on this spirit and passes on the legacy to those daughters growing up today.—MS

"... because there's no place I'd rather live."

Two hundred years have passed since West Virginia was settled by European immigrants so starved for freedom and land that they were willing to brave an uncharted world where danger and uncertainty lurked around every bend.

These early settlers endured many hardships but they held on to their dreams. Their progress was slow; they had to battle fierce Indian tribes, overcome disease and learn to live in a new environment. But they persevered. And in so doing, they changed their lives and created a new nation.

Today a new wave of pioneers is sweeping across our land. Like the original European settlers, they too, are looking for a new beginning; they've gone back to where it all began in hope of finding a better world.

These new pioneers, many of whom are young and idealistic, have settled in almost every county of the state. They come from the four corners of our land

and many have found homes in the hills and hollows of Lincoln County, attracted by reasonable land prices and the easy-going rural lifestyle.

Many of these new folks, such as Pete Shew and Margie Sayles, have built their own cabins and have carved out homesteads on long-abandoned farms. They're living much the same as the early pioneers, working the land with horses and mules, bartering goods and services and moving towards self-sufficiency.

Pete and Margie grew up in New York State. Today they live three miles up a narrow hollow with their daughter, Josie, who was born in the loft of the cabin her parents built. The two-story structure is made of pine and oak logs and sits on a little shelf just under the western ridge of a natural amphitheater that slopes down to a tiny stream where Pete and Margie get their water. The hillsides are covered with oaks, sweetgum, dogwoods, elms, poplars, pines and maples and a profusion of wild flowers.

Pete and Margie had both been to college when they arrived in West Virginia some five years ago. But they were ill-prepared for homesteading. They spent the first winter in a lean-to and devoted all their time to learning the finer points of plowing, growing vegetables, handling animals and constructing buildings.

"Since there's no paved road to our place," recalled Pete, "the first thing I did was buy a team of ponies. Paid $75 apiece for them. It took us eleven days to plow our garden that first year. The stumps were murder and I'll never forget that first day.

"A couple of our neighbors came up to help me. I thought I'd learn by watching but it didn't turn out that way. They did all the watching and they really got a kick out of seeing me struggle with the horses. We finally ended up with me holding the plow and Margie holding the reins and I guess those ponies ran away from us at least a half dozen times a week—they knew a whole lot more about what we were doing than I did."

Since those early days, this pioneering couple has added chickens, pigs, a milk cow and a large vegetable garden. Pete does a little horse trading, plows for his neighbors and says there's no place else on earth he'd rather be.

Similar sentiments are sounded a few miles across the county, at the farm of Chuck Smith and Sandy Adams, a couple of rugged young men who blazed the trail into Lincoln County. Chuck and Sandy were the first of the new pioneers to settle in the county and they had to prove themselves to their neighbors who sniffed suspiciously at this pair of bearded city boys.

Like Pete and Margie and the dozens of others who would follow, they had to learn by trial and error. They took up goat raising and established a newspaper, *The Green Revolution,* in which they wrote of their experiences and of the philosophical reasons that had led them back to the land.

By the spring of 1976, they were experienced goat herders who were making their own cheese and breeding a quality herd. They had built two cabins and often made them available to other prospective pioneers who wanted to come and sample the country life.

Mike Kreyhi and his two year-old daughter, Jessica are pioneers. Mike cleared the land on which he built their cabin (background) and began rearing Jessica in the spirit of the original pioneers who settled in the same Lincoln Co. wilderness.

"We've offered to make homesites available but so far nobody has decided to stay," said Chuck, a Kansan who came to West Virginia as a community organizer for the Office of Economic Opportunity back in the 1960's. It takes a certain type of person to make the commitment that this type of life requires."

It was a sunny morning and a soft tinkle of goat bells provided the background music as he talked. But the conversation was soon cut short when Sandy, who grew up in Wheeling, called that one of the nannies was about to give birth.

Chuck ran for the barn to get his delivery kit while Sandy attended the bleating nannie. A few minutes later, two little black and white spotted kids joined the herd.

In addition to farming and raising goats, Chuck and Sandy are also working to create a community land trust so land will be kept away from developers and will be available to others who want to come to the country. And they are working with their neighbors to establish a self-sustaining community based on trust and sharing.

"Soon after coming here I grew to love the people of the mountains and the spirit of freedom that permeates our life here.

"When I am asked why I chose to settle down here," says Smith, "my answer is always because there's no place I'd rather live."—SD

Spinning, weaving, potting and woodcarving are skills employed by the new pioneers. Maggie Hennesse is knitting on the stoop of the house she and Bill Regatti built.

Chuck Smith (left) and Sandy Adams (right) hand-feed a new-born kid at their pioneer homestead in Lincoln County.

TRIALS AND ERRORS

" . . . the only newspaper in the U.S. under solemn oath to never smell bad!"

Some folks think the unique mountain newspaper, *The West Virginia Hillbilly,* will last only as long as Jim Comstock, its tireless Editor-Publisher.

They point to the delightful, free writing style and the colorful character displayed in his unabashed and opinionated "Comstock Load" and say, "When we subscribe to *Hillbilly* we subscribe to Jim Comstock. Like William Allen White's *Emporia Gazette,* it will die with him."

"That's the craziest thing I have ever heard of," says Comstock. "The only thing I have that a lot of people don't have is stamina."

Beneath the humor and endearing writing style are stamina, determination, optimism, and a boyish, undaunted belief that the impractical is possible . . . these, more than anything else, are the reasons why there *is* a *Hillbilly* in the first place.

Jim Comstock was the fourth, fifth and sixth grades in a one-room schoolhouse on Hinkle Mountain when

teacher George Long planted the seed of newspapering in him.

He dabbled in the profession throughout his school days, but became a teacher after graduating from college during the heart of the Depression. "I guess I was a good example of George Bernard Shaw's observation. . . . 'Those who can, *do,* and those who can't, *teach.'"*

Comstock "couldn't" because it took a great deal of money to be a newspaperman in those days.

While Comstock was in the service on Guam, a newspaperman from Minnesota described the advantages of his profession:

"How on Monday you didn't do anything but rest up from Sunday or Saturday. And on Tuesday you just sat around thinking about what you were going to do on Wednesday. And then on Wednesday you just go down and do it. On Thursday you rest up from Wednesday and on Friday you start thinking about what you're going to do Saturday night."

Said Comstock, "God will punish this fellow, because never have I found the kind of life he painted up to me."

No one could have painted the kind

of life Jim Comstock was about to fashion for himself.

Back in Richwood after his service years, Jim formed a partnership with Bronson McClung and began publishing the town's new newspaper. They called it *The News Letter* because it was to be a very personal newspaper. But the Postmaster General suggested they'd have to put a stamp on it if they were going to call it a "letter."

The resulting name change set the stage for one of the wackiest careers in journalism.

"We decided to change the name to *News Leader.* We had a place in town called The Leader Store that had gone bankrupt. They had left a nice copper engraved sign in the stone outside with the word 'Leader' on it. That way we could use that nice sign. And besides, we thought we were a leader in the

Jim Comstock in a research room located in the building behind the Hillbilly office. The rooms house specific book collections— a West Virginia room, for example, a U.S. Presidents room, and a Virginia Room.

community . . . and 'Leader' was a lot like 'Letter' anyway."

They already had made the decision for *News Leader,* but:

"In America you don't change the name of anything without a contest. And you've got to have a prize.

"So we asked the readers to submit suggestions for a new name. We got 360 letters. And one came in suggesting *News Leader,* as we knew it would, and we accepted it because that's what we'd already decided to call it.

"We called the woman up and told her how lucky she was and that the prize was a year's subscription to the paper. Well, she said she already got the paper, so I said, then you can do one better—you can send it to a relative in Ohio (everybody in this town has relatives in Ohio). I checked the subscription list for the *News Leader* just the other day and found the paper is still going to that relative so we made out alright on that one."

Comstock, the wacky newspaperman, existed long before *Hillbilly.* Most vividly remembered among his early capers is the now-famous ramp episode.

Comstock was impressed by the use of aromas in the inks of Charleston and Beckley newspaper ads in selling perfume and coffee. Richwood had long been accustomed to the aroma of ramps in the spring and Comstock was quick to see a natural opportunity to promote this mountain delicacy.

"These chickened-out West Virginians in Akron come home each spring to eat ramps. Why not take the ramps to them?"

Ramps, in case you haven't heard, are wild onions (sometimes described as a stronger cousin to the European leek) that possess a strong and lasting odor that has been known to send many a school-

boy home with a "lingering ramp breath."

"We sold ads for a special ramp issue. We took pictures of the ramp in bloom, the digging and washing of them in the stream (that's the only stream pollution we have here that I know of). We even chose a ramp king. We got in touch with a chemist and asked him if he could produce a smell like ramps."

The chemist created the "essence" and it arrived one day in a little vial.

"Vile is as good a description as you could choose, because it was certainly the vilest-smelling stuff you ever smelled. The directions said to use it sparingly, and I guess we should have.

"We inked up the press and dropped in the little drops and immediately it was wonderful. You couldn't stay in the room with it. It was just a perfect imitation of the ramp smell."

The young boys who came to fold the papers didn't mind the smell since they liked ramps, and open windows and doors made the pressroom work tolerable.

"Trouble of it was the Post Office needs an act of Congress to open a door. And the worst thing I remember was the close confines on the B&O mail car. It was terrible and one fellow resigned his job and wrote a letter to the Postmaster General." Later a letter from the Postmaster General to the local postmaster was brought to Comstock. It read in part: "It is beyond the call of duty for any postmaster to accept obnoxious or offensive mailing pieces."

Comstock, fearing a loss of postal privileges, quickly promised that he would never do it again.

"In other words," said Comstock, "I am the only newspaper in the U.S. under solemn oath to never smell bad! That means I have lost my inalienable right to compete with the New York press."

Later Comstock received a letter from National Geographic requesting information for an article they were thinking of doing on the use of "perfumes in order to sell products." They had heard that Comstock had used a "perfume" to sell his paper. He replied: "To call the ramp a perfume would be a terrible libel to the ramp and a slander to the people who eat them."

There have been many other humorous episodes in the life of Jim Comstock, including his Kinsey-style report on the "Sexual Behavior of the Richwood Female" or his informative "You Can Remove Your Own Appendix."

But in spite of the sometimes flippant style of this country editor, Jim Comstock has provided much more. The pranks and the satire often are remembered best because of their flamboyancy. But Comstock's journalism has always aimed at something more meaningful . . . pride, heritage and even leadership.

Comstock has been a relentless crusader—defeated often, but the victor in many cases—physically alone in his fights, but armed with thousands of devoted readers.

Hillbilly began in the mid-fifties, and he chose a name that seemed to fly in the faces of the too sensitive mountaineers he sought to serve.

"At the outset I didn't really understand that West Virginians didn't like to be called hillbillies. But we've been a bit too self-conscious about ourselves and I think in twenty years I have made 'hillbilly' a respectable word."

The *Hillbilly* has carried reviews of literary works, sophisticated satire and extensive histories to give the publication and the word a sense of dignity. "Head and shoulders, this state is better than any other state I know of," Comstock said. "We have nothing to be ashamed of. I wanted to preserve some of the things we were losing, including the vernacular."

After considerable criticism, Comstock polled his readers with the idea of changing the name. "The vote was thirty to one to keep the name *Hillbilly*," Comstock recalls.

After its first thirteen months the *Hillbilly* folded. In spite of 10,000 new subscribers, Comstock and McClung found that their $10,000 investment was gone.

A year later, Comstock resurrected the statewide newspaper and has piloted it through troubled seas ever since. At one point, in the early 1970's, Comstock became so discouraged, he wrote the longest "30" ever, announcing the death of *Hillbilly*.

"My readers came to the rescue. They sent in subscription renewals for several years. They bought the paper for friends. They told me to raise my price. The coal operators thought they had rescued me, but it was the readers."

Many people believed the coal operators rescued Jim Comstock . . . or bought him. The coal industry did offer cash, but Comstock refused and suggested they purchase subscriptions for every miner in West Virginia. That offer was agreed upon, but Jim Comstock says the coal industry never "came through."

In the meantime, Comstock began sending his newspaper to the miners and continued his part of the bargain, even though he was never paid. And readers began to notice that Comstock was (probably always had been) pro-coal.

Although many are still critical of him, Comstock says, "I can truthfully say that nobody ever bought me off for anything. "I know people still hold me suspect. I'm supported by my readers but I'm not

enormously respected in the state. I ran for Congress and didn't even carry my own precinct. With all that I have done I am still an odd ball, still not accepted."

By 1976, Jim Comstock was beginning to "talk tired," speaking of selling, yearning for retirement and a world cruise that would be more leisurely than his Mountain State traveling that saw him scribbling the next issue of *Hillbilly* on a notepad in the back seat of a car, or on a plane, or at some dinner meeting or other.

"I'll be pushed some times and the paper has got to come out next week and I'm the only man to do it. I can have no holidays. I can't afford to become sick. Nothing can happen to me. Who would take over for a week?"

Yes, Mr. Comstock, and who would take over for the years to come?—JA

The genius of a "natural damned fool" from Harvard

Ask a West Virginian where a place called Salt Lick is and he's likely to point in nearly any direction. Almost every corner of the Mountain State has a "Salt Lick" and it was the salt springs that caused many a mountaineer to discover the wonder and mystery of oil and gas.

In the late eighteenth century, the pioneers of western Virginia were a great deal more interested in the natural flow of "brine springs" than they were in the oil and gas that often accompanied them.

When the supply of salt became inadequate, men began to dig pits and wells. The value of gas was soon gauged by the amount of salt water it might propel from the ground.

As pioneers moved west through the Appalachians, they became increasingly familiar with and fascinated by the properties of natural gas. General George Washington said it would "burst forth as freely as spirits" when he first visited the famous "burning springs" near Charleston.

In 1843, some western Virginia gentleman bored a 1,000 foot well (several rods deeper than General Washington's "burning spring") and struck a great gas reservoir that forced the 1,000 pound auger and shaft out of the well like an arrow from a crossbow.

With it came a column of salt water 150 feet high that roared a mighty roar which could be heard for miles around.

News of the fantastic sight spread far and wide and it became the custom of stage drivers to stop and let the passengers look at the spectacular display.

On one occasion, a Harvard professor was among the passengers. And so the report goes:

". . . being a man of investigating and experimenting turn of mind, he went as near the well as he could get for the gas and spray, and lighted a match to see if the gas would burn. Instantly the whole atmosphere was ablaze, the professor's hair and eyebrows singed and his clothes afire.

"The professor, who had jumped into the river to save himself from the fire, crawled out, and back to the stage as best he could, and went on to Charleston, where he took to bed, and sent for a doctor to dress his burns."

The engine house and wooden derrick were also burned and the owners instructed a courier to seek out the offender and have him arrested "unless you find that the fellow is a natural damned fool, and didn't know any better."

Later confronted with the choice of a law suit or declaring himself a "damned fool," the professor swallowed his pride and admitted he didn't know any better.

Few people *did* know better though, and the professor had unwittingly paved the way for the successful use of natural gas in the manufacturing process.

For years after the professor's mistake, natural gas lifted the salt water from the bottom of the well, forced it a mile through pipes to a salt furnace, raised it into a reservoir, boiled it in the furnace and lighted the premises at night.

No one can say for sure who ushered in the Gas Age. But it was either that bumbling Harvard professor near General George Washington's "burning spring" . . . or another surprised chap just like him! —JA

"Powder Puff" takes the hoot owl

Carol Jean Bain is a young woman with a soft voice, warm brown eyes and long, long black hair. But those are only surface aspects of her personality. Like all of us, Carol Jean Bain is many things.

For one, she's a pioneer; a person who has trodden a lonely path leading deep down into the bowels of the earth to a dark, dangerous forbidden world once considered the exclusive domain of men.

For another, she's a woman who has known the pain of divorce and the uncertainty of poverty.

She's also a mother; a woman who loves her daughter and dreads the darkness which each night takes her away from her little girl. She always peeps in at her daughter before donning her heavy coveralls and picking up her lunch pail and hard hat.

These are the clothes of a coal miner. They're also the clothes of Carol Jean Bain.

She became the state's first woman miner back in the fall of 1974, a time when groups of women throughout the coal fields were protesting that they didn't want any women down there in the darkness with their men. But Carol refused to listen. She needed the money and was determined to prove that a coal mine wasn't necessarily a man's world.

It didn't take her long to prove her point, and to earn the respect of her tobacco-chewing partners.

"The men watch their language and treat me well," she said after only three weeks on the job at the Eastern Associated Coal Corporation's mine at Affinity, near Beckley.

The women took a little longer, however, and a few of them congregated at the mine mouth for several days. They heckled and harassed her and made snide insinuations about what would happen down there in those dark, lonely shafts.

Carol Jean's lips curled upward at the memories.

"They've stopped all that now," she said. "But I just wish one of them could come down in the mine and see what it's like. Why, sometimes I'm in water and mud up to my knees. And if you don't watch what you're doing all the time, you'll hit your back on the roof."

Carol Jean's boss also agreed that a mine is no place for monkey business. And he was outspokenly delighted with the way the state's first woman miner worked out.

"She's doing a good job," said Jack Rowe, Carol Jean's foreman at the time. "She's a lot stronger than I thought she would be and she tries hard. I had two trainees on that belt crew and the other one wasn't doing as well as Carol so I transferred him."

In addition to criticism and praise, Carol Jean's new job also brought her a measure of fame. She was a celebrity at her daughter's school and newsmen from across the country beat a path to her door.

When she followed her father and brothers into the mine, Carol Jean was put on the hoot owl shift—from midnight to eight—as a member of the belt assembly crew. This crew is composed of members who, while crouched over almost double, hustle around assembling portable conveyor belts from fifty-pound metal rollers.

A year later, Carol Jean was still on the hoot owl shift. But she was no longer on the belt crew.

"I'm a roof bolt helper now," she said, "It's the top paying job in the mines. I make $58 something a day. Some people say it's a dangerous job but I don't mind it."

She said she gets along fine with her fellow workers and doesn't mind the occasional teasing she still gets.

"They'll still offer me a chew every now and then," she said, her eyes twinkling. "And they tease me about keeping clean.

"I tuck my hair up underneath my hat and put a couple of napkins in my pockets. I keep wiping my face all night to keep off the dust. The men have started calling me 'Powder Puff.'" —SD

LEGENDS, HEROES AND HEROINES

The West Virginia hall of fame ranges in scope from the first colonies—to the Civil War—to the Twentieth Century. One of the smallest states has indeed generated more than its share of greats.

If you have a few minutes, we'd like you to sit a spell, while we tell you about just a few . . .

Daniel Boone was a frontiersman held in esteem by both Indians and settlers. He was rightfully regarded as "the Great Pioneer of the West." It was said of Daniel, "heroes and legends of West Virginia come and go, but Daniel Boone stands far ahead of any frontiersman who ever tossed a tomahawk or fired a minuteball. Others were to follow and become famous but in their brightest hours they never held a candle to Boone, the yellow-haired old pioneer who fought a thousand battles and died a poor man."

Daniel Boone was born around 1734 in Bucks County, Pennsylvania. Daniel was said to have inherited from his parents, "a constitution insuring longevity, a frame fitted for a long career of toil and exertion and desperate adventure and sad suffering." But his heroic char-acter was made by the circumstances he had to deal with.

He was almost nineteen when he first came to western Virginia with the army of the English General Braddock on his march toward Fort Pitt.

Lord Dunmore, Governor of Virginia, later solicited Daniel to conduct a surveying expedition to the Falls of the Ohio. After this sixty-two day exploration, marked by the tragic death of Boone's son, he was assigned a military command and ordered to take charge of three garrisons on the frontier. He commanded these outposts during the war with the Indians that ended at the Battle of Point Pleasant.

The Indians regarded Boone as a man responsible for their loss of lands because of the expeditions he organized and settlements he began, but he never gave them cause for personal hatred or revenge. He was never a professional Indian killer though he battled them many times defending white settlements. He often tried to outwit his opponent, rather than shoot and shot only in self-defense.

Boone was classed with the wild hunters, Indian fighters, and border scouts but his real character was mild and simple-hearted. He was slow, almost impossible to anger and carried no grudges; bold and determined but not impulsive in courage; always inclined to defend rather than attack.

When Daniel was stripped of his land holdings in Kentucky, he moved to Point Pleasant, West Virginia, then to the south bank of the Great Kanawha, just outside present-day Charleston. These twelve years he spent in West Virginia were probably the most peaceful, at least the most settled, years of his life. In 1789, by popular petition, he was appointed

At thirty-three Daniel Boone led a pioneer caravan westward through Kentucky's Cumberland Gap in 1767. Some twenty years later, he settled along west Virginia's "Kanhowway" River. He represented the region in the Virginia assembly and commanded its military defenses. His seven years in the valley, which included the Ft. Lee and "Pint Pleasant" areas, netted him five hundred acres, two horses and one slave. (George Caleb Bingham's romanticized painting is from the Washington Univ. Collection in St. Louis.)

71

Lt. Colonel in command of the county militia and in 1791, represented Kanawha County in the Virginia Legislature. He served only a short term as lawmaker; the confinement of city life and politics did not suit his nature.

Daniel Boone's most lasting monument in West Virginia is the rich industrial county named for him. The naming of Boone County is a story in itself. In 1786 before the Boones came to Kanawha Valley, the family of John Flinn, living at the mouth of Cabin Creek on the Kanawha east of Charleston, was attacked by Indians.

The parents were killed and a son and daughter, Cloe, were carried off as captives. Cloe was rescued by Boone and reared in his home until she reached womanhood.

In 1847, when a new county was being formed from Kanawha and Logan counties, Mr. St. Clair Ballard, son of Cloe Flinn, asked that the county be named in honor of his mother's benefactor, thus paying a debt of gratitude to the great frontiersman. And so Boone County was named.

Stonewall Jackson, another famous fighter, was a military man who began his career at West Point, but ended it as one of the South's most effective Confederate generals.

Born Thomas Jackson at Clarksburg in 1824, he soon was without parents. His father died when he was three and his mother died four years later. Young Jackson was raised by his stepgrandmother at what is now called Jackson's Mill near Weston.

But in spite of his difficult family history, Jackson grew to be a "natural born" leader, serving as a constable in Lewis County while just 17. The following year he was conditionally appointed

to West Point where he graduated in 1846.

During his six years of service in the Federal Army, he attained the rank of

major. But in 1852 he resigned to pursue a teaching career associated with the military.

He and a company of cadets from Virginia Military Institute attended John Brown's execution at Harpers Ferry in 1859, and in 1861 Jackson took command of another group of cadets, this time as colonel in the Virginia volunteers.

Jackson soon earned his nickname "Stonewall" as one of the most formidable military men in the South. His was a triumphant campaign, but it was his own men's bullets that cut Jackson's Civil War short.

Stonewall's men were among the troops at Chancellorsville May 2-4, 1863. He attempted to carry out a flanking strategy that had worked well for him at Bull Run. Jackson, then a major gen-

eral, had come in on a reconnaissance mission behind General Joseph Hooker's right flank at twilight. His own men mistook Stonewall and his scouts as the enemy and opened fire.

Severely wounded, Stonewall Jackson died a few days later.

His talents might have been useful the following month at Gettysburg.

Near Stonewall Jackson's birthplace, another special West Virginian was to make a contribution to American history.

Anne Bailey came to America as Anne Hennis in 1761. Four years later, Anne married Richard Trotter who was killed by Indians at the Battle of Point Pleasant in 1774.

Learning of her husband's death, Anne Trotter vowed revenge on the entire In-

dian race. Forsaking the role of woman, mother and widow, Anne abandoned her home life and took up a "military career," spying on Indians, carrying messages from fort to fort, looking out for the safety of settlers and killing her share of red men.

Anne was short but sturdy, a fearless young woman who learned to love her life in the wilderness where she slept at night in a hollowed-out log. With ax and gun and hunting knife, she became a terror to the Indians who believed her most formidable weapon was her tongue. She made the Indians believe she was "guarded by spirits and if the Indians harmed her, the unseen powers would destroy the whole tribe."

She married again in 1785, this time to a distinguished border leader, John Bailey, who was sent three years later to Fort Lee at the present site of the West Virginia state capitol, Charleston.

Anne Bailey wasn't to become the typical "home body" though. In 1791, when Fort Lee was besieged by Indians, she volunteered to ride a hundred miles through dense forest to Lewisburg to replenish ammunition. She became an important Indian scout at Fort Lee and it was the settlers there who finally branded her "Mad Anne," as much for her screaming, high-pitched voice as for her daring exploits.

Mad Anne dressed and acted like a man. In those rugged times, frontier living often provoked a certain callousness in its women.

Betty Zane, however, is described by historians as a frontier beauty. But hers was no less a fearless story.

It was in 1782 that Elizabeth "Betty" Zane became a frontier heroine at Fort Henry, located at the site now called Wheeling.

Fort Henry, formerly a British bastion, was renamed for Patrick Henry, first governor of the Commonwealth of Virginia, which included the Ohio River settlement. Indian attacks, aided by the British, had continued on Fort Henry for several years after American independence had been declared and the last siege came in September, 1782, a confrontation that

is now regarded as the last battle of the Revolutionary War.

Forty British soldiers and 230 Indians attacked Fort Henry by surprise. Settlers were barely able to reach the fort and it wasn't long before they realized they had not brought enough powder.

It was Betty Zane, demure and innocent of face, but mischievous and with a fiery temper, who saved the day.

Several men volunteered to make a dash to the Zane cabin to get more powder, but Betty Zane insisted she go: "There is not one man to spare. If one should fall on this errand, the fort might be lost. The loss of a woman will not be so critical."

As she ran the 60 yards to the cabin, the startled Indians held their fire, shouting "squaw!" But they suspected her mission as she returned with powder wrapped in a tablecloth. Bullets struck all around her but she reached the fort

with no more than a bullet hole in her skirt.

The settlers were able to hold the fort and reinforcements arrived the next day.

The courage of Betty Zane lives on today through the biographical account written by her great, grandnephew—Zane Grey.

Indians were almost always portrayed as the "bad guys" in such historical accounts, but West Virginia numbers among its heroes at least two famous Indians.

Chief Cornstalk is one of them.

His Shawnee name was Keigh-tugh-qua, meaning "stalk of the maize." As a young man he earned a reputation as a ruthless military strategist who murdered women and children in his attempt to defend Indian territory. He was charged with many massacres including one in 1763 in a Greenbrier County settlement that left over fifty settlers dead.

But as he grew older, Cornstalk preferred peace to conflict. He was tall and muscular and always stood erect with his head thrust high. With his voice loud and powerful, Cornstalk began to speak with a wisdom that earned for him a new reputation, that of statesman.

He repeatedly sent messages to Lord Dunmore, governor of Virginia, to cease hostilities against the Indians, but finally felt forced to renew military conflict.

Eventually Cornstalk was defeated at Point Pleasant and peace was made with the signing of the Treaty of Charlotte. But peace did not last and Indians, antagonized by English soldiers, prepared to attack Fort Randolph.

Chief Cornstalk, still hoping for peace, went to the fort to warn the settlers.

Wary of the famed treachery of the chief, the settlers took him, his son and two companions hostage.

The next day, November 10, 1777, a soldier was shot and killed outside the fort. The soldiers rushed to avenge the death by killing the four hostages.

Legend has it that as eight bullets ploughed through Cornstalk's body, he silenced the enraged whites with these words:

I was the friend of the border-man. Many a time I have saved him and his people from harm. I never warred with you save to protect our wigwams and our lands. I refused to join your enemy. I came to your house as a friend, and you murdered by my side, my son, the young chief Elinipsico.

Unmoved by fear or pain, standing even taller, Cornstalk went on:

For this may the curse of the Great Spirit rest upon this spot; favored as it is by nature, may it ever be blighted in its hopes, its growth dwarfed, its enterprises blasted, and the energies of its people paralyzed by the stain of our blood.

Even in the 1970's, residents of Point Pleasant remember Cornstalk's Curse, and wonder if the Silver Bridge collapse that killed forty-six motorists in 1967 might not be somehow linked to the chieftain's dying words.

Chief Logan was another famous West Virginia Indian and his life closely paralleled that of Cornstalk.

Logan was a friend of the white settler until one day he returned from a hunting expedition to find that his entire

family had been massacred by the white man at Yellow Springs, near Steubenville, Ohio. He vowed the revenge of ten scalps for every murdered kinsman and began conducting relentless raids on settlements up and down the Ohio River.

He refused to be present at the signing of the peace treaty after Cornstalk's defeat, but he sent a letter that is judged to be the most eloquent statement ever made in defense of the American Indian. Written on the back of white man's wampum, it said:

I appeal to any white man to say, if ever he entered Logan's cabin hungry, and he gave him not meat; if ever he came cold and naked and he clothed him not. During the course of the last long and bloody war Logan remained idle in his cabin an advocate for peace. Such was my love for the whites, that my countrymen pointed as they passed, and said, "Logan is a friend of the white man."

But then he recalled the total destruction of his family and he wrote,

There runs not a drop of my blood in the veins of any living creature. This called on me for revenge. I have sought it; I have killed many; I have fully glutted my vengance; for my country I rejoice at the beams of peace. But do not harbor a thought that mine is the joy of fear. Logan never felt fear. He will not turn on his heel to save his life. Who is there to mourn for Logan? Not one.

Still another personal tragedy followed: Logan acquired a taste for rum and eventually sank into obscurity.

Anna Jarvis vowed over her mother's open grave in 1905 that she would establish a memorial day for mothers, living or dead. Seven years later she had done it.

The idea of a "Mother's Day" was not new. Julia Ward Howe had made the first recorded suggestion in 1872.

Sometime earlier, Anna's mother, Anna Marie (Reeves) Jarvis had organized a Mothers' Friendship Day in Pruntytown in the late 1860's to help relax postwar tensions in the community.

But it was Anna Jarvis, through appealing letters to politicians, businessmen

and other influential people, who was able to organize an actual observance and create a nationwide holiday for mothers.

The Andrews Methodist Church of Grafton was the site of the first memorial service held in honor of Anna Marie Jarvis one year after her death. Two years later, on May 10, 1908, the first official Mother's Day service was held in Grafton.

West Virginia Governor William E. Glasscock was the first official to proclaim the second Sunday of May as Mother's Day and by 1914, the day was given national recognition by President Woodrow Wilson who signed a joint resolution of Congress.

The following year the President proclaimed Mother's Day as an annual national observance.

Even though Anna Jarvis had fulfilled her promise, she lived to regret it and

spent the latter part of her life fighting against the commercialization of what she meant to be a most reverent holiday.

She died in 1948, blind and penniless, never having experienced the blessing of motherhood.

A mother who has opened her heart and door to children the world around, was born in Hillsboro, West Virginia, on June 26, 1892:

Pearl Comfort Sydenstricker, a product of two cultures, born in West Virginia and reared in Chinkiang, China, on the Yangtse River, wrote of her early childhood—"I had almost ceased to think of myself as different, if indeed I ever thought so, from the Chinese."

But Pearl came to realize her foreigner status when she and her family had to flee China during the Boxer Rebellion. They returned to Chianking as soon as peace was restored.

Pearl returned to America to study at Randolph-Macon College in Virginia, then went back to China and in 1917 married Dr. John Lossing Buck. They went to live in a small town in North China which years later was vividly recalled in her novel *The Good Earth.*

However, at this time in her life she was occupied with her home, her children and parents and teaching English literature at the University of Nanking and later, Chung Yang University. Though she was not yet writing, she was framing stories in her mind. In 1922, the *Atlantic Monthly* published her first article on China. Later, on a ship bound for America in 1925, she wrote the story which became her first novel, *East Wind: West Wind.*

When *The Good Earth* was published in 1931, it met with critical praise and popular success. Pearl was awarded the Pulitzer Prize for the best novel of the

year by an American author. She continued to write about her two worlds and in 1938, she was chosen to receive the Nobel Prize for Literature, the highest honor given in the world of letters and she was the first American woman to be so honored.

In 1935 she divorced Dr. Buck and married Richard J. Walsh, president of the John Day Company, her publisher. They settled on a 400-acre farm in Bucks County, Pennsylvania and along with her writing she took on many humanitarian projects. She founded the East and West Association: "an educational experiment designed for friendship and mutual understanding between the peoples, especially of Asia and the United States."

In 1949, she founded Welcome House, Inc., a non-profit organization for the care and adoption of children of mixed Asian-American bloods, which has had a liberalizing effect on the field of adoption.

The house in which Pearl Sydenstricker Buck was born stands beside the state highway on the edge of Hillsboro, a peaceful village in Pocohontas County. The unpretentious home, still called "The Stulting House" (after her mother's family name) is now a museum operated by the Pearl S. Buck Birthplace Foundation and stands as a living monument to a most distinguished descendant.

Sam Snead used to delight in knocking hickory nuts a country mile with a big stick, while growing up on his folks' farm along the Virginia-West Virginia border. And he made a fortune doing the same thing to golf balls a few years later.

By the time Samuel Jackson Snead was in his early 20's, he had evolved

from barefoot boy into one of this country's most promising young golfers.

His powerful, fluid swing—considered to be the finest the game has ever seen— helped him win the state championship

in 1935 and within two years he had become one of the brightest stars on the fledgling professional circuit.

His witty ways won for him the love and admiration of the state and the entire sports world and when you hear the phrase, "You ain't just whistlin' Dixie," you have to think of fun-lovin' Sammy Snead.

Snead became host pro at The Greenbrier at White Sulphur Springs in 1936 and once shot an unbelievable 59 on the "Old White" course which set a PGA record for tournament play that has remained unbroken. A born competitor, Sam was famous for fleecing suckers by playing with only one club, usually a two or three iron.

Although he had to use a full set of clubs, Snead did almost as well on the PGA tour where he won a record 84 titles.

His epic battles with Ben Hogan in the 1940's and 50's helped popularize the game and made this former farm boy into a modern American Folk hero. He left The Greenbrier in 1975, but he's still "slammin'" on the national golf circuit.

Jerry West became one of the greatest basketball heros of all time, not only for the state but for the world.

Jerry, the fantastic sharpshooter from Cabin Creek, began his legendary career at East Bank High School.

He was a hero long before he ever got to West Virginia University. Once he was invited to visit the state's chief executive. He went up to the receptionist and shyly said, "I'm Jerry West. I have an appointment."

"You don't have to tell me who you are," replied the receptionist. "You're better known than the governor."

Championship was the name of Jerry West's game. He took his high school team to the state championship, became

a three-time All-American at WVU, led his team to the NCAA finals in 1959 and co-captained the greatest U.S. Olympic team in history to resounding victory in the 1960 games.

After graduating from college in 1960, Jerry West rejoined his old coach who had become head coach of the Los Angeles Lakers, Fred Schaus.

Jerry West's years with the pros were filled not only with glory, but with injury after injury. Writers in the early years refused to believe that this frail-looking six-foot-three, 175-pound frame could stand up to the pounding it would receive.

But the sports writers were wrong. They had misjudged the pride and the mental toughness of this mountain boy. By the end of the 1960's Jerry West had broken his nose four or five more times, sprained his ankle at least three times, and sustained frightful batterings under the basket from his larger, more powerful opponents.

But he had a will of iron and his trainers had to nearly strap him in bed during the 128 games he missed in nine seasons.

During that same period, however, Jerry West was busy compiling other statistics . . . among them an overall average of nearly 28 points per game.

It's ironic in view of the battering West took to know that one of his opposing coaches once said, "He's a killer."

"This guy is the greatest clutch player ever," that coach went on to say. "In the last few minutes of close games, I tell my guys if you let him get the ball you might as well go home."

"Mr. Clutch" finally retired in the mid-70's, a decision that he hadn't looked forward to. In an interview in 1970, Jerry said, "It'll be the hardest thing I'll ever have to do in my life. It'll kill me."

It didn't kill him. It didn't even dim his hero image. His fame lives on, influencing every West Virginia kid who ever tacked a hoop up to a tree or a barn.

Booker Taliaferro Washington, a slave-born black, was one of three West Virginians elected to the *Hall of Fame for Great Americans.* (The others were Daniel Boone and Stonewall Jackson.)

Booker was born on a Hale's Ford, Virginia plantation in 1856. When few blacks could read or write, he learned to read from a *Blue-Back Speller.*

After the Emancipation Proclamation, Washington came with his family to Malden, West Virginia (Kanawha County). He attended a Negro elementary school, but economic needs forced him to leave classes and get a job.

He worked for the Ruffner Salt Works but earned his education at night through the help of a sympathetic teacher. Mrs. Viola Ruffner recognized Booker's

abilities and encouraged him to continue his education. She employed him as a servant in the Ruffner home, which permitted him to attend school one hour a day and to study evenings.

In 1872, he left Malden and walked 500 miles to enroll at Hampton Institute in Virginia. He graduated from Hampton in 1875 and then moved to Connecticut, where he found employment as a waiter.

He returned to Malden to teach school for two years. In 1877 he toured the state campaigning for Charleston as the state capital.

In 1881 he took charge of Tuskegee Institute in Alabama. By 1895 Washington had built Tuskegee into the nation's model black industrial, vocational and agricultural college.

His vocational education methods not only served to draw his race out of

ignorance and poverty, but received wide white acceptance as well. In 1895 he told a white audience in his Atlanta Exposition speech that blacks would accept social segregation and disenfranchisement in exchange for educational and economic opportunities. For this, he was hailed by blacks and whites alike.

He encouraged his race to be aggressive scholars, to be industrious and not to fear relocating to achieve better opportunities: "Cast down your buckets where you are."

His efforts resulted in strong economic support from whites for the advancement of Negro institutions and higher employment for qualified blacks, but some feel that he traded too much black political and social advancement for gains in economics and education.

Some blacks today regard his compromises as a necessary maneuver for black advancement.

Others regard him as an Uncle Tom. But History can't change the legendary innovative accomplishments of this former slave who believed in what his race could do for the country and themselves—given a fair opportunity to prove their abilities.

For his own opportunity, he gave credit to Mrs. Ruffner, back in the Kanawha Valley.

Greasy Neale was one of the state's first superstars, not only as an athlete, but as a strategist and coach who played or coached in many of the nation's biggest athletic contests.

Alfred Earle Neale was born in Parkersburg in 1891. He became one of West Virginia Wesleyan College's all-time great athletes and graduated from there in 1913.

By then he was known as "Greasy" and he held several coaching jobs including ones at Wesleyan, Marietta College and Washington & Jefferson at nearby Washington, Pennsylvania. He piloted the W&J team to the Rose Bowl in 1922 where he battled a tough California team to a 0-0 tie. Coaching also took Greasy Neale to Virginia, 1923-28, West Virginia, 1931-33 and Yale 1934-40.

From 1940 to 1951 Greasy Neale coached the Philadelphia Eagles, winning

Greasy Neale's sports career spanned over fifty years, during which time football, earlier considered a ruffianly sport and in danger of being outlawed, was emerging as a spectator sport that rivaled baseball (Neale's other love). Confident Wesleyan rooters (opposite) march through Fairmont streets to another game with rival WVU in 1913. A year before, Neale starred with the undefeated Wesleyan team that beat WVU 19 to 14.

two league championships and five division titles.

Greasy Neale, therefore, holds the unusual distinction of having played on a World Series championship team, having coached two professional championship football teams, and having coached a small Eastern college team to the Rose Bowl.

Greasy was honored in 1951 by the West Virginia Sports Writers Association who chose him as one of the first inductees into their Hall of Fame.

This story has no end.

As long as there's a West Virginia, there will always be a small factory for producing some of the greatest of great Americans . . . . —MS

BOMBS AND BULLETS

**"This is a beautiful countryside.
I never had time to notice it before."**

A hush fell over the crowded courtroom in Charles Town, West Virginia, as John Brown, head wrapped in a blood-stained bandage, rose from his cot to make the most of the situation.

Thwarted in his effort to spark a slavery uprising at nearby Harpers Ferry, facing a certain death sentence from this stern-faced judge and jury, John Brown was far from defeated as he used the chamber for a stage from which to preach his dying message to a world that focused surprised attention on the man who raided a U.S. arsenal.

Although wounded and ill, John Brown's frail but wiry body quaked with determined energy and his eyes pierced all with hard, steely glances as he gave these western Virginians a preview of the struggle for emancipation.

The year wasn't 1859. It was 1975. And this John Brown was an actor.

The Anvil, a historical play by Julia Davis, was performed in the very courthouse where John Brown was tried. and convicted.

The place, and the close following of actual court records, created awesome realism. And courtroom spectators sat in a different mental time, wondering, "Is this man a hero or a madman?"

In 1975, this man was really Neal Randell, the fourth "John Brown" to perform the role. Director Charles Wood, who also supervised the Broadway version, called Randell his best "John Brown" and he was no doubt the most knowledgeable. Randell, a "student of Brown," was a member of the U.S. Park Service at Harpers Ferry where his job was to present to thousands of visitors each year this historical story.

Nearly a dozen decades after the famous raid, Harpers Ferry seems to be as authentic a step back in history as almost any spot in the country, not only during that play in the nearby courtroom, but along every street where preservation and restoration have recaptured the spirit of the times.

One of those "spirits" is the continuing heated debate over the merits or demerits of John Brown. The arguments make you believe he lies "a molderin' in the grave."

John Brown is still misunderstood and mistrusted in Harpers Ferry.

"When I came here three and a half years ago, I was asked to give a talk about John Brown at the local high school," Randell, a native of Boston, said.

"In this lecture, I actually stole a quote from a historian who referred to John Brown as an Old Testament hero, meaning a man with a single purpose.

"Well the word 'hero' stuck in their craws and just a few hours later I was walking down the street in Harpers Ferry and a woman stopped me to complain that I was telling her son that John Brown was a hero."

The feelings about John Brown in Jefferson County, West Virginia, are strong and varied. Some would like to forget the revolutionary ever visited the area; others willingly capitalize on the hundreds of thousands of tourists who visit the Eastern Panhandle community.

The Anvil, produced primarily for and

Harpers Ferry's transition from a tranquil village to a disaster scene began with John Brown's raid and culminated during Civil War exchanges. Now a National Monument, it is extensively restored.

by members of the local community, seemed to impart to residents a new awareness of John Brown.

"A happy thing happened to me at the cast party following our last performance," Randell said.

"A man who had been on the jury for four nights approached me, and he said, 'You don't know me, but I've been on the jury since Wednesday night, and I've really enjoyed the play.'"

The jury member continued:

"But I want to tell you something else. When I came home from work on Monday evening and my wife told me that Charles Wood had called to ask me to serve on the jury, I said, 'Well, he must be crazy. He ought to know that I would just like to walk in that courtroom with a shotgun and blow that old man away.'"

Yet the same man told Randell, "Wednesday night I watched you as John Brown and that night I didn't get a wink of sleep." The play made him think about who Brown was and what his motivations were.

Thinking about the past is what Harpers Ferry and the efforts of the U.S. Park Service is all about. Visitors to this community are given the unique opportunity to experience Nineteenth Century western Virginia first hand . . . perhaps not by meeting the personification of John Brown, but by walking the very streets, seeing the infamous Engine House where John Brown and his small band stubbornly fought the U.S. Militia, where some of his sons and many of his friends were killed.

Park Service employees, in period dress, are seen everywhere—some sweeping the sidewalks in front of authentic shops—a bearded hulk of a man wielding the blacksmith's hammer as he fashions hinges, iron decorations and dinnerware for this and other parks across the country.

And now, the historic storefronts of Harpers Ferry are no longer locked, but open to the visitor who may walk into a dimly-lit general store, correct in every detail, stocked with authentic merchandise, not for sale, but marked with one-hundred-years-ago prices.

The "presence" of the past in Jefferson County keeps many of the issues of a long-gone era alive, and it is significant that many of the facts and many of the debates that surrounded John Brown still exist today.

The Anvil was presented in Charles Town as a benefit for the "Friends of the Old Opera House" who are restoring that facility in Charles Town, one of only a few opera houses still in operation in the U.S.

In addition to refurbishing the opera house, at least one important architectural change is being made. In its original construction, two doors once beckoned the theater-goer . . . the big doors for the Whites who would sit at floor level, one small one for the Blacks who might be allowed to enter and leave the balcony area. But now, twelve decades after Brown, his words in the famous courtroom were being uttered again . . . this time by an actor to help restore an opera house that would have just one door, open to Blacks as well as Whites.

John Brown is, of course, an important part of Black history whether you consider him a hero or a "madman."

The folks in Jefferson County, Virginia, were unaware (even during his trial) that Brown and his men had often engaged in the anti-slavery battles of Kansas and Missouri. They were also unaware that it was Brown who was credited with the midnight murders of sleeping men along Pottawatomie Creek in Kansas—an apparent demonstration that Brown believed abolitionists must give up debate and resort to violence if slaves were to be freed.

It was in those earlier conflicts that Brown first heard of Harpers Ferry—a template, bearing the name, was found on a rifle butt that indicated it was from the "U.S. Arsenal at Harpers Ferry."

When John Brown finally invaded that arsenal, he was a desperate man, tired of debate and ready to free the slaves by force. He needed guns and he believed the black slaves would help him get them . . . help him use them later to precipitate a war.

But for some unexplained reason, the Blacks let him down at Harpers Ferry. Perhaps because they didn't believe he could succeed, perhaps out of fear of reprisal from their masters, perhaps because they were unaccustomed to taking the initiative—they didn't show up in John Brown's most important hour. Perhaps it was because this thing seemed to be a white man's crusade with "no place" for them.

Neal Randell, John Brown reincarnated, also carried a deep interest in Black welfare as he entered that Charles Town courtroom in 1975. Under the auspices of the U.S. Park Service, Randell had spent much time organizing a Bicentennial Black History program for Harpers Ferry and he strongly believed John Brown was an important chapter in Black history.

But at the 1975 re-enactment, Blacks again failed to show up, a fact that was as puzzling to Neal Randell as to John Brown in 1859.

"I see almost a million people come and go here at the National Park each year," Randell said, "and one of the most

gratifying things is the depth of interest that we find in Blacks who come here. They want to know about John Brown. They consider Brown and the raid and the trial as a very significant milestone in the history of Black Americans.

"Yet, when we did the play in Charles Town, I would guess over nine nights in the courtroom, I saw no more than ten local Black residents. I don't know what that means. But I was a bit concerned why more members of the Black community locally didn't come to see the play. I wish they had."

Why didn't they come?

"That's a tough one. But I would guess

Neal Randell (foreground, left picture) became "John Brown" in The Anvil, a true story drama based on the original trial of the legendary John Brown (above).

this: Most of the plays I've been involved with are attended and produced and directed and acted and financially supported by white middle-class Jefferson County, W.Va., residents. Perhaps Blacks don't feel they have a stake in all these activities."

That's probably the way it was in 1859—Blacks not certain the drama was for them—citizens arguing strongly over the merits of John Brown and the dynamic words of the most famous abolitionist.

Those words still echoed as Neal Randell acted it out again as John Brown. Turning with his watch to the kindly jailer he spoke *The Anvil* lines:

"Mr. Avis, you have been most kind to me. I should like you to have this."

"But, Captain Brown—!"

And Brown's reply, "You will need it now more than I."

Then John Brown's quiet comment as he looks out the jail cell window:

"This is a beautiful countryside. I never had time to notice it before."—JA

"I'd rather have this medal than be President of the United States . . ."

West Virginians live by the creed that "mountaineers are always free" and history has proven that no other people have ever been more willing to see to it that this freedom is preserved . . . no matter what the cost.

This has been true of West Virginians since the first settlers pushed across the mountains in search of a life they could call their own. Many of these early residents took part in the Battle of Point Pleasant, which ranks as one of the bloodiest conflicts ever to occur between the Indian and the white man.

West Virginia was a battleground again during the Civil War when many residents served with distinction and gallantry . . . on both sides. It was not unknown to have father and son or brother and brother face each other on the battlefield. More than 3,000 West Virginians serving in the Federal Army lost their lives. And in the Confederate service, approximately 1,000 died in this tragic conflict.

This history of sacrifice and service has continued into the present century. In the past thirty-five years alone, no less than 150,000 West Virginians have borne arms for their country, as the tombstones in many a hillside cemetery will attest.

One of these is Hershel Williams, from the hills of Marion County; West Virginia's only living recipient of this honor. It would be out of character for this mild-mannered and soft-spoken man to initiate any conversation leading up to that incredible day back in 1945 when he defied unbelievable odds and danger to lead the American forces to victory on Iwo Jima.

But let's go back a few years before that, to the days when Williams was just another West Virginia farmboy on his family's small dairy at Quiet Dell, seven miles east of Fairmont. Born in 1923, he was pitching in with the chores almost as soon as he could walk.

"I was the youngest boy," he recalls, "and from the time I was five or six, it was my job to get up each morning at four o'clock and, along with the collie, go out into the hills and roundup the herd. Then, when I'd get them back to the barn, I'd help with the milking.

Each of us boys had certain cows he was responsible for."

It was a simple, good life and Williams still has visions of those frosty mornings, and of putting the Model T Ford pickup into reverse and backing up the hills enroute to Fairmont to deliver the milk. After the last delivery, he would scoot off to class at Fairmont East High School. In the evenings, the family would gather around the radio and listen to the shows and to the news of the spreading war in Europe, where Hitler's goose-stepping legions were setting into motion events in which young Hershel would soon play such a dramatic and deadly role.

"But the European battlefield seemed so far off from Quiet Dell," he said as he recalled those times with a sad little smile. "After I finished high school, I joined the Civilian Conservation Corps and went off to Morgantown to work. I had been transferred to White Hall, Montana, when the Japanese attacked Pearl Harbor in December of 1941."

Williams returned home during the summer of 1942 and went to work in a steel factory at Sharon, Pa. He also joined the Marines but couldn't get in right away.

"Everybody wanted in back then," he recalled. "They couldn't take me until May of 1943 because their quota was filled. After I was sworn in, I went to San Diego for training and then was shipped to the Pacific."

He saw his first combat a few weeks later, during the invasion of Guam in the summer of 1944.

"I was with "C" Company, First Battalion, 21st Marines, Third Marine Division. We were among the first waves to hit the beach. There were twenty-five of us in the landing craft and we went ashore

under heavy machine gun and mortar fire. No sooner had we landed than the Japanese hit us with a banzai charge. We were in hand-to-hand combat before I knew it."

Guam was secured in August, 1944, and Williams returned to Hawaii for some much needed rest and relaxation. Although he had no way of knowing it, fate would soon provide him with his magical moment in history.

"They were getting ready to invade Iwo Jima," Williams said as he let his memory slice through the years. "Our division was supposed to be held in reserve and we were told they probably wouldn't need us."

When forty thousand marines hit the Iwo Jima beach on a cold and gloomy February morning in 1945, Williams and his comrades were aboard a troop ship a mile offshore. They had a ringside seat at one of the fiercest fights in our nation's history and they soon ceased to be spectators.

The invasion force was unable to establish a beachhead and was taking terrible casualties. On the second day, the Third Division was sent in through the bombs and bullets only to be forced to turn back because there was no room to land on the littered beach. So back they went to the ship only to try again the next morning, after the initial two divisions had spread out under cover of darkness.

"We went right back into the center of things," said Williams. "We became the spearhead division."

The Japanese were dug in some five-hundred yards back of the beach. They had constructed a line of concrete and steel bunkers that were armed with canons, mortars, machine guns and something the marines called "screaming nellies."

"I can still hear those things, Williams said. They were fifty gallon drums full of explosives launched from a ramp a few hundred yards back from the beach. You could see those barrels come tumbling through the sky and they made the gawd-awfullest noise you ever heard. One of those things could wipe out a whole squad."

But the Third Division wasn't to be denied. The marines overran the first line of defenses and promptly ran into a second line of pillboxes. This time they were caught in a withering fire.

"Every time we tried to charge, they'd knock us back. I had a team of six flamethrowers and six demolition men and it was no time before all my flamethrower men were gone, either killed or wounded. They were hitting us with everything they had and we were all on the ground trying to find some cover."

Hershel Williams' moment had come. The man who set the events into motion was his company captain, who asked the twenty-two-year-old corporal if he thought he might be able to take a flame thrower and knock out enough pill boxes to open a gap in the Japanese line.

"I'll try," replied Williams, who at

that time weighed about 155 pounds and stood no more than 5 ft. 7 in. in his combat boots.

The Japanese bunkers were about one-hundred-fifty yards away, across a stretch of no-man's land. In order to use his flamethrower, which had an eleven-second supply of fuel, Williams had to get within ten or fifteen feet of the pillboxes. He swung the seventy-two-pound device on his back and, accompanied by six riflemen, began crawling over the powdery ground.

"When the Japanese saw us coming, they really opened up. I could hear the bullets ricocheting off the back of the flamethrower."

But Williams and his riflemen made it. Then they returned for more fuel and made the deadly crossing again. And again. And again. And again. And again. And again. Seven times, in all.

After the last trip, the marines poured through the gap and the battle tide suddenly turned. Although three of his riflemen were killed, Williams was untouched.

A few weeks later, he was given sealed orders and was told to report to Marine Headquarters at Washington, D.C. There, on October 5, 1945, this bashful farm boy was awarded the Congressional Medal of Honor.

Hershel Williams is one of sixty-two West Virginians to ever earn their country's highest award since it was first presented during the Civil War. The six-pointed bronze star today holds a place of honor in the Williams' home near Huntington, where he is the chief of the Veterans Services Division of the Veterans Administration. The circumstances under which he won the medal "now seem like a dream."

But not the words of President Harry S. Truman, who draped the medal around Williams' neck on that October day in 1945.

"I'll never forget those words," he said softly. "When he presented me with the medal, Truman stepped up close to me and said: 'I'd rather have this medal than be President of the United States.'" —SD

"Siren of the Shenandoah"

The facts of Belle Boyd's historical contribution have always caused discussion and debate. She was called "The Siren of the Shenandoah" and "The Rebel Spy." Whether or not she influenced history, she certainly made an impact on the people of her day.

Isabelle "Belle" Boyd was born in Martinsburg, Berkeley County, on May 9, 1844 into a "genteel" but not exceptionally monied family. She had a spirited, active youth and at age sixteen was

prepared to make her debut into the Capital social whirl of dance balls and official dinners.

But the times were desperate; the Capital was divided and potential young beaus had to choose loyalties. The choice was not difficult for Belle. Her place was no longer in Washington—she hastened back to her valley.

Anxious to help in any way possible, many women "shelved" the conventional passive "Southern Belle" role and backed the South with the same high courage as their men. They defied the occupying Northern troops, were ready to scout and spy on the enemy, run the Union land blockade, and care for the sick and wounded. Their infectious devotion, unflagging faith, and true grit fueled the flaming spirit that helped sustain the Confederate forces to the very end.

It was the irrepressible aggressive spirit of the women of the Shenandoah Valley in particular that impelled General Shields to wire Secretary of War Stanton in the Spring of 1862: "I can retake the Valley and rejoin General McDowell, but you must send new men to keep it. The women will take it if we don't."

Belle was a full-grown woman of seventeen when she began free-lance undercover activities for her beloved Confederacy.

Following the occupation of Martinsburg by General Patterson's army, Federal soldiers overran the Boyd's home and one particularly drunk and disorderly soldier offered offense to Mrs. Boyd. Sensing that violence was soon to follow, Belle reacted instinctively: "I could stand it no longer. My indignation was aroused. My blood was literally boiling in my veins. I drew my pistol and shot him." He was carried away, mortally wounded.

From thence on fighting for the Confederacy became a personal crusade with Belle. She smuggled letters, clothing and quinine through the lines. At least once she eavesdropped on a Union command council and regularly she beguiled Federal officers and men into divulging military secrets. These she forwarded with the help of her body servant Eliza Jane Corsey Hopewell.

Belle's most celebrated exploit occurred during her stay at Front Royal, Virginia. Knowing Federal troops were weak and unprepared with no reinforcements due, she raced across Union occupied fields under a constant barrage of artillery fire to carry the news to General Stonewall Jackson. She did reach the Confederate advance guard, warned them and Front Royal was promptly taken by the Confederacy with negligible losses.

Belle was glorified as Woman Spy incarnate but the question remains as to how significant her information was and whether or not she actually met "Stonewall."

Belle, of course, said the General gallantly offered her a horse and escort home, but according to Major Harry Douglas, Belle confided her message to him and disappeared with "one wave of her white bonnet" never to see Jackson.

General Taylor, commander of Jackson's advance guard unit considered Belle's information vital to the Front Royal victory, but years later, ex-private John Robson wrote that Belle's daring only confirmed information already ascertained.

In any case, it was the woman—not the news—that always made the greater impression. Descriptions of her physical appearance vary but there seems to be unanimous agreement on her perfect figure, vivacious manner and disarming

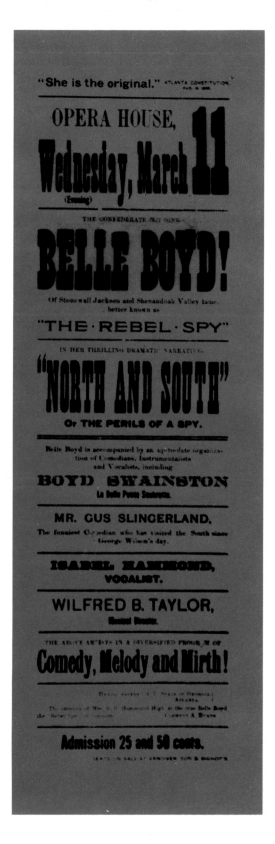

"She is the original." ATLANTA CONSTITUTION AUG. 15, 1888

OPERA HOUSE,
Wednesday, March 11
(Evening)

THE CONFEDERATE SPY GIRL

BELLE BOYD!
Of Stonewall Jackson and Shenandoah Valley fame,
better known as

"THE · REBEL · SPY"

IN HER THRILLING DRAMATIC NARRATIVE

"NORTH AND SOUTH"
OR THE PERILS OF A SPY.

Belle Boyd is accompanied by an up-to-date organization of Comedians, Instrumentalists and Vocalists, including

BOYD SWAINSTON
La Belle Poule Swainston

MR. GUS SLINGERLAND,
The funniest Comedian who has visited the South since George Wilson's day.

ISABEL HAMMOND,
VOCALIST.

WILFRED B. TAYLOR,
Musical Director.

THE ABOVE ARTISTS IN A DIVERSIFIED PROGRAM OF
Comedy, Melody and Mirth!

Harry Swainston U. S. Stage of Expositions, ATLANTA.

The adventures of Mrs. N. R. Hammond High as the true Belle Boyd the "Rebel Spy" is complete. — Clement A. Evans

Admission 25 and 50 cents.
SEATS ON SALE AT VANCOUVER SON & BISHOP'S

attractiveness to all manner of men. Even while imprisoned in the Old Capital in Washington, D.C., she captivated guards and fellow prisoners alike.

Belle was set free, only to be arrested and imprisoned again. She caught typhoid fever, however, and Secretary of War Staton commuted her sentence.

She journeyed to England and married Samuel Widle Hardinge on August 25, 1864. They had one daughter, Grace, but their union did not last long. Belle was widowed and in rapid succession became author, actress, wife again (this time to John Swainston Hammond in 1869) and mother of three more children.

Belle eventually returned to the states and toured in stock companies from New York to St. Louis to Galveston as "Nina Benjamin." An amicable divorce terminated her second marriage and in January of 1885 she married again. This time she chose a young actor, Nathaniel Rue High, only twenty-four years old and seventeen years her junior. But this marriage seemed blessed and she continued touring the country giving dramatic recitals of her war experiences and adventures.

Attracted by her success, a number of spurious "Belle Boyds" appeared, much to her discomfort and annoyance. To overcome this nuisance, Belle had to carry special credentials to establish her authenticity.

Belle was in Kilbourn (now Wisconsin Dells), Wisconsin on June 9, 1900 when she suffered a sudden heart attack—she never recovered.—MS

RESORTS AND HIGH LIVIN'

The surest way to land a proper bachelor...

West Virginia's good for what ails ya.

People have believed it for centuries. Generations from the time of the red man to today have been mysteriously attracted to the mountains for physical and spiritual rebirth and for relaxation.

To the Indians, it was the land of warm springs that brought miraculous relief to aching joints, a land of boundless plenty where clear water ran in mountain streams and plant and animal life furnished healthful food.

To the colonists, it was a place where transplanted gentlemen could escape the problems of English tyranny and the troublesome thoughts of revolution.

To Civil War leaders, it was a place of respite from the emotional rigor of the strife in a house divided.

At the turn of the century, it was still a place where the unfortunate victims of tuberculosis might seek "the cure" by the icy hand of West Virginia's pure mountain air.

And today, it is the pleasant destination of young people in quest of the challenging mountain slope or the unspoiled woodland trail or the roaring wild river. It's escape for harried businessmen and blue-collar workers who need to flee the bustle of city life. It holds its magnetic force for retiring people who want to slow down and live.

General Robert E. Lee returned to West Virginia after the Civil War was over. His had been one of several forces from both North and South that had occupied the White Sulfur Springs resort facilities.

When the war ended, "Old White" (one of the first grand facilities there), became the summer home for General Lee and White Sulphur Springs soon became the "marriage mart" of the entire South. Because of the war, young men were scarce and Southern belles (debutantes) flocked to "Old White" to attend the general's frequent balls since that was the surest way to land a proper bachelor.

Today this world-renowned resort, known as The Greenbrier, can accommodate 1,100 of its guests to dine at one time in the elegant Colonial Hall. The all-time guest list has included hundreds of personalities of international, social and historical significance.

The Greenbrier is the pinnacle of West Virginia's resort appeal. But leisure facilities have continued to spring up for resort seekers of every social and economic means: State Park lodges and recreation facilities, commercial lodges, conference and recreational centers, State and commercial campgrounds (there are even camplands in West Virginia where you can purchase your own piece of mountain nature), hunting lodges and camps. The list goes on.

Recreation and tourism stand today as two of West Virginia's most important industries . . . so it was two-hundred years ago. —JA

"Ye Famed Warm Springs"

A young itinerant Methodist minister, Francis Asbury, called it "that seat of sin." Historically, it is esteemed as the "Las Vegas of the Eighteenth Century." The Indians long revered it for its wondrous curative effect on aching joints. And, historian Fred Newbraugh believes it was exactly what Ponce de Leon was looking for—the fabled fountain of youth.

America's founding fathers knew it as Bath, Virginia.

Today this historic resort community is known as Berkley Springs, West Virginia.

The natural warm springs, located in what is now known as the Eastern Panhandle of West Virginia, was already famed as a health resort long before white men began to settle here or even dream of the "new world."

Almost every Indian tribe along the Eastern coast and throughout its inland mountains knew of the springs and had for unmeasured time trekked hundreds and thousands of miles to seek relief and even cure for tribesmen who were often racked with the pain of arthritis.

It was the Indians' most troublesome affliction, due largely to a primitive life that required living and sleeping on the cold, damp ground.

The springs were so important to all the tribes that it became the custom to allow Indian pilgrimages to pass unmolested even in time of war when it was known the destination was the famed warm springs.

Groups of Indians heading to the springs marched under a flag or symbol of truce. It is believed that early settlers soon learned of the great values of the warm springs of western Virginia and the place grew quickly into a colonial resort that closely paralleled the birth of a new nation.

The springs fell within the proprietary of Lord Fairfax who had been granted thousands of acres in colonial western Virginia.

It was a 16-year-old lad in a Fairfax surveying party who noted in his journal in March of 1748, "This day we visited Ye Famed Warm Springs." That was young George Washington and he was one of a succession of famous patriots who

would walk the streets of Berkeley Springs in the next three decades leading to the Revolution and birth of a nation.

Washington was to return again and again to the warm springs: in 1750 and 1751 with his ailing brother, Lawrence; in 1761 to regain his own health after the French and Indian War; in 1769 with his wife, Martha, and his stepdaughter, Patsy Custis, who was in poor health; and, frequently, from then to the Revolution, to participate in the social activities that began to take place there among the rich and well-bred gentlemen of the Colonies.

A community began to develop at the springs. Some of the dwellings were established by the blue-blooded gentlemen of the Colonies, others by "less desireable" settlers. They were all "squatters", however, and Lord Fairfax at one point became displeased with the developments on his land. But how could Lord Fairfax argue in those times with such prominent squatters as the Washingtons in the James Merser House, whose guests often included James Madison (who was sent to the springs by his physician), or Luther Martin who was later Attorney General of the United States and defense attorney for Aaron Burr?

In spite of Fairfax (or with him), a community grew.

They called it Bath because it bore a striking resemblance to the town of Bath, England, once branded by John Wesley as "The Devil's Headquarters."

Rich British subjects had often "resorted" to Bath, England, on the pretense of healthful repose, but only as an excuse to "revel" and gamble away idle hours. So it was natural that families like the Fairfaxes, the Carters and the Willises would establish a similar retreat at these warm springs.

Soon Bath, Virginia, was more than a resort for health. It was a resort for high livin'.

Colonial Bath was not fancy, or as fashionable as its English counterpart. Homes in the mid-eighteenth century town were rough-hewn log cabins. The warm springs bath was a hollow scooped out of the sand and privacy was provided by a screen of evergreen trees cut from the nearby forest. First the ladies, then the men, took turns as the baths continued to be valued as a relaxing treatment for all sorts of ailments.

George Washington liked to gamble in those days and enjoyed the upper class excitement of Bath where day and night it was eating, drinking, bathing, fiddling, dancing, reveling and gambling in great excess. Horse racing took place as a daily amusement and there was even an occasional duel at the race-track grounds.

It was the combination of relaxation and the thrill of high livin' that placed Bath prominently in the minds of this country's founding fathers.

Bath was finally surveyed, streets laid out, and the town chartered in 1776. Among the signers of the petition for the charter was John Hansen, who is claimed by some to be the *real* first President of the United States, as he was the first President of the Continental Congress.

"Surveyors were laying out the town while the Continental Congress was declaring the country free and independent," Fred Newbraugh said, "and what those surveyors and those fathers were thinking of at that time is shown right here in the town map.

"The main street through town was named Washington Street, after the general, who by the way, didn't sign the petition because he was off fighting the war.

"The first street coming into town from the north is Union, for the fight for "Independence," the name of the next street.

"The very next street is Congress . . . their faith was in the Continental Congress which was meeting at the very time this survey was going on to consider the Declaration of Independence.

"Fairfax was named after the owner of the land; not all the Fairfaxes were Tories, you know. Then comes Liberty . . . that's what the Revolution was all about.

"The next street was Market. That's what it was *really* all about, they wanted freedom to trade with countries other than England to avoid paying taxes.

"The next street was Warren. General Joseph Warren had lost his life at the battle of Bunker Hill. Merser Street was named after James Merser, a member of the Continental Congress and a war hero. Montgomery Street was named for General Richard Montgomery who had lost his life on the last day of 1775 at the Battle of Quebec.

"Wilkes Street was named after John Wilkes of England. He's the guy who got up in Parliament and advocated that England give us our independence and not require us to fight for it.

"One of the opposition party members then got up and said, 'I fear my friend shall either die on the gallows or of a venereal disease.' Wilkes got the floor again and replied, 'I suppose that would depend on which way I would

A young George Washington strikes a dignified pose, musket ready and "order of march" protruding from vest pocket. ("Washington as British Colonel 1772," Charles Wilson Peale.)

History, rustic charm and occasionally a touch of flair prevail at West Virginia's better known resorts, inns and restaurants. Some are modern, but most are traditional. (Upper left) Drover's Inn, located in the northern panhandle city of Wellsburg was built by John Fowler in 1848 and used to house the Fowlersburg Post Office. (Circling clockwise) "Lock, Stock and Barrel" of Williamson, in the heart of the coalfields, offers a unique bill of fare and decor with a taste of Tug River Valley frontier. The Wells Hotel, built in 1894 by Ephraim Wells, still flourishes with turn-of-the-century charm. Today it's known as Wells Inn. Shaded riding trails wind through the woods at Wheeling's Oglebay Park. Its 65 acres include 3 golf courses, a museum, a lodge, swimming pool, an amphitheatre, the Good Zoo, nature trails, Oglebay Institute and other accommodations. Pipestem Resort is a combination of luxurious lodge accommodations (night view), restaurant facilities and uncrowded outdoor beauty. The Scollay Hall dining room (Middleway, W.Va., 8 miles east of Charles Town) specializes in dishes like Old Virginia Ham and corn souffle. An 1858 antique Knabe piano is used as a serving table. From December to March, Eastern skiers congregate at Canaan Valley, Snowshoe, Oglebay Park, Alpine Lake and Chestnut Ridge. At Berkeley Springs, visitors can walk the same paths traveled by the country's founders as well as take the "cure." In 1890, (center, top) the B&O Railroad brought streams of guests to the Hilltop House in Harpers Ferry. Today both American and foreign visitors savor "Hilltop Fried Chicken" and stewed tomatoes while enjoying the view. The Mountaineer Dinner Theatre in Hurricane (lower center) offers year-round entertainment with professional casts.

leave this world, embracing my friend's policies or his mistress.'

"And on the other side of what is now the park was another street named Henry Street . . . after a rabble rousing patriot named Patrick."

It continued to be a favorite spa of this young nation with President George Washington building a summer White House there and many other early government officials adopting it as a health and social retreat from the rigors of running the nation.

Bath, alias Berkeley Springs, has continued as one of America's most famous resort communities to the present day, surviving periods when gambling flowed out-of-bounds into the hands of professional bilkers and when liquor by-the-drink was a more important elixir than the healing waters of the warm springs.

All those eras have come and gone. But those constant 75-degree waters still flow and countless hundreds still are drawn to the springs to discover what Ponce de Leon once mistook from Indian accounts to be the "fountain of youth."

The old spring house at Red Sulphur Springs in Monroe County was the center of a flourishing health resort in 1832, and the buildings (empty now) were used as a Confederate hospital during the Civil War.

"I believe this really was the fountain of youth Ponce de Leon was looking for," Newbraugh said. "And unlike others who claim it, I think I've got proof."

"Ponce de Leon was asking the Indians about these things. Communication was difficult," Newbraugh said. "The Indians told him they had such a fountain up north. And Ponce de Leon traveled well into the Carolinas before he finally turned back, fearing he and his men were being led into ambush.

"To the Indians it was the fountain of youth. Getting old to them didn't mean wrinkling skin or failing powers. It meant aching joints, and this warm spring eased the pain."

Of course there is no such place as the "fountain of youth." But there is such a place as Bath, governed by a town council that still operates under the original 1776 charter. But outside those chamber walls, on its streets, in the state maps, they call it Berkeley Springs.—JA

TROUBLE AND TRAGEDY

The afternoon of December 15, 1967 will be long remembered by Point Pleasant residents. Folks in the quiet, peaceful little river town still speak in hushed tones when they refer to the day which began amid so much hope and ended amid so much sorrow.

Until dusk the day had been a happy one for most residents. Main Street was gaily decorated and the Christmas spirit prevailed. People greeted one another as they passed, their arms laden with bundles and packages for friends and loved ones.

As the day wore on the temperature began to drop. The air was freezing cold by the time the sun sank into the hills across the Ohio River. The mood of the

Passing towboat pilots can remember the peaceful moonlit scene in this rare photograph, but no one will ever see it again. The Point Pleasant Silver Bridge opened to traffic on May 19, 1928 and was busily traveled as part of the east-west Ohio route U.S. 40. It was the first bridge project to employ heat-treated eyebars in place of standard suspension cables.

shopping crowd had changed from casual and friendly to rushed. Shoppers were now hurrying for home when suddenly everyone stopped—frozen in their tracks by a long, loud, sighing roar coming from the direction of the river just two blocks away.

"What was that?" they asked one another, in simultaneous astonishment.

A youth came running down the street screaming, "The *bridge* has fallen! The *bridge* has fallen!"

At first, folks refused to believe their ears. But as the crowd rushed to the river, they couldn't deny the horrible sight their eyes beheld. Instead of the Silver Bridge, their eyes found only emptiness—until they looked down at the river and saw the cars and trucks slowly sinking into the murky water.

Sixty-four people fell helplessly into the river that December evening. Only eighteen came out alive. Two bodies were never found and West Virginia—a state born amidst trouble—had recorded yet another terrible tragedy.

Some people said the collapse of the bridge fulfilled the curse placed on the community nearly 200 years earlier by the murdered Indian Chief Cornstalk.

Others pointed out the irony that the Ohio Valley's worst modern tragedy should take place just a few hundred feet from the site of the bloodiest battle ever fought between the Indians and the early settlers—a bloody baptism for a territory that would know so much pain and suffering.

West Virginia's formal birth came ninety years later during a war made even more tragic by the fact that it often pitted father against son and brother against brother.

After the Civil War, fires and raging rivers continued to cause heartbreak. But these periodic problems were mere primers for the industrial tragedies that were to come. When the state's natural resources first were tapped, the process involved trial and error, and some of the errors were devastating.

The worst of these mishaps took place in 1907 at the tiny West Virginia community of Monongah, where 361 miners died in a methane gas explosion. The tragedy still ranks as the worst coal mine disaster in our nation's history.

Many more tragedies occurred throughout the years but none more awful than the one which took place in 1967 just

a few miles from Monongah in the community of Farmington.

The date was November 20, and the hour was 5:30 a.m. It was a cold, dark morning and most folks were still in bed when a loud, rumbling roar filled the air. It was a sound that would herald a waking nightmare for the folks of Farmington. The word was soon circulated: there had been a methane explosion at Consolidation Coal's No. 9 mine.

Dozens of friends and family members gathered at the portal. They heard more explosions and watched fire and smoke pour from the mine which by now was a roaring furnace. After nine days all hope faded and the mine was sealed. For the seventy-eight men still inside, No. 9 had become a tomb.

The deaths were not entirely in vain, however. A shocked nation had waited along with the families and the ensuing outrage prompted Congress to enact some much-needed new mine safety legislation. But new mine laws were of no avail the next time tragedy struck the state.

It was a rainy Saturday night on November 14, 1970, when supporters of the Marshall University football team were gathered at Huntington's Tri-State Airport to await the team's return from a game in Tennessee.

The chartered DC-9 never made it back home. Instead, the craft plunged into a hillside a half mile from the airport, killing all seventy-five persons aboard and virtually wiping out the football team and coaching staff. A shocked population went into mourning.

Dec. 8, 1907 was called a "day of funerals" in Monongah. The overflow of wooden coffins literally filled the street.

The dreadful impact of sorrow caused by the plane crash was still fresh when another shocking disaster took place in a little valley deep in the heart of Logan County coal fields just a little more than a year later. The stream that flows through this valley is known as Buffalo Creek. Some sixteen coal camps are scattered along the creek, which begins as a trickle far up in the hills and grows into a full-fledged stream 20 feet wide and 6 feet deep before it flows into the Guyandotte River at the community of Man, some seventeen miles down the valley.

One of the communities furthest up the valley is Lorado, the home of Larry and Ailene Peters. And on the morning of February 26, 1972, the Peters, like most folks in the valley, were worried. Rain had been falling steadily for three days and people were concerned about the big slag dam at the head of the valley—the dam where Buffalo Mining Co., a subsidiary of the Pittston Co., dumped its coal waste.

Larry Peters went to work that morning but he didn't stay long. It was only mid-morning when he and some other miners came tearing down the valley, honking and screaming and blinking their lights.

"They were hollering that the dam had busted," recalled Mrs. Peters. "I grabbed the baby and we drove off in our car. You could look back and see the water coming."

The Peters won a desperate race down the valley but many of their neighbors weren't so fortunate. A wave of black water, ten feet high, swept down the narrow valley. When it subsided, 125 people were dead, 500 homes were gone and $50 million worth of property had been destroyed or swept away.

Ailene Peters returned home the next day. "Everything was gone," she said. "The railroad track was all twisted and sticking up in the air. Our house was gone. It was over there."

She pointed to a grassy field where a group of boys were playing.

"And right over there," she added, once again pointing to the field, "over there where that pipe is sticking up, that was where the Dillons lived. They were a family of nine. Every one of them was lost." —SD

97

FOLKLORE AND FABLE

"If you shut your eyes, you can almost hear the hammers ring . . . "

Three of the most popular legendary figures to emerge from the founding of our nation were Paul Bunyan of the Pacific Northwest, Pecos Bill of the Southwestern desert and West Virginia's John Henry, the heroic black man who died with his hammer in his hand, Lawd, Lawd, while proving a human being is better than a machine.

There's a difference between John Henry and the two other folk heroes mentioned above, however. They were mythical characters while John Henry was a real man who worked on a track gang in West Virginia during the 1870's when the C&O Railroad was boring a mile-long tunnel through the Big Bend Mountain in scenic Summers County. He was one of the hundreds of freed slaves who helped build railroads throughout this area in the reconstruction period that followed the Civil War.

There are no accurate records of John Henry's life, but authorities believe such a man really worked on the Big Bend Tunnel. They are skeptical, however, about the death of John Henry as a result of the race with the steam drill.

"That part's not true, says Edward Cabbell, director of the John Henry Memorial Foundation at Princeton and author of a forthcoming book on West Virginia's black heritage. John Henry wasn't a giant like Paul Bunyan; he was a big, strong black man who worked on the railroad and who probably was killed in a rock fall, but we don't know for certain."

Like many other epic stories, the John Henry legend was born of need. It gave the newly-freed blacks of that time a strong, positive model with whom they could identify and look to with pride. And his legendary victory over the steam drill gave them tangible proof that a human being was inherently worth more than the machines which were beginning to take their jobs.

The legend was first developed and passed along in work songs and ballads sung beside flickering campfires after the day was done.

According to these songs, John Henry was the son of slave parents in the Old South. He was given superhuman powers that enabled him to walk and talk at birth and to prophesy the future, including his own death, with a hammer in his hand, Lawd, Lawd.

By the time he was a teenager, John Henry stood better than six feet six and weighed more than 250 pounds. He could outwork any nine men with ease, whether the job was picking cotton or stripping tobacco.

Following the Civil War, John Henry and his beautiful Polly Ann left the plantation and drifted north to West Virginia, where the C&O was pushing westward across the mountains. John Henry got a job on the track gang driving long, steel blasting rods into the rocky mountainside. His great strength and endurance soon became legend among the work crews and it was only natural, according to the storytellers, that he would be the one to challenge the steam drill brought in by a salesman who claimed the machine could do the work of ten men.

The race pitting man against machine began early one morning and John Henry, with a twelve-pound hammer in each hand, drove steel into the rocks all day long without pause. Legend has it that the sparks flew like lightning and his hammer rang like thunder. When dusk came, the race was over and the machine was defeated, Lawd, Lawd, and the workers' jobs were safe.

But they had lost their hero who, according to the ballads, sank down and died of exhaustion, his head cradled in Polly Ann's lap and his hammers still in his hands.

James Twohig, a foreman on the tunnel project, has told historians the John Henry legend is part fact and part fiction.

Twohig said a study of old records revealed there probably was "a big, strapping man named John Henry who weighed 275 pounds. He was a very valuable worker and the contractor paid him $1.50 a day instead of the usual $1.25. His father came directly from Africa but there's no indication there was any such contest as described in the ballad."

Twohig also said he thought John Henry had outlived his days on the railroad and had died of old age near the community of Gap Mills in Monroe County.

No matter how John Henry died, Cabbell says the legend has become one of our nation's favorite stories, one that is told and loved around the world. He says the story is important historically because it deals with the contributions made by blacks to the construction of our nation.

"Although most people aren't aware of it," says Cabbell, "more than five thousand black slaves lived and worked in what is now known as West Virginia during the latter part of the Eighteenth Century. Black men also made important

contributions during the days the salt industry was flourishing in the Kanawha Valley."

"Also," he adds, "the story is important because as far as I know, it is our only positive legend about a black person."

The location of John Henry's grave is not known but visitors to the Big Bend Tunnel area can see a large metal statue of the famed steel-drivin' man, with his hammer still in his hand. And if you shut your eyes, you can almost hear the hammers ring while the track gangs sing:

Ain't no hammer
Rings like mine.
Rings like gold, Lawd,
Ain't it fine?

Rings like silver,
Peal on peal.
Into the rock, Lawd,
Drive the steel.

If'n I dies, Lawd,
I command.
Bury the hammer
In my hand. —SD

Dusty and his friends

Dusty Rhodes was never the ideal image of a spit 'n polish U. S. forest ranger.

They tried for years to get him to wear that dern uniform with its wide-brim ranger hat but Dusty always kept them hanging on the cabin wall, alongside the faded calendar with the pictures of the different kinds of turkey feathers on it . . . and the hat with all the holes in it.

Now there was a real hat . . . one of

those billed caps, grey in color and with a story under it that even the most skeptical hunter had to believe.

"Well, sir," Dusty said as he reared back in his rocking chair, "there was the fella that'd been killin' game outa season. I kept trackin' him in hopes I'd ketch him with the goods, but he was a slick one.

"So one day I got in the woods before he did and hid behind this tree. Then I commenced to make a few sounds like I was a squirrel a-playin'."

Dusty made a few such sounds for effect and then said, "That ole boy heard me and commenced to stalk. When he got close enough I took this ole grey hat of mine and just ran it up and down the tree just so it'd look like a squirrel a-playin'.

"Then I'd duck it behind the tree. Well sir, he was a fast shot, alright, and shot holes right through my hat!

"Well sir, I just let 'er drop like as if the squirrel was dead and that hunter just stayed still for awhile hopin' he'd see another squirrel. Finally he gave up and came up to get his game. Was he ever surprised when I jumped out!"

The hat with all the holes in it was the proof of his story this time and few of the fond listeners to this master story teller would guess that Dusty might have put those holes in that hat himself.

But there were other stories that just couldn't be believed . . . like the time Dusty was out in fifty-seven inch snow feeding the turkey, and Dusty's pet deer (Fanny) kept stepping on his snow shoes, throwing him down. (If Dusty needed snow shoes to get over the deep snow, how was Fanny able to stay aloft on her tiny feet?)

Whether or not his stories were true didn't matter much to the thousands of hunters and hunters' families and teachers and Supreme Court judges who journeyed into the mountains between Elkins and Spruce Knob to visit a most unbelievable man . . . even when the truth was known.

And it was true that this man, Dusty Rhodes, was as close to West Virginia nature as any man has ever been or will ever be.

His cabin at the base of Middle Mountain became a wondrous spectacle each day at sundown when wildlife of every description would gather in . . . deer by the herd, turkey by the flock, 'coons, possums, foxes and more.

It was a real-life woodland ritual as animals of every description clustered around their loving friend Dusty to be fed.

Dusty's cabin was right on the edge of a wildlife preserve. Out his front door his animal friends were in grave danger . . . out his back door they were safe in the preserve or within the fenced area where Dusty kept Fanny and others penned up during the hunting season for their own protection.

Though these hunters and their friends were enemies to his animal family, Dusty delighted in their visits . . . enjoyed showing off . . . basked in the beams of their amazement as he fed and caressed these wild animals and called them all by name.

One summer evening Dusty's visitors were disappointed when the animals (well fed by summer's plenty) did not show up.

"Oh, I know someone who'll come to see me," he said. Then he scurried into his cabin, returned with a handful of bread and headed for the banks of Glady Fork.

"Now, you probably don't believe this, but I can call the fish," he said. Then

he began stamping his right foot dramatically on a flat rock that jutted into the water.

Immediately the water began to churn with fish and the bread crumbs disappeared as quickly as they hit the water.

Dusty loved the animals . . . spent all his time looking after them . . . feeding them at his cabin . . . spending days and nights in the field feeding them in winter . . . rescuing them from drifts and crevices . . . giving hunters bad advice on where the "best hunting was" to spare his friends.

And the animals loved him.

Fanny in particular. Fanny was a beautiful doe who loved sweets and did not fear people. Dusty had rescued her when she was a motherless fawn . . . nursed her and protected her for twelve years.

Fanny spent more of her life at Dusty's cabin than she did in the wilderness,

though she strayed many times to become a mother. She was a modern scavenger who would even get into parked cars while visitors talked to Dusty, sometimes feasting on the tourists' picnic lunches.

"Fanny's my second wife, you know," Dusty used to say. "I found her right after my first wife died and she fusses over me just like she was my woman." It's true that Fanny would kiss and caress

Dusty's weather-beaten face and follow him through the wilderness with unending devotion.

Dusty always kept Fanny penned up during hunting season. But the season

for bow and arrow was too long and Fanny became restless.

The hunter killed her just a few yards from Dusty's cabin. "That hunter surely knew it was Fanny," one fellow mourned. "Dusty was never quite the same after that."

A few years later Dusty "retired" from the forest service and built another home further down Glady Fork. For several years thereafter he tried his best to train his animal friends to find him at his new place. But they kept going back to the old place on Middle Mountain. They just couldn't understand why Dusty wasn't there anymore.

Then one day Dusty's mountain wilderness took him . . . a jeep loaded with feed for the animals . . . a tree on the side of the road.

Dusty's gone. Yet Dusty's stories and stories of Dusty live on.

Like the time two hunters were sitting in his cabin, listening to some outlandish, but exciting tale.

There were repeated scratches at the door.

"Go 'way now," Dusty said. "Go 'way. I've got company now."

Soon the animal pushed her nose through the door . . . paraded through the front room . . . into Dusty's bedroom and curled up on his bed.

To anyone who knew Dusty Rhodes, such a sight never came as a shock—not even the fact that this privileged resident happened to be a skunk . . . —JA

"Well, we don't want this little scrape to cost you anything," the robber said. . .

September 6, 1875 dawned cold and clear above the newly-settled town of Huntington. The day was Monday and the brisk morning air held no hint that the most exciting event in the bustling little community's short history was about to occur.

Cashier Robert T. Oney was alone in the Bank of Huntington as he looked out a window and saw four horsemen coming down the dirt street. The men were all strangers to Oney. One rode a dark brown horse, two were on bays and the lead rider was atop a dappled gray stallion. Oney also noticed each man wore a long linen duster over a heavy winter coat.

But the cashier had work to do. He turned away from the window and resumed recording deposits in the big blue ledger. He had made only a few entries, however, when his attention was again diverted, this time by a fusillade of gunfire in the street.

He looked up just in time to see two of the strangers come bounding into the bank. Each man was waving a

long barreled pistol.

Oney made a desperate lunge for his revolver but the men beat him to it.

"Hold up your hands," ordered one of the men, pointing his gun at the cashier's head.

"Open the safe," they demanded.

"No!" Oney replied.

"If you don't, we'll kill you!" snarled one of the gunmen.

"If you do, you'll never get the money," Oney stammered as the men closed in. Just as they were about to pull their triggers, the cashier turned and opened the safe. Then he stood back and watched as the men quickly cleaned it out.

"Any of this money yours?" asked one of the bandits.

"Yes," replied Oney. "About seven dollars of it."

"Well, we don't want this little scrape to cost you anything," the robber said as he counted out seven bills and handed them to the stunned cashier.

A bank messenger walked through the

Notorious bank robber Frank James, accused of a visit to the Huntington Bank in 1875.

door at that moment. The bandits immediately took his bag. Then they bound Oney and the messenger and carried the loot out the front door.

John Hooe Russel, the bank president, came around the corner about this time and watched the bandits gallop down Third Avenue, firing their pistols into the air and driving folks to cover.

Russel immediately ran to the livery stable and got his horse. Five minutes later, a posse of nearly ten men thundered down the street headed west after the robbers who had fled with nearly $20,000.

The chase lasted for days and Huntington residents kept abreast of the events via telegraph. One of the bandits, a man identified as Thomlinson McDaniels, was shot and killed. Another bandit, Thomas J. Webb (alias Jack Keen) was apprehended in Fentress County, Tennessee and taken to Louisville, Kentucky. Oney went to Louisville and identified the man as one of the robbers. He returned to Huntington with about $4,000 of the bank's money.

Webb was brought back to West Virginia for trial and convicted, but the other two robbers were never arrested due to lack of evidence. However, statements subsequently made by Webb left no doubt that Frank James had been with him and probably Cole Younger.

Time has shrouded many of the details of the exciting events of that day but the old bank building still stands—preserved as part of Huntington's Heritage Village. And on display at the Huntington galleries are two pistols believed to have been dropped by the bandits while making their escape—a French pinfire revolver and a Remington Army model six-shooter—long barreled reminders of the day the James Gang came to call.—SD

The Kanawha Valley Demon

Early European immigrants brought to this country a love of ghost-story telling and an ability to dream up the most eerie of monsters.

During the colonial period of early America there was no better setting for such fantastic stories than the "border country," the perilous frontier that stretched through the mountains of western Virginia.

One of the most compelling stories was published in 1878 by "Beadle's Dime Library" of New York. Titled, "The Wolf Demon; or The Queen of the Kanawha," author Albert Aiken entwined in his fictional tale many not-so-imaginary characters including frontiersmen Daniel Boone and Simon Kenton.

The great round moon looked down in a flood of silver light upon the virgin forest by the banks of the beautiful river which winds through the richest and fairest valley in the wide western land.

A frightened deer came crashing through the forest, stalked by an Indian warrior, a brave of the great Shawnee tribe—lords of the Ohio Valley from the Allegheny to the great river of the New World, the winding Ohio.

The warrior crossed the glade and entered the thicket, unaware that as he was following the deer, another form followed him through the forest. The form moved noiselessly and cast behind it a gigantic shadow. It skulked around in the darkness as though it feared the moonlight.

The brave guessed not that the dreaded demon of his nation—the terrible foe who had left his red 'totem' (an arrow carved in flesh with the point of a knife) on the breast of many a stout Shawnee brave—was now on his track, eager for that blood which was necessary to its existence.

The demon slipped up behind the red man and felled him with one blow of its tomahawk.

The dark form bent over him for a moment and with three rapid knife slashes, the mark of the destroyer was blazoned on the breast of the victim.

Through the forest stole the dark form. As it crossed the glade, the rays of the moon fell upon it. The figure was that of a huge gray wolf that walked erect and had the face of a human. The Wolf Demon carried a tomahawk which glistened with the fresh blood of the Shawnee brave.

Daniel Boone learned about the Wolf Demon when he visited the Point Pleasant settlement. While there, rumor arrived that the Indians were about to attack the outpost and Daniel Boone was appointed commander.

With a companion, Boone crossed the Ohio to discover the plans of the Shawnee. Instead, he was himself discovered, captured and held hostage in the camp.

Boone was saved from his fate by a daring rescue staged by a mysterious friend. Held prisoner in the Shawnee chieftain's wigwam, he could hear the sound of a knife cutting through the skins that formed the walls.

Boone gazed in astonishment at the tall figure, shrouded in darkness, that he could barely distinguish standing in the center of the lodge.

"Who the deuce can it be?" mused Boone.

Then Boone felt two powerful arms seize him, and roll him over on his side.

As the hands of the stranger touched him, Boone felt a cold shiver creep all over him. The hands of the stranger seemed to be armed with claws like the paws of a beast.

"Jerusalem, stranger!" muttered Boone, "you ought to cut your fingernails; they stick right into a feller . . . ."

Strange as his savior seemed to be, Boone accepted his help and reached out in the dark to take his hand.

"By hookey!" he muttered to himself, "either your hunting shirt's made of bearskin, or else you've more hair on your arm than I have on my head.

"I wish the derned critter would say something," muttered Boone, slightly uneasy. "If he wasn't acting so much a human I should think that it was a pet b'ar that had hold me."

Boone's rescue was complete when it dawned on him that the beast was the fabled Wolf Demon.

Boone, stout woodsman that he was —a man that laughed at danger and faced death coolly and without shrinking— felt a cold shiver come over him as he watched the movements of the mysterious being who was so free in his actions. And so sparing of his words:

"Jerusalem! Is it a spook after all?"

The hair on his head rose in fright as the thought crossed his mind.

Later, in the Shawnee camp, the great chief Ke-ne-ha-ha, worried about the Wolf Demon, asked the medicine man to tell him about the Demon and summon the spook so that Ke-ne-ha-ha could destroy it.

"The Wolf Demon is far down below the earth," the medicine man said.

Then, to summon the Demon, the medicine man cast a stick into the flame:

"See, the green stick is burning," the medicine man said, staring into the fire.

"When it is ashes, the chief will stand face to face with the Wolf Demon. He will tremble like a squaw when he sees the white man's devil."

"The Great Medicine is wise, but he lies when he says that Ke-ne-ha-ha will tremble!" cried the Shawnee chief.

As the green stick burned, the medicine man spoke:

"The Wolf Demon is a white devil, and he hates the Shawnees."

"But why should he hate the warriors of Ke-ne-ha-ha?"

"Because when the Wolf Demon was on earth they did him wrong."

The chief started.

"The Wolf Demon has lived, then, a human?"

"Yes, listen," The Great Medicine paused for a moment as if to collect his thoughts:

"Twelve moons ago a songbird dwelt in the wigwams of the Shawnees . . . She was as fair as the rosy morn, as gentle as the summer wind, as lithe and graceful as the brown deer. She was called 'Red Arrow.'"

The medicine man told how the Indian maiden had wandered from the tribe and had fallen in love with a paleface.

"She left home, kindred, all, for the sake of the long-rifle. She became his squaw."

"The Great Medicine knows the fate of Red Arrow?" Ke-ne-ha-ha asked.

"Yes; the Shawnees found her in the lodge of the paleface. They asked her to return to her people. She refused, for she loved the white hunter. Then the red chiefs went away, but when the sky grew dark . . . again the Shawnee warriors stood by the lodge of the paleface who had stolen from her home the singing-bird of the Shawnees. They gave to the fire the lodge of the paleface, and while

the flames roared and crackled, they shot Red Arrow dead in their midst."

"The Shawnee woman who forsakes her tribe for a paleface stranger deserves to die," said the chief sternly.

The mark of the red arrow became understandable now, and the vengeance of the Wolf Demon was clear.

"When the lodge of the white hunter was burnt to the ground, the body of Red Arrow, disfigured by flames, lay before the warriors. They looked for the hunter, but could not find him."

"He was not in the lodge when my braves attacked it," interrupted the chief.

"Ke-ne-ha-ha is wrong," replied the medicine man. "The white hunter was

in the lodge. He saw the singing-bird fly from life to death, and was wounded by the bullets of the Shawnee warriors; then, when the lodge fell, he was buried beneath the ruins. The eyes of the red braves were sharp, but they did not discover

104

the wounded and helpless whiteskin under the blackened logs.

"The white brave lay between life and death. A huge gray wolf came from the forest. He found the senseless man under the logs. The forest beast was hungry; he thirsted for human blood. The great gray wolf ate up the wounded whiteskin. The body of the white went into the stomach of the wolf; it died, but the soul of the white hunter lived."

So the white man's soul took up residence in the body of a wolf and began its plan of vengeance.

The ten braves who had murdered the Indian maiden had been killed by the Wolf Demon. Only their leader, Chief Ke-ne-ha-ha, remained.

The medicine man turned his back to the chief, and as the burning green stick died out, he turned to face Ke-ne-ha-ha again. The medicine man had been transformed into the Wolf Demon!

A vicious battle ensued between the Wolf Demon and Ke-ne-ha-ha. Thinking he had fatally wounded the Chief, who had suffered a mere flesh wound, the Wolf Demon raced through the village and went screaming into the wilderness.

Ke-ne-ha-ha's experience was unsettling to him and when a young brave asked for his daughter's hand, he charged the youth with the duty of killing the cursed Demon in order to win the right.

The brave's name was White Dog and he eagerly pursued the strange Demon until one day he lured it into battle in a forest clearing.

Daniel Boone and scout Simon Kenton witnessed the fight and saw the dreadful thing accept the challenge. The demon quickly overpowered the young brave and stood with one foot on the fallen warrior's breast, tomahawk raised, ready to deliver the fateful blow.

Just then, the Shawnee girl Le-a-pah, Ke-ne-ha-ha's daughter, appeared in the clearing and walked toward the Wolf Demon.

The paw of the Wolf Demon which clenched the tomahawk remained poised in the air as the girl advanced.

The phantom form, motionless as one of the forest oaks, glared upon the Indian girl with its eyes of fire as if struck dumb with horror.

The scouts looked on with awe-struck eyes. They expected at any instant to see the tomahawk descend and the Indian girl to fall lifeless at the blow.

Steadily for a few moments the Demon form glared at the brave and then, taking its foot from the breast of the downtrodden brave, it retreated backward with slow steps, toward the forest, still, however, keeping its eyes upon the face of the girl as though under the influence of some terrible enchantment.

The Wolf Demon gained the shadow of the thicket, and then—as if the spell that had bound him had been broken—with a terrible cry, that rang through the forest like the wail of a lost soul doomed forever to eternal fires, he vanished amid the darkness.

Daniel Boone and his companion, Kenton, had been searching for their friend, Abe Lark, and they continued their search after witnessing this scene. Soon they found Lark's blood-drenched hat and feared he had been killed by the Wolf Demon.

The Demon, in the meantime, had returned to Ke-ne-ha-ha's camp where he fought a return bout and killed the chief. With a hoarse cry of joy he knelt beside his victim and said:

"Inhuman dog, more like the wolf in heart than I, thus do I mark you! Eleven red demons slew Red Arrow; eleven Shawnee warriors have I slain."

When the Wolf Demon retreated into the forest, he was watched by two whites, Boone and Kenton, who assumed their friend Abe Lark was dead. Holding the Wolf Demon responsible, they waited in ambush for him.

As the Demon passed by they noticed the signs of conflict very apparent on him.

"Just look at his face! It's kivered all over with blood!" whispered Daniel. "It's a terrible thing to attack this awful critter, but the death of poor Lark must be avenged."

They followed the Wolf Demon with cautious steps as he swayed from side to side through the woods. His steps became more and more irregular until finally he stepped into a little glade and stopped. The scouts dashed toward him. But the Wolf Demon fell sideways to the ground. The jolt knocked the wolf-head from its fastening and the two men, astonished, wiped the blood from its quite human face and discovered it was Abe Lark, the friend they were searching for.

Lark, dressed in wolf skins and dying, spoke of strange dreams that were in reality the actions of the dreaded Wolf Demon; dreams he had had since the day he lost his Indian wife to the cruelty of savages.

With their hunting knives, the two scouts scooped a shallow grave beneath the boughs of a hollow oak and there, by the pale light of the dying moon, they laid to rest the mortal remains of Abe Lark, the terrible Wolf Demon, the white husband of the Indian girl—Ke-ne-ha-ha's daughter—Red Arrow.

The soul of Abe Lark, once filled with devout love, then shattered by heartbreak and the insane madness of revenge, was at last restored to peace.—JA

MOUNTAIN ART

Showtime

Thursday night at the Capitol City
Music Hall in Wheeling, West Virginia
. . . crowds press through multiple front
doors . . . the noise level rises as sequined
matrons greet old theatre friends with
flourish . . . men in tails scurry back-
stage to make ready for the Wheeling
Symphony Orchestra's first Bicentennial
concert.

Saturday night in the same hall . . .
crowds again gather . . . the din builds
as visitors from Nova Scotia and Canada
and Pittsburgh tell the roaming radio
announcer why they traveled so far to
the famous WWVA Jamboree.

The symphony crowd, mostly local
folks . . . hostesses in hoop skirts, gold
brocaid, pearls and furs . . . but some
more casually dressed, one young boy in
a football jacket.

Dozens of flags on balcony stairs . . .
straight-backed boys from Linsly Military Academy and sweet young girls from
local high schools escort all to their seats
with ceremonious decorum.

Showtime.

But Saturday night, the country music

AND CITY ART

show, and the fans arrive in tour bus-
loads from West Virginia, Ohio, New
England, Canada—some coming as far
as 150 miles—ready to see what they
have heard every Saturday night for years.

Sales people hawk cowbells, charms
and license plates . . . there's a wall full
of long-play albums hawked in person
by the Blue Ridge Quartet. Young boys
hustle ticket-holders to seats while others
roam the isles with armloads of program
books and newspapers full of country-
western music stars.

Showtime.

Thursday night the stage bursts forth
with violins—not fiddles—and other "up-
town" instruments . . . brass, percussion
and rhythmic baton.

And the favored singer among West
Virginia opera fans, Eleanor Steber, em-
phatically punctuates the symphony

Wheeling's Capitol City Music Hall hosts a
gamut of entertainment: on Thursday night
opera star Eleanor Steber (right) performs with
Arthur Fiedler, guest-conducting the Wheeling
Symphony. On Saturday night, country-western
singer Darnell Miller (left) performs on the
same stage in the WWVA Jamboree.

sound with her long-famed Metropolitan Opera voice . . . a triumphant return to her native Wheeling after fifteen busy years at the top of the classical scale.

Poised, yet warmly human, Eleanor Steber speaks lovingly from the stage to her many friends who pack the house . . . reminiscing of other years when she returned annually for "Eleanor Steber Day" at the Wheeling Symphony.

Champagne flows during intermission accompanied later by hors d'oeuvres at the completion of the performance. Newly-won fans and old friends, mingle . . . seeking conversation with Eleanor Steber who will dash off in the morn to nearby West Liberty College for a voice workshop.

But Saturday night is a different scene as mirrored lights splash through the audience and dozens of country performers begin belting out love songs, sad songs, work songs, happy songs, all beamed live over 50,000 watt WWVA radio. A slide projection of a tobacco ad . . . the announcer booms, "And now time out for this commercial message from our own Bloch Brothers Tobacco Company, makers of good old Marsh-Wheeling stogies."

This show is packed full of many faithful jamboree regulars . . . including the grand old man of Wheeling country music, Doc Williams. Still at it after forty years . . . Doc, singing pure and traditional songs, worrying deeply about the

The Charleston Ballet achieved its status as the Official West Virginia State Ballet in 1972. Andre Van Damme, who conceived the idea for the troupe in 1955, continues to serve as its artistic director, choreographer and principal artist. Pictured is a scene from "The Red Death" premiered in October, 1975 at the Charleston Civic Center.

"seamy" and suggestive music now being played by radio stations across the country, not knowing that his campaign would succeed and that the Wheeling station would agree to return to tunes of a "more wholesome nature."

Intermission is wholesome with popcorn and hotdogs and the buying of trinkets. After the show it's an all-night jam session for those who still crave the sound of strings after the three-hour show.

"Highbrow" and "down-home" entertainment have existed side by side in West Virginia for years. In Wheeling, the Symphony began a few years before the Jamboree. But Wheeling is only one example of the cultural melting pot.

They call that *culture* in West Virginia and the divergent range of entertainment extends from the Northern Panhandle to the southern tip of the sprawling state. The curious fact one might observe is that people's interests often extend all the way from the compelling strains of Bluegrass bands and the heritage art of quilting bees, to the opera, ballet and dinner theater. —*JA*

" . . . give them time—and love"

The Wolfgang Flors are an outstanding example of artisans who have come to West Virginia in search of an environment, a sympathetic and compatible habitat where peace of mind can give birth to art of the highest quality and deepest meaning.

Wolfgang Flor emigrated from Germany to America in 1951 after acquiring an interest in wood sculpture at a fairly late age, 21.

He traveled in many areas of the country before settling in Cleveland to work temporarily as a carpenter and refinisher of antiques. It was to that city that Wolfgang brought his wife, Maria, also from Germany, but it was to West Virginia that this special family would eventually come.

In 1960, the Flors selected a modest farm in Upshur County after considering settlement in several other states. They chose West Virginia because they could afford it, and because they believed it would eventually provide the self-sufficiency, the climate, the materials and the economy of living they would need.

During the first year, the Flors visited their West Virginia farm whenever they could, cleaning up the underbrush and attempting to make the run-down farmhouse livable.

Then one day Wolfgang and Maria, with their young daughters Veronica and Ulrika, packed up their most precious belongings and left the city and the security of a job for the promise of a dedicated life in the mountains.

Theirs was a strange baggage.

"Our most important possessions were Wolfgang's logs," Maria recalls. And the

bigger portion of what the Flors moved to West Virginia consisted of logs and salvaged timber the wood sculptor had managed to save over the years.

To this day the Flors still value the stockpile of precious logs over all other worldly possessions because it is from this rare and diminishing supply of wood that Wolfgang fashions his unique style of sculpture.

That first farm was along a well-traveled road, and the Flors soon realized they hadn't yet found their mountain retreat.

So when they were given the opportunity to acquire their present farm they took it, in spite of the fact that it had no dwelling, was difficult to reach by car and was littered by junk autos and other debris.

The Flors were starting over—this time from an even more primitive beginning, but with a vision.

Today that vision is nearly complete. The sign back at the main road points to Eden, yet the Flors do not live in Utopia. Their life in this new place has been one of ardent toil and loving togetherness as they have literally scratched out a beautiful artist's habitat.

No flat places existed on the farm three years ago when the transformation began. Mostly by hand, Wolfgang and his family, with help from a few friends, dug the earth away from a shelf of rock

Maria, Wolfgang and daughter Veronica in the family dining room, at table made by Wolfgang. An Advent wreath of native hemlock branches hangs above. Flor's magnificent carvings (left) reveal his keen sensitivity to human characteristics. From left to right, the sculptures are: "Taking Care of the Aged," "The Miser," "Mother and Child."

on one side of a hollow. They wheeled that earth to the bottom where a fairly large flat area took shape. The house was placed on the rock shelf. Wolfgang used part of that outcropping for his living room floor and the rest became his foundation.

Using rough-cut lumber and salvaged timber, the Flors created a unique home that is, in itself, a work of art.

"You see that the house is located in consideration with the sun," Wolfgang tells his visitors as they tour the home. "Every room gets the full benefit of the sun which remains longest on this side of the hollow."

Soon a kitchen will make way for a master bedroom, a cistern will provide running water from the nearby spring and Wolfgang Flor can devote greater attention to his art.

"My work has been slow in the past few years," Wolfgang admits. "I have been too busy working on this house."

Wolfgang is a unique sculptor with a powerful style and many meaningful messages. He carves his figures from logs of varying sizes, some weighing 200 pounds or more. The style, using a balance of both strong lines and soft lines, is finished off by endless hours of waxing and polishing. Lighter woods are stained by a natural use of sulphur and acid from mine water.

"I use only the materials of the area," Wolfgang says. "If I were in the Philippines I would look for mahogany. But here I choose the wood of this place—chestnut and walnut, sometimes cherry. I could use oak, but I like walnut best."

Wolfgang's most extensive work to date has been the twelve disciples, twelve separate pieces now on display in the chapel of nearby West Virginia Wesleyan College at Buckhannon. To perform that commissioned work, he made extensive studies of the characters of each disciple before depicting them.

Most of his efforts carry an important message.

"The log he chose for 'The Miser' was just perfect," Maria said. "Barbed wire had become imbedded in it and lightening had struck it."

Wolfgang selects his logs carefully for each of his works, making certain the natural grains of the wood will complement the contours of his carving.

About "The Miser," Wolfgang said, "It represents greed for money, the root of evil in our society—not money, but greed."

An inseparable companion to his "Miser" is a work called "Poverty," a figure of a woman begging help for a child.

Looking at another of his creations, "The Return of the Son," Wolfgang spoke of it as an admonition to parents not to spoil their children. "I think we should not give our children all the material things, but give them time—and love."

Another of his sculptures, "Taking Care of the Aged," portrays a son holding the head of an aged mother; "A helping hand is all that old people need, not to be pitied, but comforted."

Thus his art gives eloquent testimony to the fact that Wolfgang Flor may live a secluded life in his retreat, but he is very much interested and involved in society, not at all out-of-touch with the world around him.

Friends who visit the Flors are treated with the same warmth and compassion that exists obviously among the family members. If the visit is by day it is likely accompanied by a mid-afternoon snack. If at lunch the guest is offered a place at the dining table. If by night the visitor may become part of an entertaining Old World evening of talk and laughter and song.

Maria is herself becoming an accomplished artisan now that motherhood makes less demands. She is learning the art of stained glass, saying "I have always liked colors."

Veronica, who graduated from high school at sixteen, makes an art of cooking which is her exclusive chore. For the past six years she has been a serious student of weaving.

Ulrika, who walks more than a mile before catching the school bus to town, has learned the art of silver smithing and applies it to intricate jewelry designs.

Together the Wolfgang Flor family is beginning to reap the fruits of this place, built by them to nurture artistic thought and talent.

In order for a flower to bloom it must have the proper environment, love and care. Is it just coincidence that Flor means flower?—JA

As a family, the Flors work in close togetherness. Creatively, each member works independently. Clockwise from the top left: Close-up of a shirt that Veronica wove, designed, sewed and embroidered; detailed shot of Wolfgang's sculpture "Taking Care of the Aged"; Wolfgang with the candle lantern that the family uses to get around the grounds at night; portrait of the two daughters, with a temporary mirror hanging on an unfinished wall reflecting Veronica (carrying coal) and Ulrika inside with Sasha, the dog; Flor home under construction—they have been building it for the past two years; stained glass window of a spider and a flower, by Maria; a still life of Ulrika's hand-made silver jewelry.

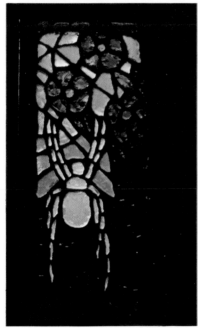

"I'm goin' to fiddle some before I die"

Imagine a moonlit night in the mountains. Shadowy figures are grouped around a flickering fire and the air is filled with wild, exhilarating music.

The moon climbs higher. The music grows more insistent. Figures start to sway and clap. Some jump up spontaneously and begin whirling, stomping jigs that lead them in and out of the shadows.

As the moon tops the sky and the music reaches a fever pitch, the dancers begin to move in a strange jerking unison, oblivious of everything but the release they've found in the cosmic clockwork of which they've become a part. It's as if they somehow have become attached to the strings of a pagan puppeteer who guides their movements with a frantic and joyful will.

Then, just as time seems to freeze, the music fades away. The figures regain their sense of individuality and sink exhaustedly to the ground beside the low burning fire. There's a pause and then voices and laughter suddenly ring out. The musicians take a bow and the spell is broken.

This moonlit scene undoubtedly was repeated many times in the mountains of ancient Ireland when the Celtic bards played their bow-like "fidels" and the young blades and rosy-cheeked colleens danced high-stepping jigs around the fire. But it's a scene that also has become rather common here in West Virginia—although the "fidels" are now called fiddles and the jigging is now known as clogging.

Many mountain music festivals are being held across the state each year, from early spring until late fall, and

fiddle music is a high point at these events. Such talented musicians as Wirt County's Glen Smith are much in demand at these festivals and their squeaky, high-pitched music invariably sets the cloggers' feet flying furiously.

Many musicians claim fiddlers are a special breed. Smith, who came to West Virginia to work for three days and stayed ten years, typifies this image.

Glen was born in the small town of Woodlawn, Virginia, where according to him, life "wasn't a'movin' too fast." He went to school up to the fifth grade but had to quit and go to work—"Them was depression days; my education what I got, I got from a saw mill."

Like most mountain musicians, Glen developed a fine ear for old country tunes by listening to his father.

"My daddy was a fine old-time banjo picker. He played fretless, that is an old mountain style. He also played the fiddle."

Glen remembers the first fiddle he ever owned. He was sixteen and "spraying varnish" at the Webb Furniture Company owned by Claude Richardson.

"I was always whistling something or singing and Claude came to me one day and wanted to sell me a fiddle. Gave him $10 for it. I was workin' for 23¢ an hour. After I bought the fiddle, I would go to his home and aggravate him till he helped me get some tunes started, and then I took over from there myself. I always liked to fiddle."

Glen used to like to sing but he's given that up. "You paint school buses ten years, you're lucky you can call hogs," he explains.

He's given up painting school buses, too. Ever since he played his first square dance and got paid, his life style was set.

Glen remembers that fateful occasion: "It was back durin' the war . . . I got $5,

and I said 'Lord have mercy, I love this'— I didn't have to work too hard for it.

"That was my first money to ever make with the fiddle, and I seen right then I was goin' like it."

Glen, who was the 1974 state champion fiddler, now takes his playing as a way of life.

"If I can get by and make a livin' for my wife and me, well, why worry. I'm goin' to fiddle some before I die!"

Whether fiddlers develop their attitude along with their skill or whether fiddling just attracts like men, Lee Triplett, a seventy-eight year old fiddle player from Clay County, also fits the mold. He admittedly would rather play the fiddle than eat and never, never misses a chance to perform.

"I was thirteen when my brother bought me an old fiddle offn' a feller," Triplett recalled one sunny, summer afternoon while attending a Morris Brothers Family Music Festival. "I sat down and learned to play it by guess. I don't know notes or chords any more than a cow does but I could always listen to somebody play a tune and I could play it back the same way."

A true mountaineer, Triplett has spent his life gardening, lumbering and playing the fiddle at the family farm on Triplett's Ridge, near Clendenin. He has also taken time "to raise twelve head of kids."

He pushed back his old battered hat and fingered the fiddle cradled lovingly in the crook of his arm. He scratched out a little tune and smiled happily. "I've been coming to these things for more than twenty years and I've been to twenty-one straight West Virginia Folk Festivals—won the first fiddlin' contest they had, in fact."

The old man was starting to wilt a little under the sun and he leaned back

against an old-fashioned iron-wheeled wagon.

"I never made much money fiddling but I had a lot of fun," he said. "The most I ever got for winning a contest was seven dollars and I had to give the banjo picker three dollars for accompanying me."

He paused again and looked at the dozens of people who had come to the music festival. When he spoke again, he seemed a little sad.

"A lot of good fiddlers have come out of Clay County," he said. "That Johnny Morris over there is one of them and he's gettin' awful good. He's a whole lot better than I am."

Triplett referred to the fiddle-playing

Old time fiddle players, Lee Triplett (left) and Glen Smith (right), perform for devoted audiences and pass along their art form to new generations of promising talent.

half of "The Morris Brothers," a pair of young Clay Countians who have worked hard to make West Virginians familiar with their mountain music heritage. Like many folks in these parts, the Morrises learned to play at home.

"We used to play of an evening," said John Morris, a red-faced, red-haired fiddler who can really get up and go. "Daddy played some and we'd pick and sing along with him. My mother also played guitar and sang and my grandpa Morris was a real good banjo player. Back twenty years ago when I started playing music, Clay County was pretty isolated and people sort of made their own entertainment. Lots and lots of people around home played music back then."

But as the Morris brothers grew up, many of the old-timers began to die off. John and his brother Dave became afraid that the old-time music would die along with them. They decided to see that this didn't happen.

"We started going around and picking up old-time songs and fitting them to our style," he said. "I learned a lot of songs from Aunt Minnie Moss. She's dead now.

"And Dave has learned a lot of old ballads from Laurie White, an old lady who lives up the hollow."

When Dave, who sings and plays guitar, left to join the service back in 1968, the family threw a party for him. The event was such a success that it wasn't long before as many as five-thousand people were flocking to the annual festival at the family's farm near Ivydale. Before long, thousands of devotees were flocking to similar festivals across the state and Appalachian region to hear the music their ancestors brought to this country three-hundred years ago.

Johnny Morris, meanwhile, has followed the path traveled by so many fiddlers before him.

"I went to college and taught school for about thirty days," he said, "but I play music full time now. Oh, I raise a little garden but I've really never done much of anything except play music."

Thus spake a latter-day bard who has inherited the ancient power to set toes a'tapping and hands a'clapping. —SD

Youthful folk dancers keep time with a flood of music at the Glenville Folk Festival in Gilmer County. The Festival was initiated by Dr. Patrick Gainer in 1950, and has since become an annual event. Glen Smith's nimble fingers (above) fret a fast fiddle tune.

BUILDERS AND BARONS

"If you want this lease, you'll pay me ten cents an acre and not a penny less."

The corner stone for a beautiful chapel had just been laid. It was the beginning of the final stage of the reconstruction of a fine cemetery in Bridgeport.

Benefactor Michael L. Benedum stepped to the platform.

"Those who preceded me have told you what I have done for Bridgeport," he said, "I would like to tell you something of what Bridgeport and its people have done for me."

The year was 1940 and the Benedum Cemetery was just the first of many projects and programs to be bestowed on Bridgeport and all of West Virginia by "The Great Wildcatter," the man who had discovered more oil than any other man who had ever looked for it.

It had been one hundred years earlier when Mike's father, Emanuel Benedum, arrived in Harrison County. Emanuel, then 22, became an accomplished cabinetmaker and general store proprietor in the rural community of Bridgeport.

He married in 1850 and was twice a father before his first wife died. Then in 1860 he was married again, this time to the niece of a neighbor. Caroline Southworth was a tall, fair-haired young woman with unusual poise and religious conviction.

Together Caroline and Emanuel Benedum earned an important place in the life of the community. Emanuel continued to toil in his woodworking shop at his home, making furniture as well as most of the coffins used in the community. His general store was a busy one, filled not only with merchandise but also with cracker barrel philosophers who loved to engage in friendly debate with Emanuel who was very good at it.

The people of Bridgeport elected Emanuel Benedum mayor for a quarter of a century. Everyone in Bridgeport affectionately called him "Squire."

At that time there were only two or three stores in Bridgeport, a blacksmith shop, a school, a grist mill and some four hundred residents. It was a typical self-sufficient agricultural town of the Civil War era. Until the railroad came in 1859, citizens received news of the outside world only by tales told by passengers on the occasional stagecoach. Soon, however, the state was to give birth to an industrial discovery that would quickly spread and affect the entire world.

Into that setting, on July 16, 1869, came Michael Late Benedum, a child timed for destiny.

What Mike Benedum was telling his friends seventy-one years later was that the events of his life and the qualities of his character had been molded by his beloved home state and that his fortune belonged to the mountains.

Mike Benedum inherited the charm of his mother, the leadership qualities of his father and the industriousness of his pioneer birthplace.

Armed with that, Mike Benedum became an oil man at an early age.

At sixteen, he had finished all schooling available in Bridgeport—ten years of four months each at Bridgeport Grade School.

If he were to fulfill his father's dream of West Point, he would have to further his education at some academy. But Emanuel had come upon hard times so Mike took a job instead. His first was at the grist mill in Bridgeport. For $16 a month, Mike worked at the water-powered mill from 6 a.m. to 6 p.m. each day. He didn't complain of the heavy work and the long hours since he was already used to working on his father's farms in Harrison and Preston Counties.

Even at mill work he excelled and by the age of twenty he was managing a mill at Lumberport for $50 a month which was more than any other young man from Bridgeport was making.

One day Mike's coat caught in the mill machinery pulling his right arm into the gears and mangling it almost to his shoulder. That ended the career of Mike Benedum, the millwright.

After long months of weary idleness, Mike was anxious to get busy again. He was a man who had definite aspirations for success but he did not know just what his method would be.

Mike had heard there were opportunities in Parkersburg so he boarded the train at Wilsonburg.

On the forty-five-minute ride between Wilsonburg and West Union, Mike met an oil man from South Penn Oil Company, John Worthington, who on that day said, "My son, how would you like to learn something about my business?"

"Is there a future in it?" asked Mike.

"Oh yes, there's a future."

"Thank you, sir; I'll do it," came Mike Benedum's instant reply and the two left the train at West Union, then an oil boom town in Doddridge County.

The future came swiftly for Mike Benedum who quickly astounded his employer with his ability to buy oil leases from wary farmers when prospects looked good and to sell out when prospects turned sour.

Farmers had good reason to hold these "field men" suspect because the scramble for oil had just exploded into a rough-and-tumble competition for leases that threw ethics to the wind.

On the other hand, West Virginia farmers had learned how to play the game to their own advantage and it was those two factors that surrounded Mike Benedum's first assignment—to obtain leases from some of the more troublesome landowners.

Mike Benedum's approach would be different from the others. He recognized that the "law of the jungle" and the "survival of the fittest" prevailed in oil country. But he reckoned that brains, not brawn, could be most effective and that an appeal to friendship, not greed, would be most successful.

Farmers were distrustful of these strangers who talked of legal papers, bank credit and other confusing things. But this Mike Benedum seemed not to be a stranger. He was at home in every West Virginia hollow. He had an honest and disarming personality. And he had his father's talent to bargain.

Mike devised his own routine for dealing with farmers reluctant to part with their land. His first step was to stop at the local bank and change his twenty and fifty dollar bills into ones. That big stack of ones always looked very tempting on some farmer's kitchen table.

Then in his frank, pleasing manner he always suggested the farmer's wife be present as the business to be conducted concerned her too.

Mike would talk about his father's farm and flour mill, discuss the weather and crops—just "down-home" country-folk talk—then come back to business. He'd count out one dollar for each acre of land he wanted to lease, making sure the money stacked up real high. Of course, he'd point out to the farmer and especially the farmer's wife, all the improvements to the farm and the home that could be made with that amount of money. He never found a woman who didn't have a million uses for that money and who didn't jump in on his side to win her husband's approval for Mike's deal.

With the needed lease consented to and signed, Mike would proceed to the neighboring farms, taking along the farmer who had already signed, who quickly convinced his "good neighbors" to follow his lead. Mike found himself returning home with what were thought to be unattainable leases.

By 1892 Mike Benedum had made a firm place for himself in the West Virginia oil regions and both the country and the petroleum industry had experienced a phenomenal growth. Mike soon moved up in the company, taking over a job like Worthington's that eventually opened up in Cameron at the base of the Northern Panhandle.

Mike had learned the oil business well from John Worthington, who proved himself a sharp yet judicious boss. Only once did Mike actually defy his superior. He was given an extremely important assignment to obtain a wildcat tract of 1,200 acres. His instructions were to pay as much as a dollar an acre if necessary.

The landowner proved to be an outspoken, hard bargain-driver himself and let Mike know the land would cost South Penn Oil Company a "pretty penny." Before Mike made his offer, the farmer continued—"If you want this lease, you'll pay me ten cents an acre and not a penny less." The deal was closed.

Mike could hardly conceal his surprise and delight, but when he phoned Mr. Worthington the good news, the big boss wanted him to try for five cents an acre. Mike was quite explicit in his reply and the offer stood at ten cents, but for years Mr. Worthington enjoyed telling of Mike's "outburst of defiance."

While with South Penn, Mike saved his money and met the man who would become his life-long partner, Joseph Clifton Trees, a petroleum engineer. It was 1895 and Trees was excited about the prospects of some oil property in Pleasants County. He wanted to buy a half interest in the royalties but lacked $1,950. With no written agreement between the two men, Mike Benedum gave Trees the money, not in the name of South Penn, but in the name of what was soon to be known as the Benedum-Trees partnership.

Three weeks later a well came in and Mike and Joe began an oil business that would take them into every oil field in

West Virginia, and then oil fields throughout the country and the world.

Mike Benedum's highest salary was $150 a month with South Penn, and it was to be the highest salary he ever earned throughout a lifetime in which he accumulated millions of dollars. He reasoned that a salary wasn't necessary. If his efforts were fruitful, he would get a dividend. If they were not, he deserved no money.

Throughout his spectacular career, Mike Benedum was a wildcatter spurred on only in the challenge of the search for oil, bored with the idea of hanging on to further develop the "find," never interested in any more conventional method of empire building.

He was a gambler, drawn like a magnet to new territories, challenged by those who would suggest "it's not there," thrilled each time by the triumph of discovery.

And money was just a by-product.

Long before Mike Benedum's death in 1959, the Benedum fortune became a West Virginia legacy. For Bridgeport he financed the cemetery, a multimillion dollar Civic Center and a multimillion dollar Methodist Church, all completed and dedicated in Mike Benedum's presence. The Civic Center is a striking replica of his birthplace, located on the very spot where Mike Benedum was born.

But the greatest public service rendered by his fortune has come through the Claude Worthington Benedum Foundation established in 1944 in memory of his son who died during World War I.

Benedum (center) knew Tyler County's heyday: families in tents, "Polecat" well No. 1, Stringtown with its derricks, and Sistersville, where wells still pump on the golf course.

Formed for "religious, charitable, scientific, literary, or educational purposes or for the prevention of cruelty to children or animals," the Benedum Foundation operates today on a large portion of the Benedum fortune and, by his direction, three-fourths of the foundation activity must be used to benefit his native state.

Because Mike Benedum's life was not based on greed and because he never forgot the love and influence of his hometown and home state, it was his destiny that Michael Late Benedum would become West Virginia's greatest benefactor. —SD

The barefoot boy from down on Pigeon Creek

Back in the mid 1930's when the Great Depression was raging, Henry Hall was just another little barefoot boy playing along the banks of Pigeon Creek. Henry loved the fast-moving stream that ran past his home just below Delbarton and he liked to go hunting in the surrounding Mingo County hills. Whenever he didn't find a squirrel or a rabbit to catch in the hills, he could always drop a line in the crystal waters of Pigeon Creek and pull out a fat bass or a quillback. His catch would help when food was not so plentiful.

Most little boys in Mingo County had to grow up fast in those days and Henry Hall was no exception. He was only in the eighth grade when he dropped out of school to help his folks. There wasn't much money to be made on top of the ground, so Henry, a short stocky young man with bright grey eyes, picked up a lunch pail and headed for the mines.

For the next eleven years he helped

Island Creek Coal Co. mine the rich, black seam of petrified vegetation that ran through the hills not far from the little frame house he once called home.

By now Henry was making almost $30.00 a day and had a wife and three strapping boys. He put a down payment on a brick home across the street from his parents' home, but no sooner had the family moved in than automation hit the mining industry.

At age thirty, Henry suddenly found himself with no job and growing children to support. His plight was shared by thousands of miners who lost their jobs in the early sixties and were forced to migrate to large industrial centers in the Midwest. Henry left West Virginia too, but only temporarily.

"It was 1960," he recalled, stuffing a big chew into his jaw and then letting the years slip away. "The mines weren't working around here so I tried truck driving for a while. I drove a rig from coast to coast."

After four years of riding rigs, Henry Hall came home. He had decided to sink or swim on Pigeon Creek.

"It was no life for a family man," he said as he sent a long brown stream of tobacco juice across the yard. "So I went back to the mines. Only this time, I went to work for myself. It was 1964 and coal was selling for $3.00 a ton. I leased some land—then I got myself a mining machine, a battery and two or three little old coal cars. The first year and a half, I worked like a dog and didn't take a cent out of the business."

Like most small independent coal operators at that time, Henry almost went broke on more than one occasion. But he held on.

"Yes, those were tough times," he acknowledged as he put a fresh chew in

his mouth and went on with his story.

"Things stayed like that for a while and then toward the end of the sixties, they began to get better. The price of coal went up to $20.00 a ton and never did drop below $6.00 after that."

Henry put his profits into more machinery. By 1973, he employed more than thirty men and was producing close to 50,000 tons of coal a year.

Billy Ray Hall, one of Henry's three grown sons who helps him operate the family mine, remembers well his father's days underground. "He always worked with the men, ever since the mine was opened," said the younger Hall, who acts as general mine foreman. "He could outwork any of the men. My dad would go into the mine at 7 o'clock just like everybody else. But then, there were lots of times when things would break down that he'd stay most of the night."

Then came the Arab oil embargo and prices began to skyrocket. When the Arabs turned off the tap, Henry was still working twelve to fourteen hours a day and spending most of his time underground down at the face of the mine. He soon learned, however, that the action was up on top.

"I've never seen anything like it," he recalled. "I watched the prices go up day after day, week after week. For me, it started at $6.00 a ton and went to $53.00 a ton in the space of a year. You had to stay on top of the market to make sure you were getting the best price for your coal. There were a lot of fast talkers coming by in those days with all sorts of deals."

But Henry turned a deaf ear to the fast talk and kept on mining coal. When the boom ended, the former little barefoot boy was still on Pigeon Creek— richer than a lord.—SD

BOOMS AND BUSTS

He didn't know it at the time, but he had tapped the richest shallow oil pool the world had ever known

European explorers entering western Virginia shortly after 1700 were dazzled by the natural beauty of the teeming forests and streams they found in the rugged land beyond the mountains. When they returned to the coastal settlements, these daring adventurers regaled their listeners with wondrous tales that were to set off what would later prove to be a continuous quest for the hidden riches of Mountain Mama—a quest that would be punctuated by a series of booms and busts which has left today's West Virginians a dramatic and exciting heritage.

Men such as Daniel Boone and Simon Kenton set the pattern when they followed those first explorers into the wilderness and began trapping beaver, otter, bear, and other animals for their luxurious pelts. Fortunes were made in the fur trade during the mid eighteenth century before the bubble burst and the supply was diminished.

But the pattern was established and the fur trade provided the impetus for a new boom; one that began at a big buffalo lick on Campbell's Creek in Kanawha County. It was 1797 when Elisha Brooks opened the area's first commercial salt operation and began scooping up the vast saline deposits left thousands of years earlier by a receding sea.

The industrial revolution brought the steam drill and the salt industry flourished. By 1850, the community of Malden was a regular stopping place for a stream of steamboats and barges which made daily runs to Cincinnati, then the meat packing center of the nation.

Other booms were taking place during this period. Lumber towns were springing up in many areas and Wheeling's glassmakers had won a worldwide following.

Then the meat packing business shifted to Chicago and the bottom dropped out of the Kanawha Valley salt industry. The decline of the salt industry coincided with a new and bigger boom, however. The Civil War was brewing in February of 1860 when Sherman Karns sank a 300-foot well in the tiny Wirt County community of Burning Springs, forty miles up the Little Kanawha from Parkersburg.

Karns was drilling for rock oil, later to become known as petroleum and he struck pay dirt. He didn't know it at the time, but he had tapped the richest shallow oil pool the world had ever known. It wasn't long, however, before word of his strike got out and the rush was on.

Oil speculators poured into the area. Towns such as Volcano and Petroleum sprang up overnight and the Ohio River community of Sistersville was soon dotted with derricks. The strike was so successful that only a few years went by before John D. Rockefeller's Standard Oil moved in and bought up all the Parkersburg refineries.

The Eagle Saloon at the corner of Diamond and Water Streets in Sistersville was a lively spot on moonlit nights. The open-air dance floor in back provided a beautiful view of the river. Around the turn of the century when the rough necks showed up and commenced construction of their wooden tower outside, the real excitement began. Then the well came in and the Eagle became a roaring spectacle inside and out. Drinkers and teetotalers alike gathered to witness the gusher which was watched from as far away as the Prater Russell farm across the Ohio.

Natural gas was next and it wasn't long before the volatile energy source, which had posed such a problem to the oil and salt well drillers in the past, was being pumped out of the ground at hundreds of sites across the state. City streets and homes were lighted with gas and West Virginia became the nation's biggest producer by 1910.

Then came coal. Boom towns sprang up along the New River and coke ovens burned around the clock. The state became the country's biggest bituminous coal producer.

After the coal boom came chemicals and it wasn't long before the plants along the Ohio and Kanawha Valleys were turning out a vast variety of compounds being used by nations around the world.

The future promises more new horizons in the coal industry with the gasification and liquefaction of coal. The oil industry has also been revived by deep drilling techniques.

No matter what happens, however, it would be safe to say that those first explorers who came into the state more than two centuries ago would be flabbergasted if they could come back today and witness the fruits of their long ago journeys into a new world.—SD

More than a century of time, a few forgotten towns and generations, and scores of fortunes separate the era of the modern, high-speed, portable drilling rig from that of the primitive, gas-fired, noisy, but faithful and productive pumping contraption . . . . But until George West died, it was still bringing out the oil at the going price. Volcano may someday errupt again.

Volcano—a name without a town

Just a few years ago the Volcano field along the Ritchie-Wood County border was a paradox.

On one hill worked eighty-seven-year old George West. With an ancient, almost comic rig, he pumped dribbles of oil out of the ground. For the last seventy-six years he had performed this ritual in the very same way.

On another hill you found a modern Texas oil man experimenting with new, more modern methods for recovering the oil that was left.

Even though hundreds of wells had been producing oil there for over one hundred years, it was the Texas oil man's belief that eighty percent of the oil was still left beneath those West Virginia hills.

Volcano, as a town, is nothing more than a name today. A highway marker on the new four-lane Route 50 east of Parkersburg informs travelers of "Volcano Road," an extremely dusty stretch that winds you over the mountain and right through the "town" before you know you've been there.

Who would ever guess Volcano's spectacular history?

A soldier, fighting during the Civil War, noted dome-shaped rock formations in the Ritchie-Wood County area and knew those formations might indicate oil.

After the war, he talked with some of his friends in Philadelphia and they decided to buy a lease in the district and drill for oil.

William G. Stiles, principal stock holder in the company, was named president, and he moved into the wilderness that would soon become the explosive town of Volcano.

Stiles was interested not only in

George West took with him to his grave the knowledge of operating the "endless cable" pumping system at Volcano, invented over a hundred years ago by W.C. Stiles, Jr. The innovation permitted twenty or more wells to be pumped from one central powerhouse. A few old timers still know the process but most of the units are dismantled.

building an oil field, but a boom town. While the first exploratory wells were in progress, Stiles was busy preparing the valley for what surely would be an influx of people.

He zoned off the hills and valleys into neat little lots quite the same as a modern city might be planned today. He designated a business district and built himself a large, three-story mansion on a high hill overlooking the town.

While Stiles was drilling his first well, another man was doing the same. The Harkness well "came in" first and the price of land soared as rapidly as the workers and speculators poured into these Appalachian hills.

Stiles' dream of a town was realized overnight. Several churches, general stores, stables and saloons sprang up. There was a bowling alley, plus lodge halls, newspapers and more. Homes appeared on all Stiles' lots and soon the boom town of Volcano was larger than the old town of Parkersburg.

Oil had to be hauled out of the remote field by mule teams to the B & O mainline until a railroad could be built into Volcano.

Hundreds of wells were drilled during the first wildcat month of Volcano and in just three months more than five thousand people took up residence there.

It was as wild and violent and tough and bawdy as the most imaginative television script writer might envision it. The rough-and-tumble oil men from Pennsylvania flocked into the town, bringing with them boisterous, lawless ways that created havoc in the town until a couple of the toughest of them were hired to keep order.

But a dozen years later the tough Molly McGuires began to threaten to burn the town.

No one knows for sure if the Molly McGuires started it, but in the early morning of August 4, 1879, a fire began that burned most of the town. A lack of water and the existence of scattered oil tanks added to the effectiveness of that roaring inferno.

The hundreds of wells in the field began, in the same period, to give less and less oil and the town was never built back. The few buildings that remained were either dismantled and moved to a new location or scavengers carried them away by bits and pieces, including the Stiles mansion which stood until just a few years ago.

George West was born three years after the fire, the son of an English blacksmith who decided to buy one of the leases after wildcatting interest had died down.

The "easy" oil already had been taken. Now it was time to squeeze out another drop. George West squeezed oil from the mountain earth for more than seventy-five years. He was the last remaining vestige of a unique era in the oil industry when diligent men toiled to build the most ingenious rigging to pump small amounts of oil from dozens of wells at one time.

The method was known as "endless wire," and that Texas oil man "over on the other hill" had never seen anything quite like it in his entire life.

The rigging was so fantastic it nearly defied description.

First, there was a powerhouse. The one George ran was affectionately called "Old Buckeye" . . . George couldn't remember how it got its name. From the outside it looked like two buildings about two and one-half stories high, connected by a one-story structure.

Inside it was fairly dark, but when

one's eyes adjusted one could see two very large wooden wheels at each end (located in the two taller parts of the building).

In the center of the building and in the rafters were several smaller wooden wheels and wrapped around all of them was a series of belts and steel cables that were attached to an oilylooking thing that resembled an engine.

It was an engine, run by natural gas. When the time came to fire up "Old Buckeye," George (even at eighty-six) lit the "pilot light" at the rear of the engine, waited for it to get hot (a primitive spark plug), and then climbed up on the large flywheel at the side of the machine. With a lunge downward, George set that wheel in backward motion.

Pow! A gush of natural gas exploded, sending the flywheel spinning in the opposite direction. A second try, and the wheel spun on with a series of Pow! puff, puff, puff, puff, Pow! puff, puff, puff, Pow!

In the meantime, George scurried to the other side of the engine to throw the entire mechanism in gear . . . belts flapped, wooden wheels cracked, steel cables began circling out of the building.

Outside, those cables went flapping merrily off through the woods. Down the line aways, the cable would wind through more wooden wheels on a primitive oil well. Coupled with cranks and rods, the walking beam on that well would begin to seesaw back and forth plunging the rod in and out of the well.

Then more wooden wheels would send the cable off through the trees and over the next hill where the same procedure would take place.

If you had traced the path of that cable through the woods, it would have taken you to the sites of a number of wells in a three-quarter mile loop back to the irregular popping power of "Old Buckeye."

George once had some forty wells hooked up to "Buckeye" and other power plants, but producing wells in the ancient field were down to less than half in the early 70's. Some wells began to pump only oily water and others just rusted full of holes and became inoperative.

When George died, the end came to the "endless wire" days because no other man knew how to hew out a pitman (connecting rod) or Sampson post or repair a broken cable without a bulge where the splice was made.

But George sold his lease to the Texas oil man a dozen years before, and as long as there was oil in those hills it was doubtful Volcano would be forever dead.

That other oil man was A. S. Parks, principal stockholder in the company that sought to produce more oil with a pioneering spirit reminiscent of the days of W. G. Stiles a hundred years before. Parks was telling friends that the nation's primary oil reserves would "play out" in the next few years.

"And when that happens," he said, "this country will either become entirely dependent on foreign countries for oil production, or the price of oil will have to rise far enough to make secondary recovery of the harder-to-get oil more profitable."

Parks invested a great deal of his money and several years of his life in the belief that the time would come when Volcano would erupt again.

He compared the wells to the results you get when you shake up a bottle of soda, letting some of the beverage out by "letting the pressure off." "But if you'd try that experiment, you'd find most of the soda remains in the bottle, and most of this oil remains down here."

With a great deal of experimentation in the water flood method of forcing oil out of the ground, Parks' operation was quite different from George West's . . . with two-way radios and computer-like electrical signals that monitored the wells, bulldozers and portable drilling rigs that replaced the quaint three-pole derricks of George's time.

In 1972, George West died. "Old Buckeye" came to a stop. But its sputtering sound was being replaced by the hum of electrical motors and the park-like setting was being preserved by the plans of the state's Department of Natural Resources.

The old ways of Volcano are just a memory now. But there's a good chance that the passing of George West, "Old Buckeye" and "endless wire" will not be the final knell for this most exciting piece of Appalachian history. It's a long shot, but Volcano could easily become a boom town again . . . one hundred years after that 1879 fire.—JA

Smoke, steam and memories

Once a year a smoky pilgrimage, including a very special list of passengers, treks through the fall-colored mountains to the Forest Festival at Elkins in Randolph County.

One of the geared steam locomotives from the restored Cass Scenic Railroad that operates over in Pocahontas County, winds its way slowly over the twisting mountain main line. The shrill, sweet sound of an overzealous engineer's steam whistle rattles the bones of history, recalling other sounds—axes and two-man

saws from the once-teeming timberlands
of Bemis, Glady and a dozen other towns
that have long since been reclaimed by
nature . . . gone, except from memory.

This train carries friends—important
people who have played some part in
the past and the preservation of a
fascinating bit of West Virginia history,
the steam-powered logging railroad. But
while they share a place on that special
list, each passenger seems to find a
unique meaning in the smell of smoke . . .
the sound of the laboring engine . . .
the memories.

C. B. Cromer wasn't invited. But he
came down to the old train station at
Durbin to stand on the rotting platform
with those who would board,
remembering his days as a fireman, and
later, engineer on a Shay locomotive
that served the timber boom of that area
during the first years of this century.

Then there was Grover Cale,
carpenter, who talked with pride of his
careful efforts in restoring the caboose
and building the cars in the early 1960's
when the state realized the importance
of preserving the Cass Railroad as a
historic and scenic monument.

There was Joe Gonzalez, railroad
buff of the first order. Like many other
buffs aboard this train, Joe tried to put
in words the dramatic feelings he had
for railroading.

"It has a lot to do with nursery rhymes
and other things you knew as a kid. Steam
engines were there, but suddenly they

A young fireman oils the bell and the engine
is fired up for the special run to Elkins.
A puff of steam, a clanging bell, a blast
from the whistle, and an "All aboard!" take
passengers back 75 years—from jet age into
the nearly forgotten magic age of steam!

128

were gone and all of a sudden we woke up and felt like we missed it.

"It's like living out a fantasy—the sound of the whistle . . . the smell of the smoke . . . talking with the crew—there's a certain kind of romance involved."

The haunting call of the steam whistle seems to cast a spell over the railroad buff, who has been known in his fanciful trance to memorize by heart every classification mark of almost every locomotive and to develop a passion for statistics akin to the most ardent sports fan.

A railroad buff often knows more about a certain steam locomotive than the people who engineered and fired it, and more about the runs it made than the people who actually worked on the line.

But the smell of smoke doesn't always conjure up visions of nostalgia in the mind of a real-life railroad man.

One crewman from the Western Maryland Railroad was introduced. "Well, actually I'm an old B & O man," he said. "I've only been with Western Maryland fifteen months."

He had started his railroading career on steam.

"I don't think it was all that glamorous. You look back and maybe you think so, but I can't see that it was—dirt in your eyes, inhaling all that smoke, tunnels that would get so hot you couldn't hardly stand it. Now we sit up there in the diesel locomotive with all the conveniences. You could never wear something like this in the old days," he said, pointing to his light-colored jacket.

Benjamin Kelly was an old steam man too, but he never made it onto one of those "cushy" diesel cabs. He remembered the days of the steam locomotive with a spirit of bravado and adventure. He began his mountaineer railroading career "working section" as a laborer on a logging line being built to the little backwoods town of Bergoo in Webster County. Later he became a fireman on a main line that wound its way to the old town of Spruce which once boasted of being the highest railroad terminal east of the Mississippi River.

Benjamin Kelly's steam locomotive, with the help of a few more, puffed its way up the twelve miles of winding mountain track from Glady Fork and then on into Webster Springs. Sometimes there were wrecks and the crew would be stranded in the cold isolated mountains for days until another crew could arrive to help.

"A lot of fellows quit because they didn't have the guts to take it. But I really didn't mind. I was used to working hard all my life. I guess I liked the days

The shrill whistle of an old-fashioned steam locomotive shatters the stillness as the train from the Cass Scenic Railroad rushes through a peaceful meadow, leaving in its wake echoes of a bygone day. A bright-eyed young railroad buff (left) plays engineer.

of steam. There was more fun to it—
more excitement."

At the end of its stay at the Forest
Festival, that same train makes the trip
to the old town of Spruce. Like the old
days, the railroad is the only way in.
But unlike the old days, the old town
of Spruce is gone—a depression in the
earth here, the remains of a stone foundation there. But the memories, the smoke,
the sound of the wailing steam whistle—
they linger on in the minds of the men
who *lived* them, and in the mountains
of Pocahontas County, where thousands
flock for one more nostalgic trip on the
Cass Scenic Railroad.—*JA*

The Cass engineer watches the trailing line of
cars as the train makes a bend on its
once-a-year Durban—Elkins run. The old
logging train is a favorite tourist attraction
during its regular excursion season at
Cass (Pocahontas Co.), West Virginia.

Lung powder, fire crackers, cackle berries, Arbuckles and pig's ears

Just moments earlier his friend had very nearly chopped off a foot, but Arden Cogar stood atop his woodblock with determination as his razor-sharp axe tore through 12 inches of poplar in seconds.

Perhaps the accident had unnerved him or he had an unusually hard block of wood. Whatever the reason, Arden Cogar wasn't the "bull of the woods" this day as he finished second best at the Mountain State Forest Festival.

Arden Cogar and 10,000 spectators who braved the cold, early morning fog to watch this competition are vivid reminders of West Virginia's colorful logging history, of the eruption of boisterous boom towns and the bravado of "good ole boys" who were proud of their nicknames—woodhicks!

But it wasn't the brute strength of man alone that caused the remote mountain valleys to echo with the thud of crashing timber.

It was steam.

By the late nineteenth century, railroad lines were penetrating West Virginia, seeking out new cargoes from its rich natural resources. Not just mainlines, but little privately-owned railroads like the Swamp Angel, powered by an upright boiler on a primitive railroad flat car, rumbled along the wooden rails of a logging tramroad built in earlier years to accommodate horsedrawn loads of virgin timber.

The Swamp Angel, tugging timber from the Cranesville Swamp, was only one of several of West Virginia's earliest logging railroads that penetrated the state's most remote territories with greater and even more powerful 14-geared locomotives.

The rise and fall of boom towns in West Virginia was spectacular.

In some inaccessible mountain valley one might first hear the straining snorts of a team of horses dragging a steam engine to the proposed site of a new mill.

Rugged woodsmen would fire up the engine, harness it to a saw blade, and begin sawing the first timber to build a shed and eventually a mill around the steam engine.

Meanwhile others would be clearing a path through the dense forest to make way for another steam engine, the locomotive, running on railroad ties and real track to the mill or running on wooden poles up some hollow or other where logging would last only a short time.

These were hardy men who were prepared to "rough it" for weeks at a time, willing workers who felled a tree with unchecked enthusiasm. "He's a lunger" present day woodsmen still say of an unusually energetic young man.

But even these rugged woodhicks demanded some personal comforts. In particular a logging company had to provide an excellent cook. "Stomach

robbers," as they were called (took away the hunger pains), provided substantial meals that were highlights of a lumberjack's daily routine.

Keeping a good cook in camp was the company's most difficult task, and if a very good cook "hit the high places" (quit) for another camp, it was likely the whole crew would follow. Arbuckles (coffee), firecrackers (beans) and cackle berries (eggs) were as important to the woodhick as a sharp axe.

If a logging camp existed for some time, other advantages sprang up, making periodic departures from the camp for the "big city" less necessary. Early in the development of a backwoods town was the establishment of a "pig's ear" (tavern where most often moonshine would be served). Soon a general store would follow where lumbermen might buy "lung powder" (snuff) or "Ritchie" clothes (heavy woolen clothes favored for their warmth and durability).

Soon camp foremen and others with the economic means and a desire to be close to their families would build homes. Overnight this wilderness camp would begin to look like a permanent community.

Today in West Virginia there are a few surviving towns that were born as lumber camps—Davis, Richwood, Cass to name a few—but most of these communities "played out" along with the timber industry that spawned them.

The town of Spruce is a good example. Located in Pocahontas County, Spruce was built along the logging railroad from Cass into Randolph County where it joined the Western Maryland. At an elevation of nearly 4,000 feet, the community once included a post office, hotel, large general store, and many homes. A pulp peeling mill supported

Muscles strain and the chips fall where they will in the tree felling contest. In twenty years, Cogar has won fifteen world championships in block chopping competitions. When asked about his national championships, "I don't count those," he said.

the community which could only be reached by railroad, but in the early 1900's the boom ended and Spruce began its decline.

Today the Cass Scenic Railroad makes a yearly excursion to the old town of Spruce. But there's nothing left there but a memory . . . a depression here to suggest someone's cellar, a grown-over stone wall there where a foundation once held someone's rugged mountain home.

These boom towns once graced almost every West Virginia "holler." Some, like Spruce and Jenningston and Burner and Curtin, are remembered in name only. Others are nameless and without memories.

All of this is unconsciously the heritage of Arden Cogar and the tens of thousands who watch him and his timbermen friends compete with the axe. Although the axe has been replaced by the raucous chain saw in his own family timber busi-

ness, he carries on a proud and colorful tradition.

He may have lost this day, but Arden Cogar still holds fifteen world championships in lumberjack competition. That makes Arden Cogar the bull of a mighty stand of timber! One bad day can't change that.—JA

"Dodge City of the East"

Thurmond is a tiny town tucked away in the rugged and remote New River Gorge in Fayette County. The Chesapeake & Ohio Railway line runs down the main street and the town, which is usually deserted during the middle of the day, has a quiet, timeless quality as if it were a still photograph instead of an actual, living community.

It's not like the deserted ghost towns on down the steep desolate gorge, however. Beury is just a collection of coke ovens and a crumbling stone mansion, but Thurmond has several dozen houses, two small groceries and a population of more than fifty. There's even a gourmet restaurant that's open in the summer when the tourists come to ride rafts down the roaring river.

Yet somehow, the feeling persists. There's an air of expectancy—of waiting. Waiting perhaps, like Camelot, to once again come alive. Waiting for the tinkling of honky-tonk piano music or for the laughter of the big-spending coal operators and the richly-gowned women who once filled the famous Dunglen Hotel.

Waiting perhaps, for the greedy gamblers, the painted ladies and the boisterous miners who used to whoop it up in the seven saloons that did a rip-roaring business during the days when Thurmond

was a wide-open boom town and one of the wildest spots on the C & O line between Richmond and Cincinnati.

Decaying storefronts line Thurmond's main street now but back in the early days of this century, the town was the biggest shipping point on the entire line, outstripping even Cincinnati. In 1910 at the height of the boom, 76,541 passengers purchased tickets at the Thurmond depot and twenty-two trains stopped there each day.

More than 2,000 people lived in Thurmond back then. The town was bursting at the seams with two banks, a newspaper, Masonic lodge, a half dozen restaurants and various other shops and establishments, not to mention the saloons. Nearly seventy coal mines were operating in the New River Gorge and hundreds of thirsty and pleasure-hungry miners each night poured into the town where their arrival was eagerly awaited by the gamblers and the painted ladies.

Thurmond had a reputation as being the "Dodge City of the East" and there was a saying among railroad men which went: "No Sunday west of Clifton Forge and no God west of Hinton."

Oren Starks can well remember what it was like in those days. A retired railroad conductor, he has lived in Thurmond for fifty years and recalls the days of wild poker games and gunshots and bodies in the river.

"Yes, this place was really something back then," he said, gesturing toward the empty sidewalk which parallels the railroad track. "You wouldn't believe it, but I can remember a time when there were so many people in this town you could hardly get up and down these streets."

Starks came to Thurmond in the 1920's, some thirty years after the community was founded by Thomas McKell, an entrepreneur whose wife had inherited several thousand acres of land in the Fayette County wilderness. McKell could see the coming need for more and more coal and he immediately set about to develop the area.

He built a 10-mile railroad spur to his mine sites, donated the line to C & O and became fabulously wealthy almost overnight. McKell was not one to hoard his fortune. He built a mansion at Glen Jean, five miles from Thurmond, and constructed a palatial opera house not far from his home.

Then, shortly after the turn of the century, he built the fabled Dunglen Hotel at Thurmond. A 100-room, three-story structure resembling a Swiss Chalet, the hotel was furnished lavishly with all the latest conveniences and opened with a gala featuring an orchestra imported from Cincinnati.

Railroads provided the nation's major form of transportation back then and

A fresh-faced young bartender, looking somewhat out of place in a fast-living coal boom town, posed proudly—drink in one hand, pistol in the other—for this faded 1912 photograph in a Thurmond saloon.

many famous singers and entertainers found themselves doing encores before pistol-packing audiences alongside the waters of the oldest river in the United States.

The railroad cars also took out tons of rich coal and Thurmond continued to grow, as did its reputation for high stakes poker games and midnight murders. More than one mine operator lost his deed at the gaming tables and many others lost their lives as they attempted to depart with their winnings.

There was so much money in the town, and so many men who wanted it, that the Dunglen ran a poker game day and night for fourteen years without stopping. The notorious Blackhawk Saloon was famous as a place where a man could get anything he wanted and some things he didn't want.

Thurmond had only one peace officer during the boom days—Harrison Ash—but he was as big as two men. He also was a skilled and fearless fighter who had several notches on his pistol and was often seen striding toward the jail with a culprit under each arm. Folks who had been out West said he was as tough as Wyatt Earp.

Mayor Leo Schaeffer was also a tough customer and a character in his own right. He gaveled his courtroom to order with the butt of a .45 and is the source of one of the town's more colorful legends.

As the story goes, a dead man was found floating in the river one morning with $80 and a pistol in his pockets. Schaeffer is said to have hauled the corpse into court whereupon he handed down a verdict that became the talk of the town. He fined the victim $80—for carrying a concealed weapon.

Thurmond's legends are many but most of them date back to the days before World War I. The town slid into a

decline during the 1920's as the boom ended and the miners, gamblers and harlots headed for greener pastures. When the Dunglen burned to the ground in 1931, the famed old hotel was just a tattered, empty ghost.

The streets are empty now and the town lies waiting. But in the meantime, Captain H.W. Doolittle, a poet and railroad conductor, tells us what it was like during its heyday.

You have heard of the California gold rush,
    Way back in forty-nine
But Thurmond on the New River
    Will beat it every time.
There's people here from everywhere,
    The colored and the white;
Some mother's son bites the dust
    Almost every night.
On paydays, they come to Thurmond
    With a goodly roll of bills.
Some gamblers get their dough
    And they sneak back to the hills.
Some, though, ne'er return alas!
    And they meet a thug—
We find them on the railroad track
    Or in the Thurmond jug.
Where handy is the blackjack
    And the price of life is low
At Thurmond on New River
    Along the C. and O.
Where men are often missing
    After the drinker's fight,
And the crime laid onto the river
    And the trains that pass at night —SD

135

FUSSIN' AND FEUDIN'

Memories of a clansman

Picture a place of breath-taking beauty, an unspoiled land where the hills abound with turkey, bear and deer and the crystal clear streams are filled with fish for the taking; a place where people live in freedom and dignity.

Logan County was such a place back in 1839. That was the year a son was born to Ephriam "Big Eaf" Hatfield and his wife, the former Nancy Vance, a lovely young mountain woman whose father, Abner, had helped drive the Mingoes from the area some decades earlier.

The boy was Anderson Hatfield, known affectionately as "Anse" to the ten of his eighteen brothers and sisters who survived infancy.

Back then, folks had to learn how to reap the natural abundance all about them. They farmed, fished and hunted to put food on the table and Anse, a strong-willed, high-tempered young man, soon became a renowned tracker and hunter who could kill a squirrel at fifty yards and follow a bear through the hills for days without tiring.

The Hatfields and Vances had migrated into Logan County from the Virginia tidelands during the previous century and by the time Anse was born, there were several branches of each family living in the area. Together, these hardy mountain families formed a powerful clan that virtually ruled Logan County, as the McCoys ruled in Pike County, Kentucky, just across the Tug Fork.

Up until the Civil War, the two clans had lived side by side with no trouble other than an occasional fist fight or argument brought on by youthful exhuberance or a little too much moonshine. But when the war broke out in 1861, the Hatfields and McCoys went their separate ways, with the Hatfields supporting the Confederacy and the McCoys siding with the Union.

Anse, by now, was a tall, strapping man of twenty-two. He promptly married his sweetheart, Levicy Chafin, and then took a commission as a first lieutenant in the Confederate Army. He quickly advanced to the rank of Captain.

The death of his close friend, Confederate General John B. Floyd in 1863 dimmed Anse's enthusiasm for the regular army and his final disenchantment came when he was ordered to execute two court-martialed soldiers—one, his cousin George Hatfield.

Anse withdrew from the regular Confederate army and turned to guerilla warfare. He organized the famous "Logan Wildcats" and this group of hard-riding sharpshooters, under his leadership, took part in several skirmishes with the Pike County militia, composed largely of McCoys and headed by Harmon, brother of Randolph "Randall" McCoy, the leader of the Kentucky clan. Anse reportedly wounded Harmon during one of these battles and later earned his infamous nickname when he single-handedly held off a Union force trying to cross a Logan County mountain known as the *Devil's Backbone.*

Quiet was restored after the war even though Harmon McCoy was found shot to death in a cave near Anse's home on Mate Creek. It was never proven that Hatfield was involved in the death, however, and although the incident caused some bad blood, the two clans still lived together in relative harmony.

But all that changed dramatically in 1878 when Randall McCoy and Floyd Hatfield, Devil Anse's cousin, argued over the ownership of a pig. The animals

were allowed to roam loose in those days and the dispute led to a civil trial in which the jury voted seven to five in favor of Hatfield. The verdict so incensed the McCoy patriarch that he vowed revenge, especially upon Bill Staton, a stocky mountaineer who had married into the Hatfield family and whose testimony had swung the jury against McCoy.

Staton was ambushed and beaten severely a few months later. He retaliated by ambushing a couple of McCoys and was killed during the ensuing fight. The bad blood was now boiling furiously and both sides became armed camps.

More killings followed and during the next fifteen years, scores of men, women and children were murdered or wounded. During the height of the conflict in the late 1880's, the states of West Virginia and Kentucky came perilously close to civil war as the governors of both states sided with their respective clans, even to the point of threatening to mobilize

Devil Anse Hatfield and Randall McCoy argue over the ownership of a hog during the famous "pig trial" in the autumn of 1878. It was the first time that the clan leaders had met face to face, with armed men supporting them, since the War. In spite of political bitterness, the two families had maintained a tense "hands off" policy following the Civil War. To the amazement of both families, the jury member whose vote broke the deadlock was Selkirk McCoy, the husband of a Hatfield. After the trial, the feud exploded and was to continue unabated for over fifteen years. From 1873 to 1890 Logan County, West Virginia and Pike County, Kentucky experienced a state of open border warfare. The two patriarchs are shown in the portraits above: Anderson ("Devil Anse") Hatfield, left, and Randolph ("Randall") McCoy, right.

their state militias.

All of the original feuding families are now gone, except for one. Willis Hatfield, in his late eighties, vividly recalls the rugged character of his father and his older brothers.

Willis was born in 1888 and when he was growing up in the 1890's, the feud had cooled considerably. He says he can't remember the last of the shooting but he well remembers what life was like on Main Island Creek where the family finally settled, away from the violence in the Tug Valley. However, new conflicts awaited Willis and his family.

"It was only a few miles to Logan from our home up Island Creek," he said. "But there wasn't any roads back then, just horse trails. My daddy worked in lumbering and he used to tell us about riding the logs down the river. He was a good man and we never wanted for nothing."

At the time he was interviewed for this story, Willis Hatfield was eighty-seven and was living with his daughter in the Logan County community of De-hue. A tall, white-haired man with twinkling eyes, he had lost none of his zest for life nor his appreciation for the ladies, a Hatfield trait that had made his brother Johnse so irresistible to Rose Anne McCoy in their fabled romance during the feud.

In the picture composite, reading from left to right (top row): Devil Anse, dressed up in hunting paraphernalia for a photograph. Hunting was a favorite form of recreation as well as a necessity for Anse (next picture), Jim Vance (with saddle bags on shoulder) and other fellow clansmen. Ellison, ill-fated younger brother of Devil Anse. The slaying of three McCoy boys, Randall Jr., Pharmer, and Tolbert in revenge for Ellison's death. Second row: artist's conception of the 1888 New Year's night raid on Randall McCoy's cabin, during which Calvin and Allifair, his son and daughter were killed; Devil Anse's arsenal of side-arms, in the collection of Henry Hatfield; Johnson ("Johnse") Hatfield; star-crossed lovers Johnse Hatfield and Rose Anne McCoy; Rose Anne in a formal portrait; actors A. D. Cover and Cheryl Stockton as Devil Anse and Levicy in the musical drama "Hatfields and McCoys," which is presented each year — alternately with Kermit Hunter's "Honey in the Rock" — at Grandview State Park, Beckley; Devil Anse and his wife, Levicy, on the front porch of their home; Willis in the uniform of a deputy sheriff; the hanging of Ellison "Cotton Top" Mounts, the only one convicted of murder for the 1888 attack on the Randall McCoy cabin.

Willis Hatfield (left column), Anse's only surviving son, maintains a jovial sense of humor, a flair for the ladies, and enjoys story telling.

"Johnse was awful bad to drink," recalled his brother. "He made lots of whiskey but so did I. I used to make some of the best you ever tasted, but I got caught and I quit."

Much the same as his father in his retiring years, Willis believes in a life hereafter and speaks of going to heaven.

Although he missed most of the feud between the clans in the early Island Creek days, life for Willis has never been dull. The Fayette County boom town of Minden was the scene of many adventurous shooting scrapes when he was lawman there. Defending his name on cue, two marriages, and a mining career until he retired at seventy-five—yes, Willis Hatfield has had a long, full life.

"I used to go coon hunting with daddy," he said. "I went bear hunting with him once and he like to run me to death. I never went again.

"Dad would live in the woods and used to stay out for a week. He'd come back and we'd all sit around the fire and listen to him tell us about tracking the bear or coon or whatever. Sometimes the dogs would be right there with us. Daddy always had a pack of dogs. They slept right in the house. My mother didn't like it but he thought a lot of his dogs.

"My father was a wonderful woodsman. He once killed four bears in one week and eight coons in one night. Mother used to parboil the coons and then bake them. They were the best things you ever tasted."

He remembers his mother as a strongly religious woman who disapproved of killing.

"She wouldn't even allow a deck of cards in the house. And there wouldn't have been any killing if she'd had her way. I've known some McCoys myself and they were pretty nice fellows. Three

This classic portrait of the Hatfield clan was taken April, 1897 (when the feud was entering its cooling stage), at a logging camp near Devon, W.Va. Back row, standing, left to right: Rose Hatfield Browning; Troy Hatfield; Betty Hatfield Caldwell; Elias Hatfield; Tom Chafin; Joe Hatfield; hired hand Oxer Damron; Shephard Hatfield; Coleman Hatfield; Levica Emma Hatfield; store clerk Bill Borden. Middle row, seated: Mary Hawes with baby Louvisa; Devil Anse; Levicy; Nancy Hatfield; William Anderson "Cap" Hatfield, Jr. Front row, seated: Tennis Hatfield; Midge Hatfield; Willis Hatfield. A life sized marble statue of Devil Anse (above) stands on his grave in the Hatfield Cemetery near Omar, W.Va. The statue faces Main Island Creek, and is turned away from the bloody Tug Fork Country.

of them stayed all night with me one time and we drank liquor and had a big time."

Willis said his father was capable of killing a man in a fit of passion, but also had a compassionate side to his nature.

"My father was well liked. He was one of the best-hearted men I ever knew and raised I don't know how many children. One time, a man from Kentucky made a raid on dad's house and took his horses. When dad came home he got his gun and went and killed the man—then took his kid and raised him up like part of the family.

"Daddy would take us up in the hills and we'd pick up bags of chestnuts. He never drank to excess but he'd take a drink of a morning to clear his throat."

He remembers also that his father loved animals and used to keep pet coons and bears.

"We used to have a couple of pet bears around when I was growing up. He kept them chained to a tree. Their names was Fanny and Bill. You could walk up to Bill but the she-bear would chew you up if you got close to her."

Willis Hatfield recalls his father's death, on January 6, 1921, as one of the saddest days of his life.

"When he died," his son said sadly, "he had one of the biggest funerals we ever had around here."

Old newspaper accounts support Willis' recollections. Devil Anse's funeral was

Willis Hatfield, lone survivor of the feuding mountain clan, spends peaceful evenings telling stories on the front porch of his Logan County home. On the porch steps, a young admirer is silhouetted in the shadows.

presided over by Uncle Dyke Garrett, a close friend. Eleven children and forty grandchildren were present. Two extra coaches were added to the train from Logan to help the overflow crowd, estimated to have been well over five thousand people.

The mighty Devil Anse was gone from Island Creek.

And an important chapter in American lore was drawing to a close. —SD

She cussed like a sailor, but the poor, the powerful and the rich heard her voice

Holly Grove is a quiet little community that sits near the mouth of Paint Creek some twenty miles east of Charleston in Kanawha County. It is a peaceful place today but in the early years of this century, the tiny town was the scene of one of the most bitter struggles in the bloody, thirty-year "war" fought between the United Mine Workers of America and West Virginia's coal operators.

Although it now seems inconceivable, federal troops and state militiamen were often brought into these struggles. They were used to quell the so-called "miners' insurrections" which actually were among the West Virginia coal miners' first, fledgling attempts to organize a union.

Labor Day 1975 found a small group of people congregated at Holly Grove to commemorate one of these struggles. They had come at the invitation of the West Virginia Labor History Association to attend a picnic in honor of Sesco (Cisco) Estep, a striking miner who was cut down by machine gun bullets fired from an armored train which steamed through the community one afternoon in the summer of 1913.

Among the picnickers was the victim's son, Clifford Estep of Lewisburg.

"I was two years old at the time my father was killed," Estep recalled. "He had stepped outside and I was in the house with my mother. She was holding me in her arms while they were shooting. She said the bullets sounded like splinters flying off the wall and there were a hundred bullet holes in the house.

"They even shot up my father's funeral a few days later."

The men who killed Estep's father were never brought to trial. He and his mother moved away a short time later and it was a half century before he returned, looking for his father's grave. "I couldn't find it though," he added. "The weeds had grown up all around."

Estep's voice trailed off and he sat listening to an old labor ballad being sung by a man in a cowboy hat. A soft rain was falling and the singer was seated beneath a canvas canopy. He was flanked by several large photographs, one of which featured a stern-faced old woman who peered out of the picture from behind rimless spectacles.

"That's Mother Jones," said an elderly man who stood in the rain staring at the faded photograph.

"I was raised right here," said the man introducing himself as Kenneth Hudnall of nearby Handley. "Why, I've heard Mother Jones speak many a time, right over there where those trees are. She cussed like a sailor."

Hudnall smiled at the memory but his voice was full of respect as he discussed the old woman who came to West Virginia and fought fearlessly for the union. She first arrived around the turn of the century and returned again and again to figure prominently in many important battles, including the Paint Creek strike of 1912-13 and the famous "Armed March on Logan" not quite ten years later.

Born in Cork, Ireland, as Mary Harris, Mother Jones came to this country in 1837 at age seven. Her laborer father then moved to Toronto, Canada, where she grew up and later became a teacher at a convent in Michigan.

But she found teaching too confining and moved to Chicago where she set up a dressmaking shop. She later went to Memphis and married an ironworker named Jones. But fate, in the form of a yellow fever epidemic, took the lives of her husband and four young children and she returned to Chicago and became an organizer for the Knights of Labor and, later, the UMW.

Mother Jones first gained attention in West Virginia when she helped the UMW organize the Fairmont District shortly after the turn of the century, a time when the state's vast lode of bituminous coal was being sought to fuel the exploding industrial revolution. She was arrested at Clarksburg in 1902 for violating a federal injunction forbidding her organizing activities. She beat the rap, however, despite the fact that the federal prosecutor at Parkersburg called her " . . . the most dangerous woman in the country today" and noted she had called the judge "a scab."

When Mother Jones came to Paint Creek in 1912, she found hundreds of striking miners living in deplorable conditions in tent cities they set up after being driven from their homes by Quinn Morton, owner of the Paint Creek Coal Co. Morton refused to go along with a general move to pay the miners another nickle a ton for the coal they shoveled into the donkey-powered mine cars. Mother Jones vividly recalled her impressions of Paint Creek in an autobiography published a few years later.

"The Paint Creek Coal Company would not settle with its miners and had driven them out into the hills," she wrote. "The strike had started out on the other side of the Kanawha hills in a frightful district called 'Russia'—Cabin Creek. Here, the miners had been peons for years, kept in slavery by the guns of the coal company and by the system of paying in scrip so that a miner never had any money should he wish to leave the district.

"He was cheated of his wages when his coal was weighed, cheated in the company store where he was forced to purchase his food, charged an exorbitant rent for his kennel in which he lived and bred, docked for school tax and burial tax and for physicians and for 'protection' which meant the gunmen who shot him back into the mines if he rebelled or so much as murmured against his outrageous exploitation."

Mother Jones rallied the Paint Creek miners and led three thousand of them over the hills to Charleston where they read "a declaration of war" to Governor William Glasscock, whom she delighted in calling "Governor Crystal Peter." The governor declared martial law in the area and dispatched fifteen hundred troops to Cabin and Paint Creeks.

Mother Jones and several miners were arrested by the troops. Although, according to her own statement, she was eighty-three at the time she was held under house arrest for five weeks and was not released until she had sneaked a telegram to Washington about the plight of the miners in West Virginia. Her telegram touched off a senatorial investigation.

Meanwhile, Henry Hatfield became governor and worked out an agreement

under which the miners agreed to go back to work, but not before they had made some gains. Their union was recognized, the coal companies' practice of hiring armed guards was criticized and partially abolished, and the miners got four of the five cent raise they were after, increasing their pay to twenty-nine cents a ton for hand-loaded coal. Small boys and old men who operated the mine ventilation doors—they were known as "trappers"—got one dollar for nine hours work.

The next real crisis between the union and the companies came after World War I. By 1920, the Kanawha, Fairmont, and New River fields were partially organized. The UMW then turned its attention to the southern coal field counties of Mingo, Logan, Wyoming, Raleigh, Mercer and McDowell.

UMW organizers went into Mingo County and immediately signed up some three thousand miners, all of whom were promptly fired. Like the Paint Creek miners, they were evicted from their coal company homes. One of these eviction episodes on May 19, 1920, touched off the infamous Matewan Massacre in which Matewan Police Chief Sid Hatfield, and a group of Matewan residents shot it out with some Baldwin-Felts Detective Agency guards, killing seven of the guards. Hatfield was gunned down by the dead guards' friends the following year on the steps of the courthouse at Welch, in McDowell County.

These events, combined with the miners' hatred of Logan County Sheriff Don Chafin, who kept out the union with a standing army of three hundred armed "deputies," led to the storied "Armed March on Logan."

The march took place in late August of 1921, a time when the Mingo strike

was still a stalemate and Don Chafin was still busting the heads of union organizers in Logan County. Frustrated by their lack of success in organizing southern West Virginia and spurred on by tales of starvation in Mingo County, thousands of miners from across the New River and Kanawha fields began pouring into the Kanawha County community of Marmet. Some seven thousand miners had gathered there by the evening of August 24 when they set out for Logan County vowing to hang Don Chafin and then go on to Mingo County and liberate their starving brothers.

Led by a young union firebrand named Bill Blizzard, the miners marched along what is now U.S. 119 in Boone County. As they walked they sang, "We'll hang Don Chafin to a sour apple tree" to the tune of "John Brown's Body." But the wily sheriff was not sitting by idly. He had recruited an army composed of dozens of state troopers and hundreds of specially deputized gunmen and citizens. It is said he even got some of his recruits from behind the bars of his always-crowded jail.

The shooting began on September 1 when an advance party of miners came upon a Chafin outpost at the foot of Blair Mountain where the sheriff had set up an eighteen-mile long battle line along the crest of the mountain. Three

Clockwise, from left: striking miners moved from company housing and lived for more than a year in tent cities; Mother Jones, "The Miner's Angel", Nov. 4, 1902; Sheriff Don Chafin, notorious hired strikebreaker; arsenal with 225,000 rounds of ammunition confiscated from Cabin Creek miners; leaders Albert and Lee Felts of the Baldwin-Felts Detective Agency were among the dead in the Matewan Massacre.

deputies were killed in the skirmish and both sides were boiling mad when the main body of miners came along a few hours later.

Although the records are sketchy, reports from the battlefield indicate the fighting raged for three days with the Chafin forces being supported by three small private airplanes which bombed the miners. The death toll was never verified but conflicting historical accounts estimate between six and six hundred men had been killed or wounded before federal troops arrived on the evening of September 3. (Neither side would divulge its casualties.)

The Battle of Blair Mountain had been a standoff but it marked the beginning of the end for the early coal field labor movement in the state. An outraged judiciary repeatedly ruled against the UMW and permitted the companies to make their workers sign "Yellow Dog" contracts which forbade union membership. By 1932, when President Franklin D. Roosevelt took office, the UMW's paid-up membership in West Virginia had dropped below five hundred miners.

It wasn't until Congress passed the Roosevelt-sponsored National Industrial Recovery Act in 1933 that the UMW was allowed to organize the coal fields and began changing the oppressive conditions under which the miners had labored for so long.

Mother Jones never lived to witness this particular victory but she enjoyed many others, including her hundredth birthday in 1930, the year she died. As she read one of the many telegrams congratulating her, she remarked, "He's a damned good sport! I've licked him many times, but we've made peace."

The telegram was from John D. Rockefeller.—SD

THE WEST VIRGINIA FRONTIER

Call it anything you like, but West Virginia is still a frontier

Respect their pride, observe their potential, hitch your wagon to their abilities. Do these things and West Virginians will give you a hard day's work for a decent day's pay.

Time has never changed the fact.

Some have paid dearly for miscalculating it.

Others are still making fortunes by understanding it.

Call it anything you like, but West Virginia is still a frontier .

It's still a frontier for the working West Virginian . . . .

Still a frontier for the capitalist . . . .

Still a spawning territory for entrepreneurs who have learned the meaning of innovation and haven't forgotten

On May 13, 1976, Intrepid iron workers connected the New River span, 876 feet above the water in Fayette Co. James E. Cutright (right), of French Creek, is one of more than 59,000 West Virginia coal miners.

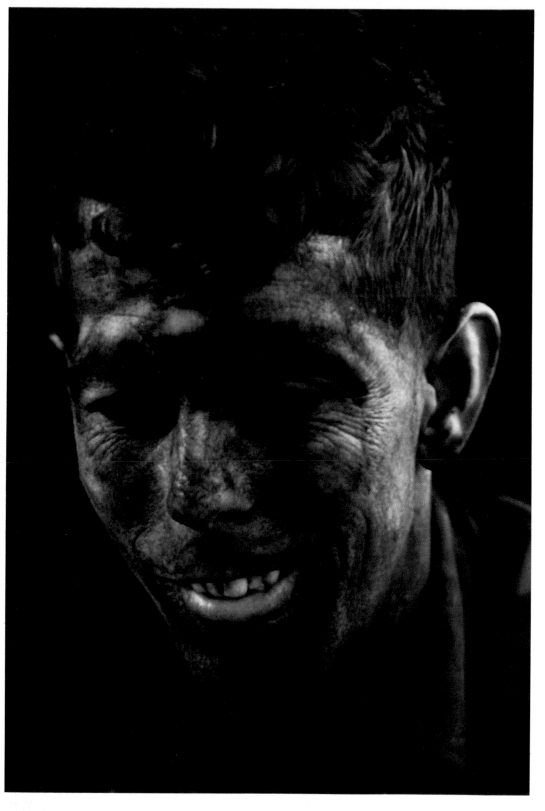

the meaning of hard work.

Great American industrialists have perpetually gazed upon her with an optimistic eye, teaming the spunk of her people with the plentiful riches of her inherent resources.

Her saga began in earnest around the turn of the century when the makers of glass, iron and chemical products gambled on obviously favorable odds and began developing thriving manufacturing empires.

A new breed of speculative opportunists (some of them having already cut their teeth on West Virginia logging and railroad ventures) launched expeditions to re-explore the hills, the valleys and the mountains and began harvesting a bountiful store of underground treasures. Oil towns and coal camps sprang up overnight and the heavy energy demands created by the manufacturers were met (often literally) "right in their own back yards."

The boom perpetuated itself. Its first impact still rings in the memories of many an old timer and in the bank accounts of industries and of estates.

With it all came still another breed of Americans . . . the immigrants. At first some were considered valuable only for their skills; others, for their strong bodies. With time, patience and understanding, their descendents would slowly emerge as proud mountaineers, the social equals of their neighbors.

Over the last three-quarters of a century, pioneering industries have been West Virginia's claim to world fame for metals, chemicals, manufacturing (from locally-produced raw materials), energy, and, due to skills handed down from some of those early immigrants, it has become the handmade glass capital of the western hemisphere.

Glass making art in the twentieth century is much like it was thousands of years ago, with similar methods, skills, and tools being employed. The earliest authenticated piece of glass, found in Egypt, dates back to about 7,000 B.C., although glass making may be as old as 14,000 years, according to a popular legend. Handcrafted items differ from machine-produced pieces in their reflection of the artisan's individual style and skill and therefore, are the most enduringly popular. The following is a list of handmade-glass plants which accommodate visitors:

Blenko Glass Co., Inc.—Milton
The Fenton Art Glass Co.—Williamstown
Fostoria Glass Co.—Moundsville
Pilgrim Glass Corp.—Ceredo
Seneca Glass Co.—Morgantown
Viking Glass Co.—New Martinsville
Rainbow Art Glass Co., Inc.—Huntington
W.Va. Glass Specialty Co.—Weston

149

Those who have recognized and invested in the work power and the integrity of the proud mountaineer are still winning on their bets.

Other speculators have ignored both the written and unwritten laws of nature's morality, leaving once beautiful green landscapes gashed with the ugly wounds of hit-and-run strip mining. Only centuries of nature's slow healing process can erase these absurd scars.

Others have recognized their debt to nature by closing up their topographic incisions and replanting.

But eighty-three percent of the state's coal still comes from underground—enough to maintain her position as the second largest bituminous coal producer in the nation. And if we continue to use coal at our present rate of 110 million tons per year, there's still an estimated two hundred to three hundred year supply (57,651,775,685 short tons) down there waiting in its 300 million-year-old grave to see sunlight again.

Still another natural resource is attracting more wealth than it exports: the magic splendor of the wilderness itself . . . and its people.

An aggressive state commerce department has discovered that the unique and often unspoiled beauty of the mountains is a salable commodity; it is staffed to answer inquiries that today run in the millions every year. Seven regional travel councils are greeting traveling adventurers, West Virginia style.

Frontier?

Yes . . . A latent frontier, re-explored!

Seventy-nine percent of the land is now green with valuable timber. The paper companies, the timber lords, the loggers, the purveyors of hardwoods have learned the hard way not to strip the earth naked but to leave the young trees

A diverse frontier—as old as America, as new as tomorrow—with industries light as exquisite crafts, heavy as steel. From top left, reading down: hay harvest in Upshur Co.; glittering coke ovens and lights on Weirton Steel's barge docks; a train of slag cars dumping their molten cargo, lighting up the night. (Slag, once a nuisance, is now a valuable by-product.) An underground power dispatch center at Appalachian Power in Huntington (top). analyzes weather forecasts and factors that determine regional energy demands; a fiery sky over the Stony River generating station (Grant Co.) operated by Virginia Electric Power. (Eastern power producers are the largest consumers of W. Va. coal.) At Marion Co.'s new Martinka Mine a surveyor (left center) lines up a precision cut for a continuous mining machine (operated by the two men below;) 19th century mining machinery on the hoof (center)—slow, but dependable (most of the time); 3 million volts (bottom picture) from an Ohio Brass Co. laboratory generator provide a rugged test for experimental equipment. The equipment is designed to transmit up to 2,000,000 volts from W.Va.'s coal-powered stations to locations throughout the American Electric Power Co. System, from the Virginias to the Great Lakes. The system's largest line now transmits 750,000 volts. A molten ingot of sophisticated metal (top) in a Huntington Alloy Products rolling mill; auctioneers (bottom) point out bidders at a Mineral Co. auction; eastern panhandle apples ready for market; elegant tableware designed by Harpers Ferry pewtersmith Don Miller; shiny metal being coiled at Kaiser Aluminum's sprawling Ravenswood Works (Jackson Co.); pigments used in making more than 15,000 ABS plastic colors in laboratory at Borg-Warner Chemicals (Washington, W.Va. plant); Union Carbide Chemicals and Plastics at Long Reach and at Institute.

(thus the good soil) and to re-forest; to preserve the beauty and to cut only the mature woods, not their own throats. (New land is no longer cheap.)

The builders and barons, however unpopular with the government bureaucrats and from time-to-time with laboring breadwinners, have brought their wealth back home to West Virginia. Witness Union Carbide's South Charleston Technical Center (which bears a close resemblance to a university campus), DuPont, and others. The name of the game is to utilize West Virginia's brain power and to discover extended uses for her resources.

The state's population is back on the increase. The frontiers are at home.

Green Bank, West Virginia's National Radio Astronomy Observatory, uses radio waves to study outer-space events that occurred millions of years before the birth of the earth . . .

The electric utility companies, still the biggest users of coal, are already transmitting more than three-quarters of a million volts from input stations close to the mines across six states. Tests are being conducted to transmit as much as two million volts to meet the energy demands of the 1990's.

Most of this is a mere five hundred miles from most of the nation's population—and its markets.

Most of it always has been—and always will be—a frontier.—*JA/HS*

The Kanawha-Cloverdale transmission line carries its 345,000-volt energy load from the coal fields through a sea of autumn fog in Summers County. In the mountains of Pocahontas County, the saucer-like telescope of the Green Bank National Radio Astronomy Observatory monitors outer space events.

152

SUNNY DAYS WITH MOUNTAIN MAMA

Seven or eight years ago I saw some kayakers on the Cheat River *and the sport looked fascinating. I loved the looks of it and decided to take it up. Later I tried out a kayak and that turned me on to it.*

Watching him maneuver his light craft with split-second precision over the frothy rapids of the Cheat River at Calamity Rock creates a hypnotic effect upon the observer. He noses the kayak straight down into a rolling hydraulic water formation which thrashes and spins the craft as though it were in a washing machine. Then, instead of tumbling into the raging waters out of control, he *balances* himself and the kayak as though it were an extension of his body.

Forty-seven-year-old Paul Felton, who lives in Rowlesburg, Preston County, became a championship kayak paddler in just three short middle-aged years after taking his first compelling ride.

I started out by getting a Vector and practicing. I taught myself to kayak and then got each of my kids one. We'd go on trips with the West Virginia Wildwater Club from Charleston. They have over two hundred members. It's a good and active club and they participate in accepted conservation practices.

He explained a few of the characteristics of the craft and then he talked about the strategy of paddling his way to championship.

The kayak originated with the Eskimos who used it for hunting and it hasn't changed as far as design. The slalom kayak is built to turn easy, has a rocker on both ends and there is no resistance to turning. The down-river kayak is built to track itself in a straight line.

I've been participating in contests now for three years. When I first started, I was overweight. I got to practicing and working on the river and lost thirty pounds. I kept working at it, paddling three or four days a week staying in shape. Most of the spectators around there thought I was crazy until I started winning races.

I figured on getting a down-river boat after taking a ride in a friend's, so I ordered one and practiced in it to be ready

Paddlers from Washington D. C., Pittsburgh and points east congregate in Smoke Hole Canyon on the North Fork of the South Branch of the Potomac River.

155

for Petersburg the next year in the championship race where you get more recognition.

So in '74 I paddled in the senior championship division and I won first place. Of course, all that kept turning me on more and after that I won two first places.

In '74 my son and I entered my old Folbot in the cruiser race at Petersburg and we won first in that race.

I've enjoyed the river all my life in one sport or another. That's probably what induced me to go into kayaking.- HS

I guess it's one of those ego-type things more than anything else. It's a lot more dangerous. I have done some rafting, but myself, I like the idea of being in a one-man boat or two-man boat—the individual against the elements.

Paddling falls isn't done very often. So far I've been the only one to run most of them. When I'm running a waterfall, I take it systematically. First, I look at the approach to the lip of the falls— a sufficient volume of water with little obstruction is needed. Next, I consider the drop itself—the actual height—and it must also be free of obstructions. Finally I examine the bottom of the falls —a deep pool is preferable, free of obstruction.

Bryan Bills, who has kayaked for four

Plunging over Kanawha Falls in his kayak, Bryan Bills, an expert paddler, touches upon the limits of the art of kayaking. At right, Paul Felton, a self-taught champion, balances his kayak in the angry white waters of the famous Cheat River.

A youngster cools off in the clear waters of the North Fork of Patterson Creek in Greenland Gap, Grant County.

Valley Falls, in a series of rushing waterfalls and foaming white rapids, stretching through a mile long gorge of the Tygart River, is eight miles north of Grafton, Taylor County, in Valley Falls State Park.

years, got interested much the same way as Paul. He met a few members of the West Virginia Wildwater Association and his fun on the water began.

If there is such a thing as a specialist among kayakers, Bryan Bills is one. His speciality is paddling waterfalls—falls that have never been run by anyone before. Even for experts, the hazards are great.

The closest call I ever had was in Birch River Falls. The approach wasn't very good at the top. When I got right to the edge of the falls, I miscued and I ended up dropping the falls almost sideways. The problem there was that I had a very narrow place, maybe five or six feet wide, that I had to go through at the bottom, and I just did make it.

The sport is very safety oriented and a person that does much of it is very safety conscious. We all wear protective headgear and of course we wear life jackets. We don't paddle alone and you don't paddle above your ability.

This sport is relatively new to the United States. There's been only one international race in this country. The Olympics no longer carry whitewater kayaking and the highest form of competition is the World Championships.

In West Virginia, primarily, the paddlers are not competition oriented. As a matter of fact, there are very, very few that have been serious racers in the past, but West Virginia has the most potential for producing people because of the water resources. We're really lucky; we've got three of the most sought after rivers in the eastern United States: The New River, the Gauley River and the Cheat River.—MS

We've paddled with people from all over the country. *I guess that's the part that's unusual in some respects.*

Dwayne Rings is a canoeist. The difference between kayaking and canoeing lies essentially in the design of the craft. The kind of water the canoeist seeks out is the same, but the technique is quite different. Dwayne, who works in the Technical Department at Du Pont's Washington, West Virginia works, has spent most of his free time over the past decade paddling West Virginia's whitewater streams, and recently has taken up the kayak but his interests lie in the esthetics and adventure of paddling much more than in championship competition. He also talks of the camaraderie among the breed of people who are attracted to the wilderness—

You find that people come to West Virginia because of the variety of water that's available. We have met people camped at Seneca Rocks who take up caving, canoeing, climbing all within fifteen or twenty miles. You can indulge in all three sports which is unusual because there aren't many places you can do this in a single weekend.

We ran into a group of Canadians from Hamilton and one couple came from as far as North Bay about 300 miles north of Toronto. They came down here because they wanted to paddle rivers like the Cheat and the Youghiogheny.

Dwayne remembered one weekend experience on New River:

Well, this was on a Sunday morning; the early morning fog had lifted. We passed through rapids and got onto this long pool between these rapids and the Quinnimont rapids. You look down the pool and about a third of the way up the hillside, buried in the greenery, is a white church. And this church had an amplifying system, playing a hymn. It came out across the water, over this absolutely still reflecting pool. Everybody

just stopped paddling—completely. It's a sensation like you could never re-create if you had tried. People just floated and listened to that music, and then, five or ten minutes later . . . we were up to our ears in water!

This is the kind of sensation that you just can't orchestrate—you don't know when it's going to happen—and you don't know how it's going to affect you . . . . —HS

I took up the bow some years back in summer camp and my interest grew in it and I started reading articles on it. Then I just broke away and went ahead and did it the way I wanted to.

West Virginia's fields and woods are heavily populated with hunters every fall and winter but from October 16 to December 31, only a certain breed that trek through the countryside are hunting in the style of the American Indian— with bow and arrow.

Jim Austin started hunting at the age of five. He had his own gun when he was six, but he didn't take up bow hunting until he was much older.

The main danger of bow hunting is gettin' up in one of these treestands . . . bow season comes in the same time as small game season and there's always some trigger happy fellow out there in the woods. Somethin' moves out there in the tree, he thinks for sure it's a squirrel and he shoots before he looks. I like to do my hunting on the ground.

Jim who usually hunts in his own

Alerted by human scent, a doe lifts her head high in search of the source. Jim Austin (rt.) conceals himself in the foliage until his game appears. To discover before being discovered and to employ unlimited patience: the not-so-simple bow hunting fundamentals.

Hampshire County, says the key to success at bow hunting is *bein' at the right spot at the right time,* but the skill most needed by the bow hunter is patience.

Jim was definitely at the right spot two years ago when he shot his first deer with the bow.

I'd been in the woods two hours—sneakin' around a little bit. I was twenty-five yards from that one, not completely broadside—just slightly—took it right behind the front fore leg. That deer ran fifty, sixty yards before it let out enough to drop.

Jim will never give up hunting with a gun, but, to *be sportin' about it,* he favors the bow and arrow. —*MS*

The trip takes six to eight hours *on a normal run; covers sixteen miles of the best whitewater east of the Mississippi . . . .*

He thought for a second. He wanted to make it sound even better—

New River is one hell-of-a-river!

He seemed satisfied that those eight words said it all.

Jon Dragan is a confident promoter when he boasts about this wild, winding stretch of beautiful water that's deeply etched into incredibly rugged, shadowed canyons and gorges.

From the point where she cuts through the border from Virginia she moves deliberately north. She slices through a corner of Mercer County into Summers, becoming Bluestone Lake, a calm water paradise for outboarders and bikinied water skiiers. She rolls over the dam in a foamy frenzy, then sensuously smiles at the bass fishermen as she waltzes on past Hinton to rub shoulders with Raleigh; does her main exhibition dance around Horseshoe Bend exposing herself in the sun at Grandview State Park where bermuda-clad city escapees salute her command performance with a volley

from their Polaroids, Instamatics, super-eights and wide-angled Nikons; wiggles right into Fayette—adorned in white lace—and literally tears the county apart.

This Fayette County display is daily attended by V. I. P.'s (very important participants): the wilderness—silent, picturesque, abandoned mine tipples, paddlers, overgrown ghost towns. Special music is provided by a symphony of C & O coal trains playing, "Black Treasure," composed in one of the richest mining regions of the world.

She accepts every dance invitation from the paddlers who affectionately call her "The New"—but she leads all the movements.

Then the lights go out as she disappears underground at Hawks Nest to change for her final act. She emerges, takes the Gauley by the hand and changes her name to the Kanawha at Kanawha Falls.

Jon applauds this daily spectacle. His enthusiasm is justified. She is *one hell-of-a-river.*

It has the highest volume of white water east of the Mississippi. But rapids can be equally as difficult with less water, depending upon the gradient and narrows of the stream.

Jon Dragan is in the whitewater business. He operates Wildwater Expeditions Unlimited in Thurmond, the first of four companies that now conduct rafting tours on West Virginia whitewater rivers.

Appalachian Wild Waters operates on the Cheat, New River and the Gauley; Mountain River Tours on the New River

Even after careful instructions, beginning rafters are surprised on contact with a new set of wild rapids. Decisions and maneuvers must often be made within a thirtieth of a second, or even sooner.

and the Gauley, and Blue Ridge Enterprises on the Shenandoah.

On Dragan's New River float trip, each raft holds ten adventure-seeking passengers plus two guides. A longer trip on the Gauley requires more experience:

We start at Summersville and run twenty-two miles to Swiss, Jon begins—over what he assures is—*very, very technical water considered to be the most challenging in the East. The trip is two days—and on that trip you are land-locked two days unless you walk about a mile and a half to a country road.*

Most of our people just sleep right down on the river.

The New River trip attracts a variety of beginners and enthusiasts—of all ages, of all backgrounds, of all countries. Then he remembered three lady customers from just downstream and across at Gauley Bridge . . . .

In the age column on her application, one wrote "Golden Years," one was seventy-three; one was seventy-five; one was seventy-six. They had a ball! They're the best sort of walking advertisement we've got.

Jon identifies with the Dwayne Rings story of the church near the Quinnimont rapids:

You're down there on a weekend; you're out in the middle of nowhere. All of a sudden it starts coming out of the PA system—you're just not certain whether you're going to heaven—or going down the river.

And that's just a heck-of-a-nice uncertainty. —HS

I'd always been of the impression that once you hooked and lost a fish, *your chances of catching that particular fish over again were just almost impossible . . . that it'd felt the sting of the hook . . . and would never strike again,*

Like a small chip on the water, a raft scoots past an abandoned mine tipple on its journey down the New River. Four commercial companies offer whitewater trips on W.Va. wilderness rivers, where permanent residents (like the raccoon) are just as startled by the visitors as the visitors are amazed by the abundance of wildlife.

at least—within a reasonable length of time . . . .

Richard Oesterle began his story, taking his time, and the small audience of friends quietly and eagerly listened.

Sporting fishermen constitute just about the largest, most loyal legion in West Virginia. Few people are more dedicated or patient.

And few, including Dick Oesterle, who fishes West Virginia from corner to corner, can tell stories with greater zeal.

Dick and a fellow dedicated angler were sharing a boat in a lake fishing tournament when Dick had a strike, but the fish got away with the bait as well as the *hook.*

Oesterle was startled, and his partner was confused, at first.

Oesterle cleared his throat and resumed his tale:

Well, this old gentleman wanted to know—' What happened?' —and I said, 'Well, apparently, I tied a poor knot and it slipped off.'

He said, "I'm gonna tie that hook on so that the biggest bass in the lake can't pull it off!'

Which he did . . . .

About my first or second cast after he did this, I had another strike. And this time I came in with about a nice, two-pound bass.

It wasn't a big fish, but it was what we call in the tournament circuit—a 'qualifier.'

This old gentleman dipped the fish for me, and I reached down into the dip net and pulled it out—(He paused for a second)—And there, in that fish's mouth, was my other worm!

Oesterle couldn't hold back his enthusiasm:

That bass—had hit that bait—it had

The first rays of dawn tint the Shenandoah River a delicate gold, silhouetting two early rising fishermen. Alexander Spotswood (lt. governor of Virginia in 1710) led a party of explorers into the Blue Ridge Mountains. They named the river they discovered the Euphrates, but the Indian name describes it best: Shenandoah; "daughter of the stars."

a hook in its mouth—It had a worm halfway down its throat—Yet I caught that fish—I know—within five minutes after losing it . . . !

We hear alot about "the big one that got away."

Now we have, for the record, a little one that came back.

This just happens to be one of those rare cases, where the story outweighs the fish. — HS

I discovered the Canaan Valley— first, indirectly through literature and also through references to it in terms of the great hunting in this unique area of West Virginia . . . .

Later, Bill Gerhold studied Canaan from the air and eventually explored its picturesque landscapes mile-by-mile over country roads.

There were frequent stops, continuing the journey on foot, carrying his paints and easel over fences, through the woods and across sloping corn fields to record other visual episodes in his collection of watercolors on his favorite corner of America.

. . . And having grown up in West Virginia—we become used to its beauty before we think about its beauty.

And it's not until you begin to suffer through living in places like New York and Cleveland, and being in and out of the busiest airports in the world, like Chicago O'Hare—or Midway—when I

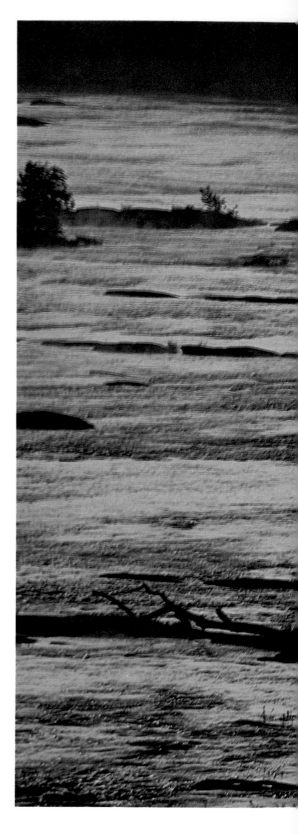

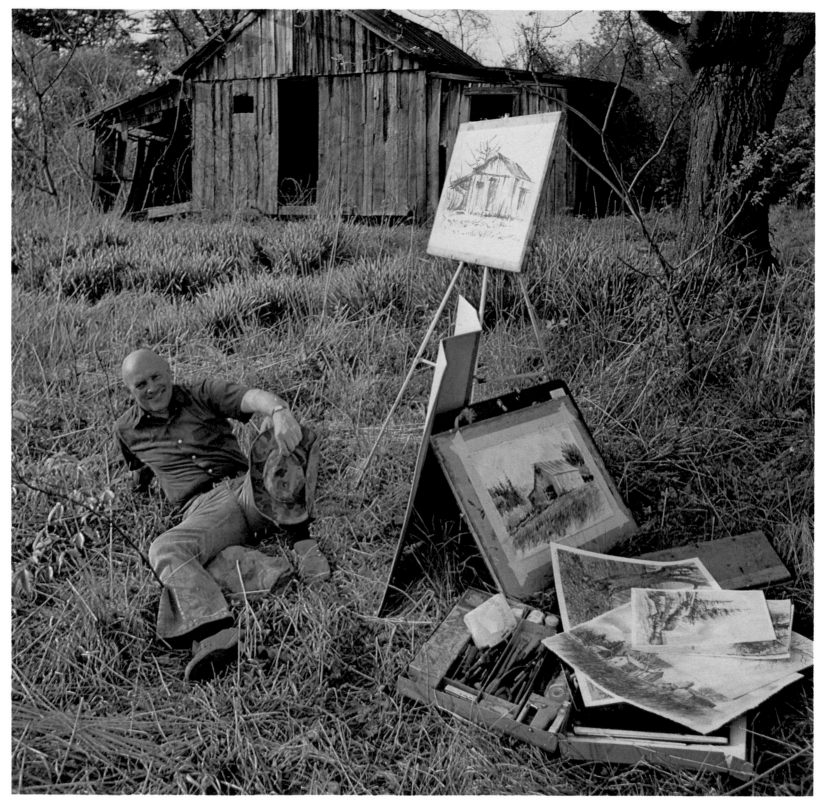

*first simmered up in an airplane, that you
begin to appreciate home and what it
is we've got here in this area of the
world . . . .*

There's authority and conviction and
warmth in Bill's voice when he talks of
home and what he wants to do with this
chapter in his life. To arrive at this he
has a number of reference points, including his years as a professional industrial pilot when there were no such things
as regular working hours, or regular
days—and *home,* more often than not,
was some far-away city or airport.

Now Bill is Director of the Art Department at Marietta College and has a *home*
in Williamstown across the Ohio River
in West Virginia. But his *favorite home*
is the family studio in the Canaan Valley.

*Little by little I've gotten more ac-
quainted with this area and for the last
several years now, we've conducted painting workshops at Canaan Valley State
Park. I think we had sixteen states represented last year in the people that came.*

*I just got back from the second of
our four workshops this summer, and in
that group of twenty-three people, twelve
had been there last year.*

*Their responses are gratifying because
once they get here—they're coming back.*

Bill Gerhold is only one of thousands
who have explored the big cities and
made an amazing discovery at the end
of a long cycle of searching—

Home. —*HS*

*Old farm homes—abandoned and weathered—
barns and other rustic rural architecture
are blended with season landscapes in
Bill Gerhold's watercolors.*

It looked like fun! I had a friend who did cross-country—I like to get out in the woods. *It's a very pleasant way to get out in the wintertime . . . it's the easiest and quickest way to travel in the woods in the wintertime.*

Cross-country skiing is a sport fairly new to the West Virginia hills, but with the resort ski slopes jammed to capacity and the United States obtaining its first Olympic medal in the sport with Bill Koche winning a silver medal, the sport seems to be gaining new advocates.

Bruce Summers, who belongs to a cross-country ski club in Morgantown, is an enthusiastic convert. The club was started by Bruce Wilson who works for the State Geological Survey.

Summers says it's difficult to compare cross-country skiing and downhill skiing. *Downhill skiing takes a lot of balance and strength, whereas, cross-country skiing is more analogous to running. But* as Bruce pointed out, *in cross-country skiing, you step, kick and glide, and traveling down these West Virginia hills, you can whip up a good speed.*

You don't really need any skills to start; all you have to do is be able to walk . . . there isn't any kind of level you need to obtain before taking the sport up. Of course, endurance and balance and learning how to use your equipment are all important.

Bruce skis mostly around the Morgantown area and Elkins. He and his friends have even taken a trip across Dolly Sods. But there are no limitations to cross-country trips.

There's lots of places to ski. You can

Bruce Summers and Mia Sleminski kick and glide through Coopers Rock State Forest in Monongalia County. The snow-laden trees, at right, are in Pocahontas County.

cross-country ski anywhere there's snow. You're not limited by anything—just enough snow to cover what's on the ground. Of course, areas where there's very deep terrain, it'll get a little more exciting and you probably need a little more skill than a place that's flat. But you can ski on the street if there's enough snow to keep your skis from going through and scratching on the street.

Mild rolling terrain is probably the most pleasant. In very steep areas, it sort of stops being cross-country and becomes another sport which is called ski mountaineering. Some people like it very flat—then you can really work on speed.

A mild slope is really pleasant because you kick—you don't have to try and ski—you get your kick in there and you can move along quite easily.

When the snow season arrives, any well-hidden trail, shady hillside or inactive country road is the cross-country skier's avenue to pleasure. —MS

We're concerned with cave conservation because it's the last frontier here in this country. *It really is a wilderness underground and we want to keep it that way.*

Kyle Isenhart and Delbert Province are spelunkers from West Virginia. The term, "spelunking," is derived from the word "speleology," which is the scientific study or exploration of caves.

Thousands of spelunkers from everywhere swarm the West Virginia limestone regions every year to explore its caves but it is rare that their individual interests are purely scientific. With many cavers, it's more of a sport.

There are three things that most experienced spelunkers seem to have in common.

First, is that most abide by certain

Life in the mountains—the rugged landscape, teamed with the charm, the traditions, the cultures of its hearty people—must be experienced to be appreciated. From top-left, reading down: Wanda Chaplin on a summer afternoon at "Oleo Acres" ("the low priced spread") in Wood Co.; Potter Scottie Wiest (Upshur Co.); John Lutz and Barbara Murphy, backpackers (Wood Co.); traditional handicrafts (Mountain State Art & Craft Fair); handmade toys (in window), Harpers Ferry; naturally made foods (Swiss cheese maker); autumn (North Bend State Park, Ritchie Co.); horse-pulling contest at Waverly's Memorial Day celebration; Blackwater Falls (Tucker Co.); harness racing at the State Fair, Lewisburg; snowmobiling at Canaan Valley State Park; boat regatta at New Martinsville on the Ohio; hang gliding club (in Mason Co. and in Summers Co.); Bluestone Lake—open to swimmers, skiers, and fishermen; the ancient sport of jousting at the Mountain State Forest Festival in Elkins; a Philadelphia climber at Seneca Rocks; a young rider at Wheeling's Oglebay Park trains her mount for show competition.

ethics and ground rules.

Second, is that most are a special breed of people with a common compassion for the underground environment.

Last, there seems to be a universal fascination for the unknown.

Every year the number increases and some serious cavers find the situation deplorable because a large number of the beginners are uninformed novices who are not only reckless with their own lives, but are reckless with nature itself by thoughtlessly defacing caves with litter and the writing of graffiti on the walls. Some commit the worst crime of all by breaking and pilfering beautiful formations that took nature hundreds or thousands of years to create.

Floyd Collins of Kentucky is commonly recognized as the greatest spelunker of all time but his tragic death might possibly have been avoided had he obeyed a basic safety rule: Never cave alone.

In order to better equip beginners with knowledge on ethics and safety, Isenhart started offering a basic course on the subject at Parkersburg Community College in the early '60's.

It's a particular problem when we carry in everything we need to sustain ourselves while we're there . . . but after we get the useful life out of them, we're obligated to carry our trash back out. There's nothing more useless than spent carbide or worn out batteries.

People have to be educated to carry out all their trash, even under fatigue.

Cave safety and ethics is a growing concern as the number of novices multiplies. The National Speleological Society and other organizations have a high code of ethics, but they are frequently abused by beginners and often passed over by experienced spelunkers as well.

Much the same as with hunting, fishing or any activity involving private property, it is important to get the property owner's permission before entering caves and extend the courtesy of informing the owner when leaving.

It also may prove to be a lifesaving gesture to inform a friend or some other responsible person of each trip plan.

Kyle insists, *skillful people don't take chances.*

When Delbert Province first began spelunking in the '50's, he recalled there were about 280 charted caves. *Now we know there's at least that many in Greenbrier County alone—not to mention Pocohontas and Pendleton Counties.*

Province, who has been in about a hundred West Virginia caves, feels that getting lost is one of the worst dangers the novice faces, when he is unaccompanied by a leader who knows the particular cave.

I've been confused a few times—for a long time—but never really lost.

You don't have to worry about gas in caves the way you do in the mines, but loose rocks and pools of water are hazards.

Isenhart says there are now around 3,000 caves in the state that have been explored. *If you don't tell anyone where you're going—that's how many places the searching parties have to look for you if you get in trouble.*

Bill Bauman, silhouetted in mid air, rappels a seventy-foot free drop into the entrance of a Pocahontas County cavern. Rappeling requires considerable rope-training. Two N.S.S. members (right) enjoy the natural wonders of a Pendleton Co. cave. Delicate formations— mineral deposits from dripping and seeping water—are "grown" over hundreds or thousands of years.

There is a lot to know about caving safety and ethics. The best way to learn, Delbert suggests, is to go *with a N.S.S. member or someone else who is experienced and responsible.*

Our motto, says Kyle, *is take nothing but pictures and leave nothing but footprints.*

You find a lot of different attitudes *among people who climb. I personally climb because I really like it. A lot are into doing hard climbing and others are into teaching. For the most part, they're a good bunch of people.*

John Markwell and his business partner, Bob Livingstone, are climbers. They operate a small store called *The Gendarme* at Mouth of Seneca, West Virginia, directly across the North Fork and the highway from Seneca Rocks in Pendleton County.

Seneca towers a mere nine hundred feet above the river but her vertical walls offer the gamut of climbing problems ranging from beginners routes to the impossible. It's considered to be the best technical climbing in the East.

The Gendarme sells climbing and spelunking equipment and serves as a hangout for climbers from everywhere, in search of climbing companions for the next day or just a willing ear to listen to their stories (not all of which are completely believable).

John is in the business much more for the personal satisfaction than for big profits.

Scaling a Seneca route named "Cockscomb," John Tollett (Texas) and Al Crouse (Ohio) rest on a ledge above the North Fork Valley landscape. A summer sun etches around the distant silhouette of Pittsburgh climber Cora Addicock, as she works her way up the third pitch to Seneca's south summit.

I wanted to move where I could climb and get a job teaching. We've been going almost five years. The shop alone won't support us so we have to work other jobs. I work for the Department of Welfare and Bob works for the Department of Natural Resources.

But we're providing a service, as well as making a business.

Part of that service includes the thoroughly unpleasant job of rescue work.

During the day and all hours of the night and under every kind of weather condition, when the emergency alert is given, Bob and John shoulder up rescue and first aid gear, recruit any experienced climbers who happen to be around, and begin climbing desperately toward the accident location.

Often the situation proves to be trapped amateurs who have worked themselves into a mess and nightfall catches them without lights. Other situations are much more gruesome.

If you're going to have a full-time rescue team you need climbers living in the immediate area and there aren't any (except for John and Bob and another climber nearby who is still recovering from a falling accident). It's a fly-by-night operation. If we're here, we're here—if not, then too bad . . . . Not much potential for a permanent thing unless the Forest Service would pay us.

Thus, it is by circumstance, not by choice, that John and Bob *are* the rescue service, for all practical purposes.

Dwayne Carling (Colorado) descends part of a 100-foot rappel in eight-foot leaps. (Extended jumping is dangerous—overheats equipment.) An Alpine-dressed climber clings to delicate finger and toeholds on "Breakneck."

We hassled the Forest Service until they bought some rescue gear. Then it got stolen. The second time the climbers bought it—set up a rescue fund.

Most folks who climb are real good people—willing to help when someone gets hurt. No climber has ever been sued for administering first aid. Climbers do have a moral obligation to help.

John lives by that obligation.

I think the prime thing all the accidents have in common, except for a couple of incidents, is a lapse in concentration. People have been climbing here since 1939. Up until November of 1971, there was never an accident that involved an evacuation.

In '71, we had our first fatality and since then, we've had thirty other assorted accidents that involved evacuations and three fatalities. The people involved run the gamut from beginners to experts.

John went on to point out the increase in the popularity of the sport and that most climbers know both their equipment and their own limitations.

The accident rate in climbing, he claims, *is lower than anything in the country. If you know anything about climbing, you have a better chance of getting killed driving down here.*

John never enjoys his rescue work but he's always ready when he's needed. And *The Gendarme* is always ready the year around to welcome a special breed of people who, for better or for worse, happen to have climbing in their blood.

It's a place for climbers to get together and exchange information. It's the first place they stop when they come and the last place before they leave.

You might say *The Gendarme* is in the people business, for better or for worse. —HS

It's not the type of thrill you get from riding a car fast or doing something dangerous. *You don't get the butterfly type of thrill, its just really pretty . . . something little ol' ladies would love if they ever tried it, but its not a scary thing to do.*

Jan Haddox met Jim McCausland on a hill one day; they sort of glided into each other. Living in different parts of the state, they had both read an article in Reader's Digest about hang gliders and each had ordered one. After that fateful encounter, they decided to work on promoting the sport and organized the West Virginia Hang Gliders. It's a professional organization with professionally-trained instructors which in Jan's words *lets people know what it's like and what it's about.*

Hang gliding has really grown tremendously. I'd say we have fifty to a hundred flyers in the state now and two years ago we didn't have any.

So what's hang gliding all about? Well, Jan, who's living in Point Pleasant, says it's the closest thing to natural flying that man has ever conjured up. The sport goes back to the days of Icarus, who attempted soaring via wax and feathers; da Vinci, centuries later, had more luck with designs of more finesse. Even nineteenth century Germans were taken with the sport.

Today there are many kinds of gliders—foot-launch and boat-towed. Jan's advice to novices is to stick with foot-launch gliding.

It's much easier to do and there's

less chance of accident. Towing—you leave that to the professionals.

People are making twenty-four and twenty-five mile flights and staying up for five and six hours. The record now is eleven hours.

A misconception that is fostered by the name "hang gliding" is that the person actually hangs on the glider.

It's called hang gliding but you're hanging from the glider in a harness, and all you do with the control bar is rest your hands on it. It's just so that you can shift your body weight. You fly the whole thing by your body—you just lean and the glider goes that way. That's what makes it so close to natural flying! You ride the lift currents.

The gliders are very, very accurate. You can put them down on just about anything and the landings are very soft. One of the things that surprises people the most is how soft they come in and land.

The only danger in hang gliding, besides the pilot, is the wind. High winds increase by the square of the difference so a ten-mile-an-hour wind isn't twice as strong as a five—its four times stronger and a twenty-mile-an-hour wind instead of being four times stronger than a five is sixteen times stronger. That's why when you fly in higher winds you really have to be careful.

Anyone interested in soaring to higher altitudes should be prepared to take a little banging and bruising but according to Jan, nothing more drastic than injured pride is usually involved.

That's what makes it really nice— you're not polluting and it's very quiet. It has the same appeal as sailboating. You're using the currents and you're using what you've learned.

Now that's a real high! —MS

It began with the mythical Icarus and was somewhat refined by Leonardo DaVinci. Hang gliding—". . . the closest thing to natural flying" is a new participation sport.

The sunny days of the Gasoline Age around Clarksburg and on Buckhannon's West Virginia Wesleyan College campus after 1911 are beautifully preserved in a remarkable collection of photographs.

A youthful, curious, energetic merchant's son, name of Ward Fletcher, acquired two cameras along about the

time he entered college. One was a cumbersome (but faithful) postcard-format reflex. The other was an occasionally-used Kodak vest pocket model.

However, Fletcher's curiosity was not confined to photography. He displayed a passion for anything mechanical—automobiles, motorcycles (see picture), race cars and even *motorized canoes*.

His interests proved to be much more than mere infatuation. Fletcher demonstrated an expertise in his activities that

Fairs and circuses were Fletcher's favorite subjects. Here his Graflex caught a bashful grin from a young sideshow entertainer. The action shot (at Wesleyan around 1912) captured a pole vaulting athlete at his apex over the highest crossbar setting, and a classic study of the amazed crowd.

ultimately ranged from photography to aviation—all within a short span of seven years.

Photographically, he documented a dynamic, flashy, booming era that has since been forgotten by all but the remaining few who witnessed it. His collection of negatives is evidence of unquestionable technical competence. His subjects were either interesting or exciting—never dull—and were always artistically composed. His varied and successful experiments were clearly indicative of his genius.

Some of the technically-difficult images he managed to immortalize on very slow, nitrate-based films would have stumped seasoned press photographers thirty or forty years hence. The subjects of those visual achievements include available light pictures at the circus, night pictures, unique self portraits, lightning pictures, trick double exposures of himself on both ends of the same ladder and excellent action shots of a boundless variety of events.

His diverse interests included athletics. Though small in stature, he managed to prove himself in football, swimming, basketball and gymnastics.

His love affair with machinery guided him into the amazing new world of aviation. As a World War I army flight instructor in Texas, he trained fighter pilots in *Jennys* (those windy crafts constructed of wire and wood and canvas that weren't

The potpourri of pictures on the left are all a part of Fletcher's dynamic youth. Among them are several portraits of Ward himself. Teammates at Wesleyan, who were reliant on his wit and humor, fondly referred to him as "Fletch."

Recovering from extensive injuries sustained in his plane crash, Ward managed a swollen faced grin for this photograph (damaged in processing). During emergency treatment, he refused anesthetic and joked with doctors.

exactly famous for their dependability). Finally he was trapped in a fateful flight—a panicked student's nose dive over which Ward seized control only a split second above that hard Texas earth. The crash left nothing intact except the *Jenny's* engine and the two badly injured aviators. Fletcher was rushed to the hospital—the broken control stick of a *Jenny* tightly clenched in his fist.

After returning to Clarksburg, Ward Fletcher settled down to marriage and a long, contented life devoted to his family.

Fletcher was a modest man in his mature years. His grandchildren never heard tall talk about his youthful adventures, but his photographs speak for themselves . . . .

The man is gone now, but those sunny days from the youth of a productive, creative, artistic genius, in brilliant, silvered images, live on.—*HS*

Ed Pitner (center), naturalist and artist, explores the mountain wilderness, studying and sketching its flora and fauna. An authority on edible plants, he also teaches a course in outdoor survival (Parkersburg Community College). Surrounding Ed is an assortment of forest closeups. From top left, to bottom: Redbud in bloom (Pendleton Co.); barn swallow (McDowell Co.); floating maple leaves (Valley Falls State Park, Marion Co.); apple moss (Hardy Co.); baby red-tailed hawks (Wayne Co.); monarch butterfly (Ritchie Co.); downy woodpecker; newt salamander (Pendleton Co.); red maple tree (Wood Co.); fiddle head fern (Middle Island, Tyler Co.); gay wings—a plant found in the higher elevations; golden trout, developed at the Petersburg Hatchery (Grant Co.); fox tail grass at full flower stage (Nicholas Co.); screech owl (Lincoln Co.); fungi growing on a log (Cathedral State Park, Preston Co.); a well camouflaged tree frog; snow covered beech tree; teaberry in Cranesville Swamp (Preston Co.); an orb-weaving spider's web (Kanawha Co.); lady fern in Coopers Rock (Preston Co.).

187

WEST VIRGINIA USA:
A CHRONOLOGY

Queen Elizabeth granted a patent to Sir Humphrey Gilbert in 1578 for exploration and discovery in North America. Though his expedition was unsuccessful, Gilbert's half-brother Sir Walter Raleigh was granted a renewal of

the patent and his expedition led to the discovery of Virginia.

From the reconstructed fort at Jamestown, Virginia, cannons overlook the James River from stockade walls.

MAN

12,000 B.C. Indians inhabited the Kanawha and Ohio Valleys. There are sparse remains of these nomadic hunters but the strongest evidence of a Paleo-Indian campsite is in the Parkersburg area. Another site is believed to be on Peck's Run in Upshur County.

8,000-1,000 B.C. During the Archaic Period, hunting and fishing attracted Indians to West Virginia valleys. It is believed that Indians entered the state from the south down the New River. They are known to have lived on the east bank of the Ohio in the Northern Panhandle and throughout the Kanawha and Ohio Valleys.

1,000 B.C.-1 A.D. In the Early Woodland Period, Indians spread throughout the central and northern portions of West Virginia and into the Eastern Panhandle.

The first rudimentary type of farming was practiced and hunting weapons became more refined. Flint knives, hoes, pottery and notched projectile points (the tip ends of either spears or arrows) made by the Woodland Indians have been found.

The Adena and Hopewell peoples of this period provide the major archaeological clues to West Virginia's past through their burial mounds. The largest single earthwork in the state and also east of the Mississippi is the Grave Creek Mound at Moundsville. It was opened in 1838 by A. B. Tomlinson.

1 A.D.-500 A.D. During the Middle Woodland Period, the Adena peoples were displaced or absorbed by the Hopewell culture. Two distinct subdivisions began to develop in West Virginia: the Wilhelm Culture in northern West Virginia and western Pennsylvania and the Armstrong Culture in central and southern West Virginia.

500 A.D.-1,000 A.D. Succeeding the Armstrong Culture in central West Virginia during the Late Woodland Period was the Buck Garden Culture. The beginnings of compact village life began during

this period. Paralleling the Buck Garden Culture were the Watson Farm Stone Mound Builders who dominated the Northern Panhandle. They succeeded the Wilhelm Culture.

1000-1700 The last period before recorded history is known as the Late Prehistoric Period. A variety of Indian cultures inhabited the state but the primary groups were the Fort Ancient peoples in the Kanawha and Ohio Valleys and the Monongahela Culture in northern West Virginia. The agricultural base of their economies allowed the Indians to settle into villages. Their staple crops were corn, beans and squash.

A special feature of this period is the rock drawings or petroglyphs carved by the Late Prehistoric peoples. The Harrison County Indian Cave Petroglyphs, the Salt Rock Petroglyphs in Cabell County and the Timmons Farm Site in Monongalia County are all Late Prehistoric sites.

THE VIRGINIA COAST

1497-1498 John Cabot (a Venetian sailing for England) explored North America probably as far south as the Chesapeake Bay thereby establishing early English claims to the American continent.

1527 An English ship, the *Mary Guilford* sailed along the eastern coast and reached the West Indies before returning to England.

1584 Sir Walter Raleigh was granted a renewal of Gilbert's charter. An expedition under Richard Grenville sailed to the New World and explored Roanoke Island and Albemarle Sound, but three attempts at establishing a colony on Roanoke failed.

JAMESTOWN

1606 King James of England issued charters to the Plymouth and

London Companies in hope of settling the eastern coast of America with English subjects.

1607 The London Company made its first settlement at Jamestown, Va.

Captain John Smith, leader of the settlers at Jamestown, was captured by Powhatan, chief of the Powhatan Confederacy of Indian tribes. Smith claimed that Pocahontas, the chief's daughter, saved his life.

Captain Smith, president of the Jamestown council, enforced regulations on industry and social organizations which saved the colony.

Christopher Newport explored the James River thirty miles west of the present site of Richmond, Va. in search of a route to the Far East.

1650 Captain Abraham Wood, commander of Fort Henry, led an expedition with Edward Bland into the Roanoke Valley, land of the Occaneechee Indians.

1651 Edward Bland's description of the Wood expedition was published in London where it aroused great interest in the frontier of Virginia and the western fur trade.

1660 The British Privy Council organized a committee to foster trade with the colonies.

1669 Rene Robert Cavalier Sieur de La Salle established amicable relations with the Iroquois and penetrated south of Lake Erie to the Ohio River.

John Lederer explored the Shenandoah River.

1670 The Hudson Bay Company was organized to participate in the fur trade. William Berkeley, the Governor of Virginia, became its first American representative.

1671 Thomas Batts, Thomas Woods, Robert Fallam, Jack Neasam and Perecute, an Appomattox Indian, explored westward to the New River. This expedition put English claims to the interior on a firmer base.

1716 Alexander Spotwood's expedition reached the Shenandoah

Statues of John Smith and Pocahontas stand in the park at Jamestown, Virginia.

Young sailors on James River waters first explored by Christopher Newport in 1607.

Valley and he took formal possession in the name of King George I of England.

FRONTIERS

1719 The Potomoke Church, the first in West Virginia, was founded by Presbyterians at Shepherdstown.

1722 The Iroquois surrendered their claims to land south of the Ohio River which included the Eastern Panhandle counties.

1726 German people from Pennsylvania settled near Shepherdstown which is now considered to be the first settlement in West Virginia.

1730 The first recorded grants of land in West Virginia were made to Isaac and John Van Meter.

1731 Morgan Morgan established what was thought to be the first settlement in western Virginia near Bunker Hill (now Berkeley County).

1742 John Peter Salley (Salling) and John Howard led an expedition that took them from the Greenbrier River through the Coal River Valley to the Great Kanawha River. They discovered coal in what is now Boone County.

The first iron furnace west of the Blue Ridge was constructed by Thomas Mayberry at Bloomery on the Shenandoah River.

1746 Thomas Lewis began surveying the Fairfax lands. The Fairfax Stone was erected, at the corner of Tucker and Grant counties, to mark the western boundary of lands granted by the Crown to Lord Fairfax.

1747 George Washington surveyed lands along the Potomac.

1749 Jacob Marlin and Stephen Sewell established the first settlement west of the Alleghenies near what is now Marlinton.

The Ohio Company received a grant of 500,000 acres of land between the upper Ohio River and the

Monongahela and Great Kanawha Rivers.

Celeron de Bienville buried lead plates along the Ohio River to affirm French claims to that valley and the interior.

1750 Thomas Walker, on behalf of the Loyal Company, explored the Greenbrier Valley and then entered Kentucky through the Cumberland Gap.

Christopher Gist, principal agent of the Ohio Land Company, surveyed lands in southern Ohio and northeastern Kentucky. He preceded the better known explorer Daniel Boone by eighteen years.

1752 Gist concluded the Treaty of Logstown with the Delaware and Shawnee Indians. The treaty recognized Virginia's claim to land west of the Alleghenies to the Ohio River.

1754 The French and Indian War began. English colonists under Governor Dinwiddie resisted French expansion in the Ohio Valley.

1755 General Braddock marched his army through Jefferson, Berkeley and Morgan Counties en route to Pittsburgh where he suffered defeat by the French and Indians.

Fort Ashby was constructed in what is now Mineral County. It is the last standing unit in the chain of forts built under the orders of George Washington.

1757 Hampshire County, the first in the state, was organized.

1758 Fort Duquesne was captured by the English under the leadership of General John Forbes and renamed Fort Pitt.

1762 Shepherdstown was incorporated and both English and German schools were opened.

Romney, Hampshire County, was incorporated as a town.

1763 The Treaty of Paris ending the French and Indian War was signed. France ceded to England all the territory east of the Mississippi River except the area around New Orleans.

The advance of white settlers was hindered by Pontiac's Conspiracy and Indian resistance.

The Proclamation Line of 1763 prohibited purchase or settlement of lands west of the Appalachian watershed to quiet Indian unrest.

1764 General Horatio Gates, who was second in command to George Washington, settled in Jefferson County where he lived until 1790.

Lewis Wetzel, who later achieved fame as an Indian fighter, settled with his family on Wheeling Creek in Marshall County.

John and Samuel Pringle deserted from Fort Pitt and settled in a giant sycamore tree at the mouth of Turkey Run, the future site of Buckhannon.

1765 Aracoma, eldest daughter of Chief Cornstalk, and her husband, Bolling Baker, came to live in the city of Logan (which was once named for the princess). She was eventually killed in a battle in 1780.

1767 Ice's Ferry, Monongalia County, was settled by Frederick Ice. His son Adam, born the same year, was the first white child born in the Monongahela Valley. Andrew Ice started the first authorized ferry in western Virginia in 1785.

1768 Ebenezer Zane and his two brothers established a settlement on the Ohio at Wheeling Creek.

The Treaty of Fort Stanwix was concluded. The Iroquois ceded all their lands and their allies' lands east of the Allegheny and south of the Ohio Rivers. The boundary line extended west to the Tennessee River.

The Vandalia Company (or Walpole Co.) was organized and included all of present West Virginia west of the Allegheny Mountains and eastern Kentucky.

1769 Isaac Williams, noted spy and hunter, founded Williamstown.

1770 Washington explored the Ohio Valley and claimed lands for himself.

"Harewood," home of Colonel Samuel Washington, the brother of

"Harewood" was designed by George Washington for his brother Samuel.

At Pricketts Fort, located five miles south of Fairmont, visitors can experience over one hundred years of frontier life by taking part in the many craft workshops.

On Oct. 10, 1774, Chief Cornstalk and his force of around 1,200 Indians attacked Gen. Andrew Lewis' army at Point Pleasant.

George Washington, was built in Jefferson County near Charles Town. James Madison later married Dolly Payne Todd there.

1771 John Floyd discovered a burning spring (natural gas) in the Kanawha Valley.

1772 Simon Kenton, adventurer and border scout and two companions spent the winter in camp on Elk River near Charleston. They were the first white men to live there. Kenton later served in Lord Dunmore's War.

Jacob Prickett, Sr. settled on land at the confluence of Pricketts Creek and the Monongahela River. A fort was built there about the time of Dunmore's War and was believed to be one of the largest and strongest frontier residence forts in the Monongahela Valley. In 1973 the Pricketts Fort Memorial Foundation began reconstruction of the fort on the traditional site in Pricketts Fort State Park, Marion County.

1774 Chief Logan's family was murdered in western Virginia across the Ohio River from their home at the mouth of Yellow Creek. Logan led his tribe on the warpath against the settlers, taking no less than 30 scalps in revenge. The *Logan Massacre* was one of the events that precipitated Lord Dunmore's War.

Lord Dunmore, in an effort to preserve white strength west of the Alleghenies and to divert Virginians from growing tensions with England, advanced against the Indians in a series of attacks known as *Lord Dunmore's War.* He led an expedition down the Ohio from Pittsburgh to join forces with those of General Andrew Lewis at the mouth of the Kanawha.

General Lewis and his men arrived at Point Pleasant and while awaiting Dunmore's troops, were attacked by Indians. The day-long Battle of Point Pleasant resulted in a colonial victory that effectively subdued the Indians during the coming revolutionary years and prevented the presence of stronger British reinforcements at the outbreak of the war.

Simon Girty served as an interpreter for Lord Dunmore during the war but from 1778 to the end of the American Revolution, he lived among the Indians leading attacks against the colonists. He became known as "the white Indian" or "white renegade." After the revolution, Girty escaped to Canada and died there in 1818.

After the decisive victory at Point Pleasant, Lord Dunmore entered into a peace treaty at Camp Charlotte with members of the Delaware, Shawnee and Mingo tribes. The Indians gave up all claims to land south of the Ohio River.

Fort Fincastle at Wheeling was renamed Fort Henry in honor of Patrick Henry, Governor of Virginia.

1775 Dr. Thomas Walker, on behalf of the western Virginia settlers, negotiated the Treaty of Pittsburgh in which the Ottawa, Wyandot, Mingo, Shawnee, Delaware and Seneca Indians agreed to a policy of neutrality.

Secure from Indian attacks on their frontier homes, many westerners answered the call of the Continental Army as the Revolution began.

BIRTH

1776 In May, the Continental Congress adopted a general resolution advising the colonies to form governments for themselves whenever the old governments had broken down. Virginia adopted its constitution in June and incorporated into it a bill of rights which was used as a model by other states.

1777 Chief Cornstalk was murdered at Fort Randolph in Point Pleasant.

A force of about 200 Indians and British attacked Fort Henry at Wheeling. According to legend, Major Samuel McCulloch, trapped

by Indians while trying to bring aid to the Fort, leaped 300 feet from a cliff above Wheeling Creek, on horseback, and escaped. The site is known as "McCulloch's Leap."

Captain William Forman of Hampshire County and his scouting party rushed to the aid of Fort Henry and were massacred in McMechen's Narrows, halfway between present-day Moundsville and Wheeling.

1778 Indians unsuccessfully attacked Fort Randolph to avenge the death of Cornstalk.

Indians invaded Kanawha and Greenbrier Valleys. The attack on Fort Donnally in the Greenbrier area was known as the 2nd Battle of Point Pleasant because after their defeat, the Indians no longer threatened settlements in the upper Kanawha Valley.

1781 The Articles of Confederation went into effect.

1782 Elizabeth Zane became a heroine during an attack on Fort Henry by carrying gunpowder while under fire from her brother Ebenezer's house to the fort.

Lydia Boggs Shepherd Cruger was also a heroine of the Fort Henry seige. She became influential in national politics through her friendships with leading statesmen. Her close alliance with Henry Clay was responsible for the route of the Cumberland Pike passing through Wheeling, the site of her mansion, Shepherd Hall.

General William Darke of Berkeley County led the Hampshire and Berkeley regiments to Yorktown and was present when Cornwallis surrendered. Cornwallis' capitulation signaled the end of the Revolutionary War.

1783 George Washington resigned his commission before Congress at Annapolis on December 23 to return to his beloved Mount Vernon and "take . . . leave of all employments of public life."

The first test run of James Rumsey's invention, the steamboat, was

conducted at St. John's Run, near Bath (Berkeley Springs) on the Potomac River. Rumsey's boat was demonstrated before an audience that included George Washington. Rumsey was not given public recognition by Congress until 1839.

1784 George Washington visited the Ohio Valley again to protect his land titles.

1785 The James River Co. was incorporated for the purpose of connecting the James River with the New and the Great Kanawha Rivers; also to construct a road over the Alleghenies to the Falls of the Great Kanawha. The first project failed but the road over the mountains was built and became known as the Midland Trail or the James River and Kanawha Turnpike.

1786 The road from Winchester to Morgantown was opened.

The Old Rehoboth Church was built near the present site of Union in Monroe County. It was frequently visited by Bishop Asbury, the first bishop in America. Today it is the oldest remaining church building west of the Alleghenies.

1787 The Northwest Ordinance, providing for government of the territory north of the Ohio River, was passed by the Congress of the Confederation.

1788 The Federal Constitution was ratified by Virginia.

Daniel Boone moved to the newly formed Kanawha County.

George Clendenin erected Fort Lee on the site of present day Charleston.

1789 The road from Winchester reached Clarksburg.

GROWTH AND GROWING PAINS

1790 The Virginia Resolutions were framed by Patrick Henry.

The first newspaper in West Virginia, *The Potomac Guardian and Berkeley Advertiser*, was established

John Murray inherited the Scottish earldom of Dunmore in 1756 and was appointed governor of England's Virginia colony in 1771.

Daniel Boone, shown in mortal combat with an Indian, was actually extremely slow to anger, preferring to trick his foes whenever possible.

at Shepherdstown by Nathaniel H. Willis.

Fleming Cobbs, Kanawha Valley pioneer, made a powder run from Fort Lee at Charleston to Fort Randolph at Point Pleasant that saved the Kanawha Valley fort from surrendering to the Indians.

1791 Anne Bailey, known as "White Squaw of the Kanawha," at age 49 made a powder run from the beseiged Fort Lee to Lewisburg.

1794 Frontier farmers staged "The Whiskey Rebellion" in response to the federal tax on whiskey.

Jay's Treaty was signed requiring the British to relinquish their Northwest posts by 1796.

The first blast furnace west of the Alleghenies was built at Kings Creek near the present site of Weirton. Connell, Tarr & Co. took over the furnace and began to produce iron in 1820. The furnace became known as the Peter Tarr Furnace and was restored in 1968.

John Chapman, who came to be called "Johnny Appleseed," arrived in Brooke County from Pittsburgh. Although Johnny Appleseed is credited with planting apple trees in this area, the true fathers of commercial fruit growing in West Virginia were Jacob Nessly of the Northern Panhandle and W.S. Miller of the Eastern Panhandle.

1795 The town of Wheeling was established by an act of the Virginia Assembly.

1796 The Old Stone Church was built by Presbyterians at Lewisburg in Greenbrier County. It is the oldest unrestored church in continuous use west of the Alleghenies.

1797 Elisha Brooks established the first salt furnace west of the Alleghenies in the Kanawha Valley.

1798 Harman Blennerhassett settled on an island near Parkersburg and built a mansion there. In 1805 Aaron Burr visited the island. A year later Blennerhassett and Burr equipped a force of men on the island but their alleged conspiracy to commit treason was

brought to an end with Burr's arrest in Alabama the next year.

Decker's Creek Ironworks was established in the Monongahela Valley.

1800 Pottery manufacturing was established at Morgantown, Wellsburg and Wheeling.

1801 John Marshall was appointed Chief Justice of the U. S. Supreme Court serving until 1835. He also served as a delegate to the Virginia Constitutional Convention of 1829. Marshall University in Huntington was named for him.

1803 Lewis and Clark began their expedition descending the Ohio River.

The first newspaper west of the Alleghenies, *The Monongalia Gazette and Morgantown Advertiser*, was established at Morgantown.

St. Joseph's, the first Catholic parish in West Virginia, was founded in Martinsburg.

1806 Robert Fulton successfully demonstrated his steamboat on the Hudson River 24 years after James Rumsey's first test run of his steamboat on the Potomac River.

1808 The Great Kanawha River salt industry gained national recognition through the enterprise of David and Joseph Ruffner. They converted a 10-mile stretch on the Kanawha into the largest salt production area in the country with distribution outlets that extended to the Mississippi River Basin.

1810 Sistersville, the only town in the U.S. by that name, was settled by the family of Charles Wells. Two daughters, Sarah and Delilah, who laid out the original boundaries were the "sisters" in the name.

The era of the steamboat was launched with the completion of the *ew Orleans* at Pittsburgh.

1812 Western Virginia sent substantial numbers of men to fight in the War of 1812.

Tanner's Crossroads in Roane County (now the town of Spencer) was named for Samuel Tanner. Later

during the oil and gas boom, the deepest well east of the Mississippi was drilled on the nearby Marcellus Hart farm, to a depth of 9,104 feet.

1813 Isaac Taylor Duvall & Co. was built in Wellsburg. It was the first glass factory in West Virginia to make cobalt blue, green and clear flint glassware.

1814 Francis H. Peirpont, the first acting governor of restored Virginia and so-named "Father of West Virginia," was born in Monongalia County.

1815 Andrew Jackson's forces won a resounding victory against the British in New Orleans in January, two weeks after the Treaty of Ghent was signed.

1816 The steamboat *Washington*, built by Henry Shreve at Wheeling, proved the practicality of the steamboat for the inland waterways.

1817 To help solve the problem of banking west of the Alleghenies, banks were established at Wheeling and Winchester.

The Kanawha salt producers formed a trust, one of the first in America.

David Ruffner experimented with coal as a fuel for the salt furnaces.

1818 The National (or Cumberland) Road was completed from Cumberland, Md. to Wheeling. This road eventually became U.S. 40.

1819 West Virginia's first theatrical entertainment, a drama called *Speed the Blow*, was held in Wheeling under the auspices of the Thespian Club in the Old Lancastrian Academy (now Linsly).

1820 The Missouri Compromise on the issue of slavery was passed by Congress.

The Monongahela and Kanawha Valleys began to supply white oak lumber to the east coast shipbuilding yards.

1823 Alexander Campbell began publication of *The Christian Baptist*, West Virginia's first religious newspaper.

1824 The Baltimore and Ohio Railway requested from the state of

Virginia a right-of-way to the Ohio River.

Thomas Jonathan "Stonewall" Jackson was born in Clarksburg.

1825 The French general Marquis de Lafayette and his son arrived in Wheeling on a tour of the U. S.

1826 In his *Biographical Sketch of the Late Michael Cresap*, John Jacob challenged Thomas Jefferson's charge that Cresap was responsible for the murder of Chief Logan's family.

1829 The Constitutional Convention was convened at Richmond. The Trans-Allegheny reformers failed in their attempts to gain the provisions which were their major concerns: white male suffrage and the popular election of government officials.

At Wheeling, William Cooper Howells established one of the country's first labor journals, *The Eclectic Observer and Working People's Advocate*.

Jesse Hughes, the ferocious Indian fighter responsible for the "Bulltown Massacre of 1772," died and was buried on the banks of the Ohio at Ravenswood.

1830 *The Wheeling Gazette* proposed separation of western Virginia from eastern Virginia.

The Virginia Constitutional Convention adjourned and the new state constitution was ratified.

William Morris' well drilling innovation revolutionized the salt industry in West Virginia. This process was used later in oil drilling operations in Pennsylvania.

Circular saws appeared in the lumber industry in West Virginia.

1831 Alexander Scott Withers published his *Chronicles of Border Warfare*.

Patrick Gass of Brooke County chronicled the Lewis and Clark expedition.

1833 A cholera epidemic struck the Wheeling district and set a record death toll of 23 in one day.

1834 The Kanawha Valley's first

The restored Peter Tarr furnace stands near the modern blast furnaces and steelmaking and finishing mills of Weirton Steel Division of National Steel Corp.

J. N. Camden was responsible for two railroad systems in W.Va., The Ohio River Railroad and the Monongahela River line. Both became part of the B&O Railroad.

The Old Stone Church was used as an emergency Civil War hospital.

commercial coal company, the Ohio Mining Company, was incorporated.

The Baltimore and Ohio Railroad, after being delayed by disputes over right-of-way in the Potomac Valley, reached its western Virginia terminus at Harper's Ferry.

1835 Steam sawmills were introduced into the state.

1837 Marshall Academy, later to become Marshall University, was founded in Guyandotte (later renamed Huntington).

1838 The Grave Creek Mound in Moundsville was opened by A. B. Tomlinson. Two burial chambers containing skeletal remains, copper bracelets, shell beads and mica were found.

Beckley was founded.

1839 Captain Anderson Hatfield ("Devil Anse"), patriarch of the feuding clan, was born in Logan County.

1840 Alexander Campbell founded Bethany College, the state's oldest college.

1841 William Tompkins used natural gas as fuel to operate his salt furnace at Burning Springs on the Kanawha River. It was believed to have been the first commercial use of natural gas.

The Staunton-Parkersburg Turnpike was completed. It extended from Staunton, Va. over the Alleghenies through central West Virginia to Parkersburg.

Henry Ruffner, of the Franklin Society of Lexington, proposed gradual emancipation of slaves west of the Blue Ridge Mountains.

1842 Wayne County was named in honor of General "Mad Anthony" Wayne, victor over the Indians (in 1794) at the Battle of Fallen Timbers, near the present Toledo, Ohio.

1849 The Wheeling Bridge, designed by Charles Ellet, Jr., was completed after two years of construction and controversy. The city of Pittsburgh contended

successfully before the Supreme Court that the bridge interferred with navigation because the clearance was not high enough, but the bridge was finished in spite of a restraining court order.

1850 The Reform Convention met in Richmond in an effort to revise the Virginia Constitution. Delegate Waitman T. Willey, born in Marion County, was a chief leader in the West Virginia statehood drive.

Lemuel Chenoweth of Beverly, Va. (now West Virginia) obtained the contract for bridges on the Staunton-Parkersburg Turnpike. This former furniture and cabinetmaker constructed many of the covered bridges in the Mountain State.

1851 The second Virginia Constitutional Convention convened. Important reforms adopted were voting privileges for all white males over 21 and the direct election of local officials and the governor. The delegates also approved a head tax to be levied on every voter to support the schools.

1852 *The Intelligencer*, West Virginia's oldest daily newspaper, was established in Wheeling. It supported Lincoln in 1860 and the Union during the Civil War and became one of the chief advocates of separation from Virginia.

The Baltimore and Ohio Railway reached Wheeling.

1854 The Wheeling Bridge was blown down by severe winds. As replacement work began, Pittsburgh again appealed to the Supreme Court but this time Wheeling won— the height of steamboat chimneys was to be determined by bridge clearances. The new 1,010-foot span was completed in 1856 making it at the time the longest suspension bridge in the country.

The Internal Improvement Convention at White Sulphur Springs supported the proposed Covington and Ohio Railroad.

1857 The Northwestern Virginia Railway between Grafton and Parkersburg was completed.

1858 Johnson Newlon Camden discovered a large quantity of petroleum on the banks of the Little Kanawha. He developed his refining business, J. N. Camden & Co. of Parkersburg, into one of the leading distributors of lubricating oils. He eventually exchanged his refineries for stock in John D. Rockefeller's Standard Oil Co. Camden also started the Weston & West Fork Railroad Co. and later became president of Monongahela Coal & Coke Co. In 1881, he was elected to the U. S. Senate by the West Virginia Legislature.

1859 John Brown and 22 followers attacked the federal arsenal at Harpers Ferry in an effort to incite a slave insurrection and put an end to slavery. Federal Army Colonel Robert E. Lee was dispatched from Washington to seize Brown. The raid failed and Brown was tried and executed.

David Hunter Strother of Martinsburg, one of the nation's highest paid writers, acted as sole reporter at the trial of John Brown and made the last sketch of him before his execution. Strother, whose pen name was *Porte Crayon,* contributed sketches and essays to *Harper's* magazine.

The Rathbone Well (first successful well drilled purposefully for oil in West Virginia) was drilled on Burning Springs Run in Wirt County.

1860 Abraham Lincoln was elected President.

WAR

1861 The Virginia General Assembly authorized an election of delegates for a state convention to consider Virginia's position within the Union. On April 17, the convention passed an Ordinance of Secession contingent on approval by popular vote.

John S. Carlile, a convention delegate from Harrison County,

Harpers Ferry as a peaceful village before John Brown's raid.

Lt. Robert E. Lee as Union Army officer in 1829, shortly after his graduation from West Point. Ironically, when he arrested Brown, he too was opposed to slavery, but his military loyalty was stronger than his personal feelings.

"Stonewall" Jackson died of pneumonia following his accidental wounding by C.S.A. troops after the battle of Chancellorsville.

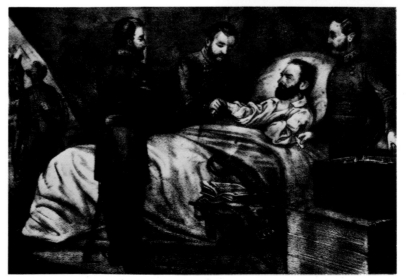

organized a protest meeting in Clarksburg to denounce the Secession Ordinance. Those present at the meeting authorized another convention to be held in Wheeling on May 13.

The First Wheeling Convention proposed that delegates from the western counties be elected to a general convention to decide the matter of secession.

On May 23, the Ordinance of Secession was approved by popular vote but on June 11, 100 delegates from 34 counties of the present state of West Virginia formed the Second Wheeling Convention. These delegates declared the Virginia Secession Convention illegal and they formed the Reorganized Government of Virginia, electing Francis H. Pierpont as governor.

The Battle of Philippi was fought as the first land skirmish in the Civil War. The Confederate forces under Colonel George A. Porterfield retreated with such speed that the battle became known as the "Philippi Races." Brigadier General Robert S. Garnett then assumed command of the Confederate forces.

The Union forces won a victory at Rich Mountain. General George McClellan prevented disruption of the B & O Railroad line which determined the Confederate boundary line in West Virginia as the Allegheny Mountains rather then the Ohio River.

Confederate General Henry Alexander Wise (ex-governor of Virginia) advanced to the Kanawha Valley to recruit troops and halt formation of the new state of West Virginia. He defeated Jacob D. Cox at the mouth of Scary Creek, Putnam County, then retreated to White Sulphur Springs.

Confederate troops under General John B. Floyd were defeated by Union forces under General William W. Rosencrans at the Battle of Carnifex Ferry.

General Robert E. Lee ordered General W. W. Loring to retreat to Lewisburg, thereby giving up the Confederate offense in western Virginia. The Confederate withdrawal gave the Union complete possession of western Virginia.

Nancy Hart, famed Confederate spy, led a surprise attack on the town of Summersville. Nancy had been captured and held prisoner at the officers' quarters in Summersville but escaped and led the attack in which Captain Starr and his Union forces were captured and most of the town was burned.

The town of Madison, located in what is now Boone County, was burned by Union troops. It was later rebuilt near the original site.

Governor Francis H. Pierpont called a convention in Wheeling to draft a constitution for the new state. The name West Virginia was chosen by the delegates.

The town of Sutton (Braxton County), settled in 1784 by Benjamin and Jeremiah Carpenter, was burned by Confederates, but was later rebuilt.

1862 The General Assembly of the Restored Government of Virginia convened and approved the formation of the new state of West Virginia from inside the boundaries of the old state of Virginia.

Senator Waitman T. Willey submitted West Virginia's application for statehood to the U. S. Senate. Both houses of Congress voted approval but stipulated that the gradual emancipation of slaves be included in the new statehood bill.

Jesse Lee Reno of Wheeling, a Major General in the Union Army, died from wounds received in the Battle of South Mountain. He was a fellow West Point classmate of Stonewall Jackson.

REBIRTH

1863 The Willey Amendment guaranteeing gradual emancipation was approved by the state constitutional convention and popular vote.

On June 20, West Virginia became the 35th state in the Union.

Arthur I. Boreman was elected as the first governor of the state.

Peter G. Van Winkle and Waitman T. Willey were elected by the West Virginia Legislature as the first U. S. Senators representing the state.

Linsly Military Institute's building on 15th and Eoff Streets in Wheeling served as the first Capitol of the state until 1870.

General William E. Jones and Brigadier General John D. Imboden spearheaded a month-long Confederate invasion into West Virginia. B & O Railroad bridges were destroyed and 150,000 barrels of crude oil were burned at Burning Springs in Wirt County.

Brigadier General Stonewall Jackson was wounded in error by his own men during fighting at Chancellorsville. His left arm was amputated and on May 10 he died from his wounds.

1865 The surrender of General Robert E. Lee at Appomattox Courthouse ended the Civil War.

President Lincoln was assassinated and Vice-President Andrew Johnson succeeded to the presidency.

1866 An amendment to the state constitution was passed denying citizenship and the right to vote to all persons who had supported the Confederacy.

Moundsville was selected as the site of the State Penitentiary.

1867 The legislature established the Agricultural College of West Virginia at Morgantown and in 1876 designated it as West Virginia University.

Francis Pierpont—responsible for raising and organizing the Union Army troops and preparing the way for statehood.

Waitman T. Willey—one of the first U.S. Senators from W.Va.

A. I. Boreman served three terms as governor of W.Va.

1868 Mrs. Francis H. Pierpont started the movement to make May 30 Decoration Day.

1869 Collis P. Huntington acquired control of the Chesapeake & Ohio Railway. Dissatisfied with Guyandotte as a railhead, he obtained land extending 2 miles west along the Ohio from the west bank of the Guyandotte River. In 1871 a city was chartered and named for Huntington.

Michael Late Benedum, "The Great Wildcatter," was born in Bridgeport. In 1900, he co-founded the Benedum-Trees Oil Co. He established the Claude Worthington Benedum Foundation in 1944 and became one of West Virginia's greatest philanthropists.

1870 The State capital was moved from Wheeling to Charleston.

A School for the Deaf and Blind was established in Romney.

1871 The Flick Amendment to the State constitution was adopted giving all male citizens regardless of race the right to vote.

Newton D. Baker was born in Martinsburg. He served as Secretary of War under President Woodrow Wilson from 1916-1921.

Henry Gassaway Davis, co-founder of Elkins, was elected to the U. S. Senate. He was the first Democrat from West Virginia to hold that office. He also served as the Democratic nominee for vice-president in 1904. In 1881, he was granted a charter for the West Virginia Central Railroad to tap the coal and timber resources of Tucker and Randolph Counties.

1872 The constitution under which West Virginia now functions was drawn up and established.

1873 Joseph Harvey Long purchased *The Huntington Herald.* He installed and operated the first sterotype and linotype in West Virginia. In 1890 he founded *The Wheeling News.*

The first coke ovens in New River Valley were built by the Quinnimont Co.

1874 Matthew Manfield Neely was born near Grove in Doddridge County. He became one of West Virginia's most enduring politicians—serving in the Congress from 1913-1920. He was elected to his first term in the Senate in 1922 and was elected governor in 1940. He was again elected to the House of Representatives in 1944 and in the election of 1946 he regained his senatorial seat and held it until his death in 1958.

1875 The capital was moved to Wheeling.

1877 A pay reduction for B & O railroad workers resulted in the first national labor strike when crews at Martinsburg halted operations and refused the passage of trains. The strike spread to Maryland, Missouri, Pennsylvania and New York.

A referendum resulted in the selection of Charleston as the permanent seat of State government.

1879 The first oil pipeline in West Virginia was completed. It ran 15 miles from Volcano to Parkersburg. Later that year the town and the oil field at Volcano were burned.

The Bloch brothers began the manufacture of Mail Pouch tobacco at Wheeling.

1880 The first telephone in West Virginia was installed at Wheeling.

Paddy Ryan defeated Joe Goss at Colliers Station in the Northern Panhandle. Ryan was the first American to win an undisputed bare knuckle heavyweight championship of the world, after 87 rounds in 87 minutes.

Nathan Goff, born in Clarksburg in 1843, was appointed Secretary of the Navy. He was elected to Congress in 1882 and served 3 terms. In 1913 he was elected to the U. S. Senate after serving as a justice of the U. S. Circuit Court and Circuit Court of Appeals.

1882 The Hatfield-McCoy feud erupted on the West Virginia-Kentucky border and continued

intermittently amid considerable national publicity for ten years.

The Wheeling electric light plant began operation. The idea of using electricity for lighting was brought over from the Paris Exposition by A.J. Sweeney.

1883 The Norfolk & Western Railway's New River Division was completed.

After experiencing the worst winter in local recorded history, the Ohio Valley suffered a great flood that swept away whole towns.

1885 The capital was moved to Charleston under the provisions of the popular mandate decided in 1877.

The National Gas Co. of West Virginia was formed, producing gas from Northern Panhandle wells.

1886 The Mountain Brook mine disaster at Newburg took thirty-nine lives.

The Elkhorn Tunnel through Flat Top Mountain was completed.

1889 The legislature created the West Virginia National Guard and authorized the Bureau of Labor.

Drilling operations near Mannington initiated an oil boom on a modern scale.

THE NINETIES: GAIETY AND ANARCHY

1890 The Office of the Inspector of Mines for the coal industry was created.

At 5:40 a.m. on October 23, a C & O train was wrecked by a landslide near Hinton killing the engineer George Allen. The accident was immortalized in the ballad *Wreck on the C & O* which was probably written by a Negro engine-wiper who worked in the Hinton Roundhouse. Several versions of the song have been passed down and it remains one of West Virginia's most enduring railroad songs.

The United Mine Workers of America organized in the U. S. and

Paddy Ryan was 28 years old and Joe Goss was 44 when they staged their championship match. The modern heavy-weight championship chain of titles date from this bout.

Stephen Benton Elkins was chairman of the powerful Interstate Commerce Committee of the Senate during Teddy Roosevelt's administration.

Pearl Buck birthplace, Hillsboro, W.Va.

quickly became an important influence in West Virginia.

Alexander Glass, Nelson E. Whitaker and E. C. Ewing formed the Wheeling Corrugating Co., forerunner of Wheeling Steel.

1892 Stephen Benton Elkins was appointed Secretary of War by President Harrison. In 1895, Elkins was elected to the U. S. Senate where he served until his death in 1911.

The first producing oil well in the Sistersville oil field was drilled and named the "Polecat." The Sistersville oil field became one of the country's greatest oil producing areas.

The Norfolk and Western Railway opened its line to Ceredo.

Author Pearl S. Buck was born in Hillsboro. She was awarded the Pulitzer Prize in 1932 for *The Good Earth* and the Nobel Prize for literature in 1938.

William T. Price established in Marlinton the *Pocahontas Times* which is still printed by hand-set type.

The first shipment of coal was made by the N & W out of Mercer County.

1894 "Big Moses," one of the country's largest gas wells, was dug at Indian Creek in Tyler County. The well produced an estimated 100 million cubic feet per day at its peak initial flow.

One of West Virginia's greatest land disputes erupted in Logan County when a New Yorker, Henry C. King, one of the incorporators of Logan Coal and Lumber Co., filed claim to an heirship of the entire county. The claim was based on a 500,000 acre government grant which had been made to Robert Morris after the American Revolution to satisfy a war debt. The fight lasted 17 years; King was defeated by a Supreme Court decision in 1911.

Louis Bennett, Jr., W. W. I flying ace and hero, was born in Weston.

1895 Postmaster General William Lyne Wilson, born in Jefferson County, established the first Rural Free Delivery service (RFD) in America.

Bluefield Colored Institute was formed with an enrollment of 523 students.

"Brick Top" was born Ada Beatrice Queen Victoria Louise Virginia Smith Duconage in Alderson. She became an international figure on the night-club circuit in Paris, Rome and later, New York.

1896 The last public hanging in West Virginia took place in Ripley when John Morgan was hanged for murder.

1897 The miners of West Virginia, Ohio and Kentucky went on strike for an eight-hour day, semi-monthly pay and an end to the company store.

1898 Two regiments were raised in West Virginia to serve in the Spanish-American War.

Lieutenant Andrew Summers Rowan, of Gap Mills, West Virginia, landed in Cuba to deliver a message to General Garcia, leader of the Cuban insurgent forces. He returned with secret information for which he was awarded the Distinguished Service Cross.

The Hope Natural Gas Co. was incorporated in West Virginia. Hope and the United Fuel Gas Co. (a subsidiary of Columbia Gas system) dominate the natural gas industry within the state.

1900 State oil production reached a peak of over 16 million barrels.

1901 The legislature appointed a Tax Commission which recommended sweeping tax reforms.

Waddington Farm was purchased by Earl Oglebay who developed it into an experimental laboratory for agriculture. Colonel Oglebay died in 1926 and willed the land to the city of Wheeling for use as a park. The City officially accepted the gift in 1928 and it became known as Oglebay Park. Today it is the nation's finest municipal park.

1902 Senator Jennings Randolph was born at Salem. He was elected to the House of Representatives in 1932 and to the Senate in 1958 and

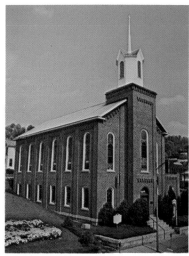

The Mother's Day Shrine (Andrews Church in Grafton) where Anna Jarvis worshipped and taught for 30 years.

W. Va. led the nation in oil production in 1911.

is still holding that office.

William H. Collidge and Albert F. Holden purchased 30,000 acres in the Logan area and began development of the Island Creek Coal Co.

Consolidation Coal Co. (incorporated in 1860) made its first acquisition in the state with the purchase of the Millholland field in northern West Virginia. Consolidation Coal Co. is the largest producer of coal in the state and one of the largest employers.

1903 The Elkins Act, sponsored by West Virginia senator Stephen B. Elkins to eliminate the railway rebate system, was passed by Congress.

1904 Logan County's coal boom was impelled by the completion of the Guyandotte Railway Company's tracks to Logan, following the route of the Guyandotte River. Engineer Neal Bishop arrived in Logan on September 9 with No. 174 pulling 3 cars loaded with feed and household goods and ironically, a fourth car loaded with coal.

Classes began at Davis and Elkins College.

The State Bureau of Archives was established.

1905 The Phillips Sheet and Tin Plate Company (forerunner of Weirton Steel) was founded in Clarksburg by Ernest T. Weir, David M. Weir, J. R. Phillips and John C. Williams.

The Homer Laughlin China Co., at one time the world's largest pottery plant, was erected in Newell by Homer and Shakespeare Laughlin.

1906 The New River Coal Co. was formed.

1907 The Monongah Mine Disaster near Fairmont took 361 lives, the worst in U.S. history. The disaster dramatized safety needs in the mines and helped spur formation of the State Department of Mines.

1908 Due to Anna Jarvis' work and devotion, the first official Mother's Day celebration was held at

Andrews Church in Grafton.

1909 Ernest and David Weir and John Williams built a steel mill in the Northern Panhandle and founded Weirton Steel. The city of Weirton grew up around it.

1910 The West Virginia-Maryland border line was determined to be the low-water mark of the south bank of the Potomac River.

West Virginia became the nation's leading producer of lumber.

A fire destroyed nearly all of Mt. Hope, Fayette County.

1911 West Virginia led the nation in the production of gasoline and continued to do so through 1913.

1912 West Virginia experienced its first major coal strike and its worst labor war along Paint Creek and Cabin Creek. "Mother" Jones, the famous union organizer, joined the miners' fight for better living conditions. Governor Glasscock called out the state militia to quell the bloody war and subdue 6,000 armed miners.

1914 Prohibition went into effect.

The Westvaco Chemical Products Plant was located at South Charleston.

1915 The State Department of Health was created.

The U. S. Supreme Court placed West Virginia's share of the Virginia debt at $12,393,926 and thus settled a 52-year old controversy.

1916 Ira "Rat" Rodgers became West Virginia University's first All-American football player. He was again chosen All-American in 1917 and 1919. A fellow teammate from W. V. U., Russ Bailey, was also chosen for the 1917 and 1919 first teams. They were followed by Bob Orders in 1953 and Bruce Bosley and Sam Huff—who both made the 1955 squad and are being inducted into the W. Va. Sportswriters Association's Hall of Fame. In 1970 Jim Braxton and Dale Farley were chosen and Danny Buggs was picked in 1973.

Eleanor Steber was born in Wheeling. She studied at New England Conservatory of Music in Boston and made her debut in *Der Rosenkavalier* in 1940. She has sung in the major opera houses throughout the world.

The Libby-Owens Sheet Glass Co. (now Libbey-Owens-Ford Glass Co.) was located in Kanawha City.

MORE WAR—AT HOME AND ABROAD

1917 The United States entered W. W. I and 45,648 West Virginians were inducted into the armed forces. The state was commended for its war effort.

The war sparked a revival of river traffic along with a program to improve navigational facilities on the Ohio and its tributaries.

Under the stimulus of the war the large resources of salt found in the Kanawha and Ohio Valleys became basic assets for the rapid expansion of the chemical industry.

The state's natural gas production reached a peak of 308,617,101,000 cubic feet per year.

The Owens-Illinois Glass Co. located the largest bottle plant in the world at Kanawha City.

1918 W. W. I came to an end with the signing of the armistice on November 11.

A legislative act required pipeline companies in West Virginia to supply state consumers before channeling gas elsewhere. This act was later held to be unconstitutional by the U. S. Supreme Court in 1923.

Child labor was forbidden by an act of the legislature.

Preparation for the miners' march on Logan began. Logan and Mingo Counties became famous for their "mine wars" in the course of union organization efforts in the coal mines.

1919 The Virginia debt was finally settled when the state paid Virginia $1,062,867 in cash and $13,500,000 in bonds.

THE BLOODY, ROARING TWENTIES

1920 In Matewan, Mingo County, Baldwin-Felts Agency detectives hired by the coal companies clashed with local miners. Seven detectives, the mayor and two union men were killed in what came to be known as the "Matewan Massacre."

Alexander Glass, founder of the Wheeling Corrugating Co., was named Chairman of the Board of the newly consolidated Wheeling Steel

A gasoline plant in Clendenin was transformed by Union Carbide into an ethylene and chemicals plant.

1921 The Capitol building in Charleston was destroyed by fire.

West Virginia became the first state to levy a state sales tax.

"Devil Anse" Hatfield, head of the feuding clan, died on Island Creek.

Sid Hatfield and Ed Chambers, leaders of the Matewan Massacre, were gunned down on the steps of the McDowell County Courthouse.

3,000 miners marched on Logan, culminating in the Battle of Blair Mountain. Governor Ephrain Morgan called in federal troops to end the strife.

The Rubber Services Laboratory started operation in Nitro. In 1929, the founders and operators of the lab spilt into 2 companies: one became affiliated with Monsanto Chemical Co. (one of the Kanawha Vallly's pioneer chemical producers). The other company became Kavalco Products, Inc. (forerunner of present day "Apex" or FMC organic chemicals plant).

1922 The Huntington Alloy Products Division of International Nickel was established.

The Reverend John Joseph Swint was consecrated as the fourth Bishop of Wheeling, the first native son to become a bishop.

A pulp plant of Viscose Co. was established at Nitro.

During World War I 60,000 West Virginians served in the military. There were 5,000 casualties from the Mountain State.

Union Carbide's 230 acres of plant properties in the Charleston area includes 100 acres on Blaine Island.

1923 The first gasoline tax went into effect.

West Virginia's first radio station, WSAZ, went on the air in Huntington.

The *USS West Virginia*, one of the world's most powerful battleships, was commissioned.

1924 John Williams Davis, a Clarksburg native, campaigned for the presidency on the Democratic ticket.

Ground was broken for a new Capitol building in Charleston.

1925 Union Carbide expanded its facilities in the state and located a plant in South Charleston and later placed some of its production operations on Blaine Island in the Kanawha River.

The United Carbon Co. was formed by a merger of 15 carbon black and natural gas companies.

1927 Virginia Ruth Egnor *(Dagmar)* was born in Huntington. In 1951, she contracted with ABC for *The Dagmar Show.*

A federal prison for women was located at Alderson, West Virginia. After W. W. II Alderson's "distinguished inmates" list included *Tokyo Rose*, infamous Japanese radio announcer whose propaganda broadcasts to G.I.'s in the Pacific were entertaining, but contained undertones and overtones programmed to lower the morale of the American forces. Rose was released in 1956 after serving 6 years and 2 months of a 10 year sentence for treason.

Alonzo Beeher Brooks, noted naturalist and philosopher, began conducting his widely-attended morning bird walks in Oglebay Park, Wheeling. After his death in 1944, a trail in Oglebay Park was dedicated in his honor.

1928 West Virginia ranked as the nation's number one producer of bituminous coal.

THE THIRTIES: HARD TIMES

1929 The Wall Street stock market

"Dagmar" charmed television audiences with her performances.

Billy Edd Wheeler spent four years researching the history of the Hatfield-McCoy feud for the script of his drama.

Eleanor Roosevelt, a frequent visitor of West Virginia in the 1930's, took active interest in its problems.

John L. Lewis became president of the UMW in 1920, the year of the Matewan Massacre. The W.Va. union of the United Mine Workers was organized in Wheeling in 1890, although it wasn't until 1935, after more than 20 years of bloodshed, that most of W.Va.'s industries had been organized.

crash sent the nation's economy into a depression.

President Hoover dedicated new locks and dams for navigational improvements on the Ohio River.

The design of the State Flag was modified by a legislative resolution.

Dolls Gap, Mineral County, was designated by the state as the reputed birthplace of Nancy Hanks, mother of Abraham Lincoln.

National Steel is formed by the merger of Weirton Steel, Great Lakes Steel (Detroit) and the Hanna Co. iron ore and mining properties.

1930 Construction began on the 16,252-foot Hawk's Nest Tunnel to divert water from the New River for electrical generation purposes.

The first Mountain State Forest Festival was held by the city of Elkins. It originated as a homecoming celebration for Randolph Countians.

1931 Bluefield Colored Institute became Bluefield College.

The gathering impact of the Depression caused widespread distress in West Virginia where large numbers of the laboring force were dependent upon a limited number of industries, particularly coal.

1932 The main building of the new state Capitol was constructed.

Billy Edd Wheeler, songwriter, singer, poet and playwright was born in Whitesville. He grew up in Highcoal, Boone County and became the star of his own syndicated TV show *Country Suite.* His drama *Hatfields & McCoys* is presented each summer at Beckley's Grandview State Park.

1933 West Virginia ratified the Child Labor Amendment.

The Arthurdale resettlement community was established in Preston County. First Lady Eleanor Roosevelt was instrumental in the planning and development of the community.

A Tax Limitation Amendment to the West Virginia Constitution, which gave relief to property owners, was ratified. It set the stage for the enactment of the state's first income tax.

A federal fiat unionized the state's coal miners after a quarter century of violence and bloodshed.

1935 Suzanne Fisher from Sutton made her debut at the Metropolitan Opera in New York City.

Walter P. Reuther (born in Wheeling in 1907) organized the United Auto Workers in Detroit. He was elected president of the organization in 1946 and became head of the Congress of Industrial Organizations in 1952. He helped the CIO merge with the AFL (American Federation of Labor), but withdrew the UAW from the organization and in 1968 allied it with the Teamsters Union. He was killed in a plane crash in 1970.

1936 Extensive flooding caused much damage to the Ohio Valley.

1937 Another Ohio River flood proved (economically) to be a record-setting U. S. disaster.

The West Virginia University football team went to its first bowl game and defeated Texas Tech by a score of 7-6 in the Sun Bowl.

1938 The state embarked on a program of sealing abandoned mines to prevent acid drainage.

NIGHTMARE AT DAWN

1941 The Japanese attacked Pearl Harbor and Congress declared war on Japan. The *USS West Virginia* was one of the first and hardest hit of the battleships: 6 torpedo hits and 2 bomb explosions sent it to the bottom but she returned to combat duty in 1944. She bombarded the Japanese coast to assist the U. S. occupation of the island and was present in Okinawa's Buckner Bay when the Japanese formally surrendered aboard the *USS Missouri*.

Bombing smoke hangs heavy over the South Pacific island of Gizo as a U.S. Army B-17, Aztec's Curse returns from its mission. S/Sgt. Robert L. Fitzpatrick from St. Mary's, W.Va., was its belly gunner. He survived 14 plane crashes during his tour of duty.

General Charles E. Yeager (pictured as a Colonel in the 1950's) was honored in 1975 by the House of Representatives in recognition of his contribution to aerospace science.

"Hot Rod" Hundley graduated from his starring position at W.V.U. to a professional career with the N.B.A.'s Lakers. He was named to the N.B.A. All-Star teams in both 1960 and 1961.

During the war years, 218,665 West Virginians entered the armed forces and 5,830 lost their lives in the service of their country.

1942 Corning Glass Works built its first plant in West Virginia at Parkersburg. It later expanded throughout the state, establishing plants in Martinsburg, Paden City and Buckhannon.

Scotty Hamilton of Grafton was chosen as West Virginia University's first All-American in basketball. He was followed by Leland Byrd—an All-American for 1948, Mark Workman, 1952, Rod Hundley, 1957, Jerry West, 1959 and 1960, Rod Thorn, 1962 and 1963 and Will Robinson in 1972.

1944 The Claude Worthington Benedum Foundation was established by Michael Benedum in memory of his son. Foundation grants have benefited many students and educational institutions, as well as religious, health, civic and service organizations in the state.

1945 Booker T. Washington who spent his boyhood in Malden, West Virginia, was elected to the American Hall of Fame. He became nationally known as administrator of Tuskegee Institute in Alabama and toured the nation speaking on educational and racial subjects.

1946 The Chesapeake and Ohio Railway acquired the Greenbrier Hotel and restored it to its previous glory as a resort and tourist attraction.

1947 Brigadier General Charles Yeager of Lincoln County was the first man to break the sound barrier when he piloted the XS-1 research plane faster than the speed of sound.

American Cyanamid Corp. began production of intermediate chemicals at its Willow Island plant in Pleasants County.

1949 The first television station in the state, WSAZ, began operating in Huntington.

Virginia Mae Brown, born in Pliny (Putnam County) was appointed Executive Secretary to the West Virginia Judicial Council. She was the first woman to serve in that capacity. She went on to become the first woman ever appointed State Insurance Commissioner in 1961; first woman ever to serve on West Virginia Public Service Commission (1964); elected vice-president of the Interstate Commerce Commission in 1969 and reappointed to the ICC in 1971.

THE ROCKIN' FIFTIES

1950 West Virginia ranked second in the South Atlantic states in the production of electricity.

Art "Pappy" Lewis became head football coach at West Virginia University. He was chosen "Coach of the Year" by the Southern Conference in 1954.

Dr. Patrick Gainer, widely-traveled folklorist and Professor of English at West Virginia University, organized the first West Virginia Folk Festival in Glenville. He gained wide recognition with his dissertation, "The Refrain in the English and Scottish Ballads."

The Korean War began with North Korea's invasion of Seoul, capital of South Korea on June 25. At the U.N.'s directive, President Truman authorized use of U. S. air and naval forces and committed ground forces under General Douglas MacArthur to assist the Republic of South Korea. A total of 899 West Virginians were dead or missing in action by the end of the war which came in June 1953.

1951 Beckley High School won the first of four consecutive state basketball championships coached to victory by "The Gray Fox," Jerome Van Meter.

Robert C. Byrd, of Sophia, Raleigh County, was elected to the U. S. House of Representatives. He was re-elected in 1954 and 1956. He served his first term in the Senate in 1958 and is currently the Democratic Majority Whip.

1953 Soupy Sales, born Milton Hines, began his rise to fame in Detroit where he became a top-rated television personality. He was raised in Huntington and earned his degree at Marshall University.

Phyllis Curtain, a native of Clarksburg and world-renowned soprano, was engaged by the New York City Opera to sing in the premiere of *The Trial.*

Monroe J. Rathbone, born in Parkersburg in 1900, was elected president of Standard Oil Co. (N. J.), the largest oil company in the world. In 1963 he was elected chairman of the board.

Major General Frank K. Everest, Jr., a Fairmont native, set the official world speed record by flying on Air Force plane 755.149 m.p.h.

1954 The West Virginia Turnpike was opened to traffic.

1955 Kaiser Aluminum & Chemical Corp. began building the world's largest fully-integrated aluminum works at Ravenswood in Jackson County. The plant was fully operating by 1959.

1956 Both the government and private sectors launched studies on how to meet the state's economic problems, with special attention being given to industrial development.

Union Carbide's Technical Center was opened in South Charleston.

Jim Comstock and Bronson McClung started publishing their unique, lightly-humored weekly newspaper, *The West Virginia Hillbilly,* in Richwood.

1957 West Virginia was recognized as the nation's glass state with 56 glass plants in operation.

Marbon (a Borg-Warner Corp. subsidiary) built its plastics division base in Washington, West Virginia. A leading supplier of rubber resins in the early 1950's, Marbon made a technological breakthrough in 1954 with the development of a tough, rigid plastic—CYCOLAC. In 1973 the company name was changed to Borg-Warner Chemicals.

A guardsman, called to duty, embraces his family. An estimated total of 95,000 West Virginians served in the Korean War. Two National Guard units were mobilized: the 1092nd Engineering Battalion and the 201st Field Battalion.

Senator Robert C. Byrd is the only West Virginian ever to have served in both houses of the legislature and both houses of Congress.

Soupy Sales started his career as a radio script writer.

1958   The National Radio Astronomy Observatory was built at Green Bank, Pocahontas County and began operating in 1959.

Lewis L. Strauss, born in Charleston in 1896, was named Secretary of Commerce. He previously served as secretary to Herbert Hoover (1917-1918) when Hoover led the vast foreign relief work. In 1953, he was made Special Assistant to the President for atomic energy matters and from 1953-58 he served as Chairman of the Atomic Energy Commission.

1959   Sam Snead at the Greenbrier Open & ProAm Tourney carded 31-28 on the par 70 course, the greatest competitive round in golf history. The tournament was renamed the "Sam Snead Spring Festival" in his honor.

Hal Greer, fresh from a record-setting 4 year career at Marshall University, began playing his first of 15 seasons with NBA club Syracuse Nationals. While at Marshall, Greer led his team to its only Mid-American Conference championship. He holds many NBA records and was picked for 10 NBA All-Star teams.

1960   The primary election victory of John F. Kennedy in West Virginia became a springboard to his election as President.

Everettsville-born John McKay was named the 16th head football coach at University of Southern Cal. A former All-State football and basketball player at Shinnston High School, he led his U.S.C. teams to 5 Rose Bowl victories.

Neil Boggs began his network career with NBC News. Born in Dundon (Clay County), Neil became well known as a newsman with various West Virginia media. He was with WSAZ-TV, Huntington, before taking his newscasting position with the NBC-TV network which has brought him 5 Emmy awards.

1961   Flash floods in the Charleston area killed 23 people.

Marshall College's growth was recognized by the state legislature

John McKay

Don Knotts

Dr. Leon Thompson

and the school was awarded university status.

Don Knotts, Morgantown native and W.V.U. alumnus, received an Emmy award for outstanding performance in a supporting role. He first gained recognition acting on Broadway in the 1955 play *No Time For Sergeants.*

1962   West Virginia undertook its first comprehensive travel survey to provide data for development of tourist attractions.

The federally-sponsored 600-foot radio telescope at Sugar Grove was abandoned because technological developments made its planned military use obsolete. In contrast, the scientific use of the radio observatory at Green Bank continued to expand as the National Science Foundation completed a 300-foot diameter radio telescope.

Phil Conley, noted West Virginia historian and author, was presented the Knight Gold Cross of the Order of George I by King Paul of Greece.

LOOKING BOTH WAYS

1963   West Virginia celebrated its 100th birthday on June 20. Celebrations were conducted throughout the state. Ceremonies at the Capitol were attended by Governor W. W. Barron and President John F. Kennedy.

During the Centennial year, a special Centennial Exhibit toured the state.

The *Rhododendron* was christened as the Centennial showboat and toured West Virginia rivers.

Kermit Hunter's outdoor drama *Honey in the Rock* opened at Grandview State Park near Beckley.

President Lyndon B. Johnson was a participant in the Forum for the Future which was held in Charleston.

1964   The voters of West Virginia approved the largest road bond issue to date for $200 million.

1965   U. S. involvement in Vietnam was escalated with air attacks on the north and commitment of

ground troops (numbering about 550,000 by 1968).

1967   The collapse of the Silver Bridge at Point Pleasant claimed 46 lives.

Charleston-born Dr. John C. Norman, a pioneer in organ transplant techniques, made an important discovery that the spleen manufactures a substance which offsets the most common type of hemophilia.

1968   On November 20, a mine disaster at Farmington killed 78 miners.

George Crumb, Jr. Charleston-born composer, was awarded the Pulitzer Prize in music. While attending Charleston High School, he won first place in the National Scholastic Awards Competition for his composition *Cradle Song.*

Cyrus Robert Vance, born in Charleston in 1917, served as U.S. negotiator at the Paris Peace Conference on Vietnam. This former Secretary of the Army (1962-63) and deputy Secretary of Defense (1964-67) also served as Special Representative of the President to Cyprus and Korea.

Wheeling Steel Corp. and Pittsburgh Steel Co. merged to form Wheeling-Pittsburgh Steel with administration offices in Wheeling.

1969   An Earth Satellite Communications Station was put into service at Etam in Preston County.

James Edward Allen, Jr., of Elkins, was appointed U.S. Commissioner of Education and Assistant Secretary of the Department of Health, Education & Welfare under President Nixon. He resigned in 1970 and was killed in a plane crash in 1971 while on vacation.

THE SEVENTIES: MOVIN' AHEAD

1970   The longest railroad car ever built—124 feet long and 12 feet wide with a capacity of 150,000 tons —was built by Amherst Industries near Charleston.

The political awareness of West Virginia's youth was officially recognized with the right to vote

In 1933 Fred M. Torrey sculpted a three-and a-half foot high model for a statue of Abraham Lincoln. The model remained in his studio for 30 years until it was brought to the West Virginia Capitol on Lincoln's birthday, February 12, 1970. The completed statue was placed outside the Capitol four years later, on West Virginia Statehood Day, 1974.

The Science and Culture Center opened July 11, 1976 in Charleston. The modern building houses the W. Va. Library Commission and the W. Va. Dept. of Archives and History.

Dr. Leon Thompson, past Chairman of The West Virginia State College Music Department, was appointed Director of Educational Activities for the New York Philharmonic.

1971   West Virginia ratified an amendment to the U.S. constitution giving 18-year-olds the right to vote.

Don Whitlatch, Parkersburg native, was designated by Governor Arch A. Moore, Jr. as the first "West Virginia Wildlife Artist in Residence."

Former Governor W. W. Barron was indicted for jury tampering. He pled guilty, was fined and sentenced to prison. He was released in 1975.

1972   Arch A. Moore, Jr. was the first governor of West Virginia to succeed himself since 1872.

125 lives were lost and $50,000,000 in property damage occured when a slag dam at the head of Buffalo Creek Valley in Logan County collapsed.

As of December 31, the unofficial count of West Virginians killed in Vietnam according to the State Adjutant General Dept. was approximately 711.

1973   On January 23, a Vietnam peace agreement was announced in Paris. By March, 8 POW's from West Virginia had been released.

West Virginia announced plans for the longest arch span bridge in the world, over New River near Fayetteville and Oak Hill.

Construction began at Morgantown on the Personal Rapid Transit System, the first of its kind in the world. The site was chosen by the U. S. Department of Transportation.

Limitations went into effect on the issuing of permits for surface mining.

Arnold Miller of Cabin Creek was elected as President of the United Mine Workers of America. He unseated incumbent Tony Boyle.

1974   Many Kanawha County public schools were closed during the 74-75 school year due to boycotts and bombings by citizens'

groups crusading against what they considered to be unpatriotic and immoral textbooks.

The statue *Lincoln Walks at Midnight* conceived by the late Fred Torrey, a Fairmont native and completed by sculptor Bernie Wiepper, was erected in front of the State Capitol in commemoration of Lincoln's role in establishing West Virginia as a separate state in 1863.

1975   On Jan. 30, U.S. District Court Judge Kenneth K. Hall ruled that the disputed books in the Kanawha County book controversy did not violate the First Amendment guarantee of the division of church and state. The suit challenged the Kanawha County Board of Education's authority to introduce the books but Judge Hall maintained that while the texts might be "offensive" to plaintiffs' beliefs, they did not violate church-state separation principle.

John Daniell Maurice of the *Charleston Daily Mail* was awarded the Pulitzer Prize for editorial writing. His editorials on the Kanawha County book controversy helped that area return to normalcy.

Two 330-foot towers on the New River Bridge construction fell and set completion of the bridge back a year.

In May, the final section on the arch span of the New River Bridge was fitted into place making the arch self-supporting. The arch span with a length of 1700 feet and a rise of 370 feet is the highest east of the Mississippi.

1976   A medical school was established at Marshall University giving West Virginia a second major medical training center.

The Boyd Stutler private collection on John Brown and West Virginia history was returned from Chicago for exhibit in the new West Virginia Science and Cultural Center, Charleston. Stutler, who died in 1970, spent 50 years gathering over 5,000 volumes and thousands of original letters, manuscripts, photographs and artifacts.

BIBLIOGRAPHY

Ambler, Charles H., *West Virginia: The Mountain State*. New York: Prentice-Hall, Inc. (1958).

Becker, Martha Jane, *West Virginia Sons & Daughters: Mountain Roots Branching Out*. Parsons, W. Va.: McClain Printing Co. (1976).

Blair, LeGette, *Man on Fire*. New York: Coward-McCann, Inc. (1944).

Bogurt, W. H., *Daniel Boone and the Hunters of Kentucky*. New York: Miller, Orton and Co. (1858).

Brehan, Carl, *The Escapades of Frank and Jesse James*. New York: Fredrick Fell Publishers (1974).

Candee, Marjorie D., Ed., *Current Biography 1956*. New York: The H. H. Wilson Co. (1956).

Clagg, Sam E., *West Virginia Fact Bank*. Chicago: Rand McNally & Company, Inc. (1973).

———. *West Virginia Historical Almanac*. Parsons, W. Va.: McClain Printing Co. (1975).

Clarkson, Roy B., *Tumult on the Mountains*. Parsons, W. Va.: McClain Printing Co. (1964).

Clendining, John, and others, *Plant Fossils of West Virginia*. Morgantown: West Virginia University (1966).

Comstock, Jim, *West Virginia Heritage Encyclopedia Supplemental, Vol. 25*. Richwood, W. Va.: Jim Comstock, publisher (1974).

Conley, Phil, *West Virginia Encyclopedia*. Charleston: West Virginia Publishing Co. (1929).

Conley, Phil, and Doherty, William Thomas, *West Virginia History*. Charleston: Education Foundation Inc. (1974).

Cranmer, G. L., *History of the Upper Ohio Valley, Vol. I*. Madison, Wisconsin: Brent and Fuller (1890).

Dushkin Publishing Group, Inc. *The Encyclopedia of American History*. Guilford, Conn.: Dushkin Publishing Group, Inc. (1973).

Harris, Theodore F., *Pearl S. Buck, A Biography*. New York: John Day (1969).

Hatfield, G. Elliott, *The Hatfields*. Stanville, Kentucky: Big Sandy Historical Society (1974).

Lee, Howard B., *Bloodletting in Appalachia*. Morgantown: West Virginia University (1969).

———. *The Burning Springs*. Morgantown: West Virginia University (1969).

Lewis Virgil A., *Hand-Book of West Virginia*. Charleston: Tribune Printing Company (1904).

———. *Life and Times of Anne Bailey the Pioneer Heroine of the Great Kanawha Valley*. Charleston, West Virginia: Butler Printing Co. (1891).

Mallison, Sam T., *The Great Wildcatter*. Charleston: Education Foundation of West Virginia, Inc. (1953).

McCormick, Kyle, *The New Kanawha River*. Charleston, West Virginia: Mathews Printing (1959).

———. *The New River and the Mine War of West Virginia*. Charleston, West Virginia: Mathews Printing (1959).

Morris, Richard B., *Encyclopedia of American History*. New York: Harper & Brothers (1953).

Newbraugh, Fred, *Valleys of History, Vol. 2, Issue 3*. Potomac Edison (1966).

Olcott, William, *The Greenbrier Heritage*. Arndt, Preston, Chapin, Lamb & Keen, Inc.

Parton, Mary Field, Ed., *The Autobiography of Mother Jones*. Chicago: Charles H. Kerr and Co. (1974).

Price, Charles, *The World of Golf*. New York: Random House (1962).

Reniers, Perceval and Ashton, *The Midland Trail*. New York, New York: Midland Trail Pub. (1946).

Rice, Otis K., *The Allegheny Frontier*. Lexington, Kentucky: The University of Kentucky Press (1970).

Schneider, Norris, *Blennerhassett Island and the Burr Conspiracy*. Columbus, Ohio: Ohio Historical Society (1966).

Sigaud, Louis A., *Belle Boyd, Confederate Spy*. Richmond, Virginia: The Dietz Press, Inc. (1944).

Stutler, Boyd, *West Virginians Awarded the Medal of Honor*. Charleston, West Virginia: West Virginia State Dept. of Archives and History (1956 ed.).

Thoene, Eugene, *History of Oil and Gas in West Virginia*. Charleston, West Virginia: Education Foundation (1964).

West Virginia State Board of Education, *West Virginia*. New York: Oxford University Press (1941).

Commerce
Gerald S. Ratliff
Steve Payne, Dept. of Commerce
Dept. of Commerce
Seawell (2 pictures)
93 Kuykendall
94 Seawell
96 West Virginia University Collection
98 Kuykendall
101 Ed McMahan
101 Courtesy of Emma Rhodes
102 Missouri Historical Society
104 Courtesy of Joe Sakach
106 Kuykendall
107 Kuykendall
108-109 Matthew Seawell
110 Kuykendall
111 Kuykendall
113 Kuykendall (all pictures)
114 Strat Douthat
115 Seawell
116 Jim Osborn
117 Seawell
120 Walter McCoy Collection
123 Walter McCoy Collection
124 Seawell
125 Arnout Hyde, Jr., Dept. of Natural Resources
126 Jerry Ash
128 Kuykendall
129 Kuykendall
130 Kuykendall
130-131 Tom Evans, Dept. of Commerce
132 Kuykendall
133 Kuykendall
134 Kuykendall
135 Courtesy of Walter Caldwell
137 Courtesy of The Logan News
137 Henry Hatfield Collection
137 Ron Fowler
138 Seawell
138-139 (left to right)
Seawell
Library of Congress (2 pictures)
Henry Hatfield Collection
Ron Fowler (2 pictures)
Henry Hatfield Collection
Ron Fowler
Courtesy of The Logan News
Henry Hatfield Collection (2 pictures)
Library of Congress
Michael Corbitt
140-141 Library of Congress
141 Matthew Seawell
142 Matthew Seawell
144-145 (from top to bottom)
WVU Library Archives (3 pictures)
Library of Congress
Courtesy of The Logan News
146 Kuykendall
147 Kuykendall
148-149 (top to bottom)
Seawell (2 pictures)
Evelyn Eddy
Kuykendall
Arnout Hyde, Jr., Dept.

of Natural Resources
Seawell
Kuykendall
Tom Evans, Dept. of Commerce
Seawell (2)
Kuykendall
Harry Schaefer
Seawell
W.A. Rogers
150-151 Seawell (4 pictures)
Kuykendall
Seawell (3)
Courtesy of Mrs. Adah I. Fletcher
Seawell
Dave Cruise, Dept. of Commerce
Kuykendall (2)
Seawell (4)
152 Seawell
153 Harry Schaefer
154-155 Seawell
156 Arnout Hyde, Jr., Dept. of Commerce
157 Kuykendall
158 Kuykendall
158-159 Jack Lowe
160 Kuykendall
161 Kuykendall
162-163 Courtesy of Jon Dragan, Wildwater Expeditions Unlimited, Inc.
164-165 Seawell
165 Seawell
166-167 Kuykendall
168 Seawell
169 Seawell
170 Kuykendall
170-171 Kuykendall
172-173 (top to bottom)
Seawell
Dave Cruise, Dept. of Commerce
Seawell
Roger L. Hughes, Dept. of Commerce
Kuykendall
Jeri Buxton, Dept of Commerce
Jim Osborn
Seawell
Jim Osborn
Kuykendall
Jack Lowe
Kuykendall
Gerald S. Ratliff, Dept. of Commerce
Robert McIntire
Kuykendall
Seawell
Kuykendall
Seawell (2 pictures)
Jim Osborn
174 Seawell
175 Kuykendall
176 Seawell
177 Seawell
178 Seawell
178-179 Seawell
180 Kuykendall
180-181 Seawell
182-183 Ward B. Fletcher, Sr.
184-185 Ward B. Fletcher, Sr.
186-187 (top to bottom)
Seawell (2 pictures)
Jack Lowe

Kuykendall
Ric MacDowell
Kuykendall
Ed McMahan
Kuykendall
Jack Lowe (2 pictures)
186 187 Kuykendall
Seawell
Jack Lowe
Kuykendall
Ric MacDowell
Kuykendall
Ric MacDowell
Kuykendall (2 pictures)
Seawell
Jack Lowe
188 Virginia State Library
189 Seawell
190 Gerald S. Ratliff, Dept. of Commerce
190 Pricketts Fort Memorial Foundation
190 Jack Lowe
191 Dept. of Archives and History, Charleston, W.Va.
191 Library of Congress
191 State Historical Society of Wisconsin
192 Weirton Steel Division of National Steel Corp.
192 Dept. of Archives and History, Charleston, W.Va.
192 Gerald S. Ratliff, Dept. of Commerce
194 Currier and Ives Painting
194 Ohio Historical Society
194 The Museum of the Confederacy, Richmond, Va.
195 Library of Congress
195 Courtesy of Monongahela Power
195 Courtesy of Monongahela Power
196 The West Virginia Hillbilly
196 Gerald S. Ratliff, Dept. of Commerce
197 Gerald S. Ratliff, Dept. of Commerce
197 Ward B. Fletcher, Sr.
198 Seawell (2 pictures)
199 Wide World Photos
199 Kuykendall
199 WVU Collection
199 WVU Library Archives
200 Air Force Photograph
200 The Logan News, courtesy of Litz McGuire
200 Seawell
201 Seawell
201 Wayne Rosencrans
201 Wide World Photos
201 courtesy of EXXON
202 From Mountain Roots Branching Out—Martha Jane Becker
202 Wide World Photos
202 Whitestone Photo
203 Seawell
203 Tom Evans, Dept. of Commerce
203 Steve Payne, Dept. of Commerce
208 Arnout Hyde, Jr., Dept. of Natural Resources

research associates
JACKIE CORDRAY
SUSAN CURRY
MARY KUYKENDALL
DEBBIE OESTERLE
PAT SCHROEDER

layout consultant
KENNETH R. HINE

research consultants
LOUISE BING
MAURICE BROOKS, Ph.D.
MAHLON C. BROWN, Ph.D.
O. O. BROWN
JIM COMSTOCK
CATHY GURLEY
A. L. HARDMAN
JAMES G. JONES, Ph.D.
ADAM KELLY
HENRY McCOY
PAUL PRICE, Ph.D.
JOSEPH SAKACH

copy consultants
SALLIE DAUGHERTY
ALYCE GOLDBERG
DOROTHY PHIPPS

color separations
FALCON COLOR, INC.
Wash., D. C. 20002
PRIMACOLOR, INC.
Parkersburg, W. Va. 26101

art associates
WALTER McVEIGH
MARY BETH METZGER
BARBELLA KUENZ
RONALD LOTT
SUSAN SHEPPARD
JAMES SULLIVAN

Stratton L. Douthat

Jerry Wayne Ash

Bill Kuykendall

Harry Seawell

Jerry Ash, a native of Bridgeport, is editor and co-publisher of a weekly newspaper in Terra Alta. As a journalist, he consistently manages a certain feeling of warmth in his well-paced, but unpressured writing.

He's a good listener and lets his subjects tell the story before he tells it. These qualities are immediately obvious in *Rebirth of a wilderness* and several other stories on these pages. As Nancy Abrams, Jerry's Managing Editor, puts it—"Jerry doesn't take West Virginia for granted."

Light humor also frequently finds a comfortable place in Jerry's story telling ("*The genius of a natural damned fool*"—"*The only newspaper in the country under solemn oath never to smell bad*"—"*The country lawyer makes his point*").

Jerry holds two degrees from West Virginia University, where he later taught in the School of Journalism. His informal style and the encouragement he gave his classes earned him much respect. Some of his students have since become seasoned professionals.

After seven years at West Virginia University, Jerry (now 37) found himself thoroughly addicted to the smell of printing ink. He formed a partnership with Rich Hopkins and purchased *The Preston County News*. He writes an editorial column ("Dear Preston:") which has won numerous national awards.

Jerry is also Vice President of The Pioneer Press of West Virginia, Inc., a printing and publishing firm in Terra Alta.

Michele (Jerry's wife, who is also active in the business) provided him with both assistance and moral support during the long, hard months that his days, nights, weekends and holidays were divided between his regular business and his inspirations for this book.

Strat Douthat (born in Huntington) has spent most of his journalistic career with the *Associated Press*. As their Huntington correspondent, he travels southern West Virginia writing feature stories that are nationally published.

Strat's mild-mannered approach wins the respect of his subjects during his relaxed interviews. His extensive experience with Associated Press has seasoned his ability to find unusual story material. "*Powder Puff*" takes the hoot owl and *The barefoot boy from Pigeon Creek* are excellent examples.

Some of his subjects also prove to be strong in character—a quality that Strat analyzes and beautifully recreates without exaggeration. This is reflected in both *Memories of a clansman* and "*I'm goin' to fiddle some before I die*".

While studying at Marshall University, he worked at assorted jobs that included truck driving, bar tending and working on C&O freighters on Lake Michigan. After finishing his A.B. degree, majoring in journalism, in 1961 he did active duty in the United States Army under the reserve plan, then joined the Charleston AP Bureau. After a year he transferred to Bluefield where he was correspondent for 18 months. He returned to the Charleston Bureau to cover politics, sports and features.

In 1966 Strat transferred to the Miami Bureau and, after a year, became News Editor, directing a staff of 35. He continued to write as well, covering a variety of events which included the tragic Apollo fire. He also freelanced as a magazine writer.

After five years in Florida he returned to his present Huntington assignment where he and Kitty (his wife) and the kids (Mark, Stratty and Chris) have their home. The family also has a farm in Lincoln County, where they are building their own log cabin.

Strat thoroughly enjoys people. It's quite appropriate that his writing efforts usually involve people in one way or another. Dick Buholz, the Charleston AP Bureau chief, admires Strat as a "top staffer" and what he calls "Strat's unique ability to find stories of good human interest" that other journalists have passed by, "and then develop these stories into top-notch features."

Bill Kuykendall, another gifted West Virginia native, born in Romney, is known across the country as both a picture journalist and an educator.

He practices what he preaches and does it with a masterful finesse.

Our selection of Bill for the book assignment couldn't have been a better choice.

Not only did he return from his travels around the state with exciting pictures to illustrate a long laundry list of stories, he took every opportunity to record additional situations that couldn't have been predicted. The dramatic shot of the New River bridge in its final construction stages (page 146) is one of dozens of examples.

His landscapes and waterscapes are as varied and as exciting as West Virginia itself.

His sensitive, but direct and dramatic handling of people borders on photographic genius. The picture of the pioneer father and daughter (pages 60–61) has all the qualities of a renaissance painting and more. His spontaneous approach to people in motion, like the kid chasing the calf (page 30), is pure photographic poetry.

After "sneaking out of WVU with an AB in zoology in 1966," as he puts it, Bill attended the University of Minnesota Graduate School to study photojournalism, and followed that with an internship with *National Geographic*. During the next three years he held a position with the *Worthington* (Minnesota) *Daily Globe* where he was voted *Newspaper Picture Editor of the Year* by the National Press Photographers Association and University of Missouri in their joint annual competition in 1970.

While with the *Globe,* he also traveled the country speaking at newspaper and magazine workshops and judging exhibitions. Then he worked $2^{1}/_{2}$ years teaching photojournalism and graphics at the University of Missouri School of Journalism, before returning to West Virginia to freelance and to give a vital hand to WEST VIRGINIA USA. Bill and Mary Kuykendall presently live in Keyser with their 3 year old son, Adam. Mary participated in the editorial program as well, by handling a number of important research assignments.

Jim Vance, one of Bill's fans, a former employer and Publisher of the *Worthington Daily Globe*, shares with us the excitement over Bill's fine West Virginia coverage. He also regards Bill as an "extremely talented and gifted photographer" whose travels in America have given him new perspective on interpreting "his native land and its people, back where his roots are planted."

This book is Bill's tribute to his homeland . . . and his homeland's tribute to his return.

The editorial staff deserves more recognition, but a few words must be managed in limited space: *Mike,* for smiles and performances when they were needed, and several Saturdays and Sundays—*Debbie,* for early encouragement and help with the cover design—*Mac,* for inspiration, tough brainstorming, heavy film work and brilliant tape editing—*Linda,* for her amazing dedication, amazing planning and endurance—*Bill,* for good clean humor, flexibility and devotion—*Don,* for lots of white collar work, wearing a dozen hats, darned good marketing work and an *occasional* barber shop song—*Jackie,* for finding facts and pictures that couldn't be found—*Maria,* for her entertaining copywriting, for her indestructable smile, determination, brilliant research and for staying cool when the Chronology had to be ruthlessly chopped to make space—*Evelyn,* for being there day and night when the going was tough in the lab, for keeping everybody in a good supply of smiles and for always being Evelyn—*Matt,* for a hundred jobs, for his photography and lab work—*Harry,* for nights and weekends, for trying new things and for printing an excellent set of color duplicates—*Marilyn, Fearless Marilyn,* for fine public relations, or whatever needed to be done—*Jenny,* for setting a pace, meeting deadlines and hanging in there, tough as rawhide.—*HS*

Harry Seawell, Producer of WEST VIRGINIA USA, is a tireless communicator whose career is devoted to the pursuit of perfection. This standard—teamed with enthusiasm, drive, curiosity and imagination—commands high

respect among editors and art directors around the world.

These qualities are reflected in this book. In its conception, its design and, especially, in the team of people Harry has assembled to make it all happen. He has the remarkable ability to seek out the right talent, and then to inspire and to lead them to levels of extraordinary accomplishment. The final result is this true gem among books on Americana.

Harry's background is diverse: a Texas-born, small-town cowpoke; painter of *Coca-Cola* signs; U.S. Marine Corps—first in China and then the Korean War; award winning photographer for the *Parkersburg News*; then Schaefer & Seawell, a partnership in publishing and photography, contributing to major magazines world-wide, as well as producers of WEST VIRGINIA IN COLOR, a best-seller in 1963.

Today, Harry is President of Seawell Multimedia—producers of photography, films and books.

His awards and honors include numerous one-man shows for both art and photography; News Pictures of the Year; Rochester Salon; University of Missouri School of Journalism; *Look* Magazine (for sports photography); CA (Communication Arts) Magazine; World Premiere International Colour Photography Exhibition; *Who's Who in the South and Southwest* (November 1976).

More often than not Harry's recreation is his work. When his seven-day WEST VIRGINIA USA weeks were interrupted by other photography assignments, he referred to them as "vacations". Other pleasure activities include his spelunking, painting, technical climbing (which he also teaches) and—planning the next six volumes of the APPALACHIA USA series.

—*Ken Hine*

SEAWELL
MULTIMEDIA

producer
HARRY SEAWELL

project coordinator
DONALD GEIBEL

design
HARRY SEAWELL

art director
JENNY MORLAN FIETSAM

publisher's assistant
LINDA MILES

research
MARILYN PASQUARELLI
MARIA SUTEJ
JACQUELINE WILLIAMS

audio visual
EVELYN EDDY
ROBERT McINTIRE
HARRY D. SEAWELL II
MATTHEW SEAWELL

office manager
MICHAEL CORBITT

publisher's representative
WILLIAM DOBBIE

Sunlight filtering through a thick canopy of trees (overleaf) illuminates a country road in Holly River State Park in Webster and Upshur Counties.